or the
more
dai
the sa
Three
looks

short of staff again. Major Watpi is M.O.
An old Sergeant was telling me about the different sorts
of shells - the German send over. He says one kind,
called the "Oil Can"- whose duty it is to upset the nerves
of the troops is most feared of all.

A Nurse at
the Front

WAR DIARIES

A Nurse at the Front

The Great War Diaries of Sister Edith Appleton

Edited by Ruth Cowen

SIMON &
SCHUSTER

London · New York · Sydney · Toronto · New Delhi

A CBS COMPANY

First published in Great Britain by Simon & Schuster UK Ltd, 2012
A CBS COMPANY
In association with the Imperial War Museum

Text copyright © Dick Robinson and Imperial War Museums 2012

1 3 5 7 9 10 8 6 4 2

Simon & Schuster UK Ltd
1st Floor
222 Gray's Inn Road
London WC1X 8HB

www.simonandschuster.co.uk

Simon & Schuster Australia, Sydney
Simon & Schuster India, New Delhi

Every reasonable effort has been made to contact copyright
holders of material reproduced in this book. If any have inadvertently been
overlooked, the publishers would be glad to hear from them and make good
in future editions any errors or omissions brought to their attention.

A CIP catalogue record for this book
is available from the British Library

ISBN: 978-0-85720-223-9

Typeset in Caslon by M Rules

Printed and bound by CPI Group (UK) Ltd, Croydon, CR0 4YY

To the dedicated women who
selflessly nursed our sick and wounded men

and

For all those silent or yet unheard voices from
almost 100 years ago

Contents

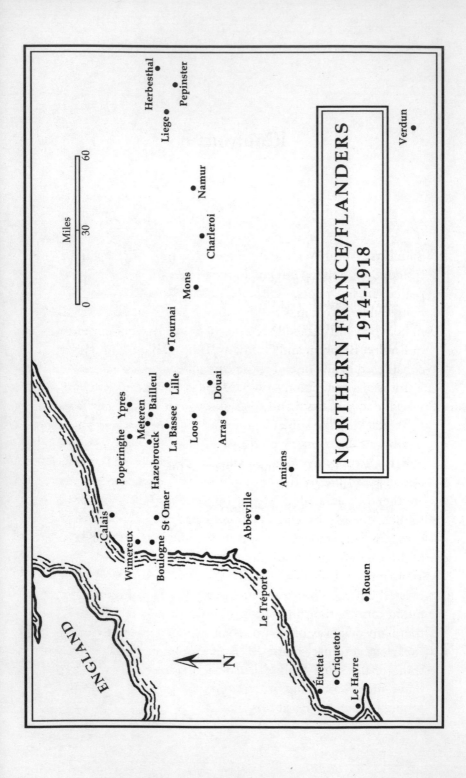

NORTHERN FRANCE/FLANDERS
1914-1918

Miles
0   30   60

N

ENGLAND

Calais
Wimereux
Boulogne
St Omer
Poperinghe Ypres
Meteren
Hazebrouck Bailleul
La Bassee Lille
Loos
Arras Douai
Abbeville
Amiens
Le Tréport
Étretat
Criquetot
Le Havre
Rouen

Tournai
Mons
Charleroi
Namur
Liege
Herbesthal
Pepinster
Verdun

Foreword

The First World War, the horror and the pity of it, still has a tremendous hold on our collective imagination. It has compelled artists, poets, writers, ordinary and extraordinary people alike. What makes these diaries so remarkable is that, in her vivid and detailed accounts of her working experience in France, Belgium and Germany, Edie Appleton might be considered in any one of those categories.

I was of a generation – perhaps the last – where it was still possible to gain first hand spoken accounts of the First War. I have tackled the subject a number of times, perhaps most notably in *War Horse*, which I wrote in the early 1980s and which – twenty-five years later – has been given a whole new lease of life by the National Theatre and now has yet another life as a film. My inspiration for *War Horse* was fuelled directly by conversations I had with a handful of octogenarians who were living at the time in my tiny village of Iddesleigh. A few of them had gone to war with the Yeomanry and recalled vividly the close relationship that existed between horse and trooper. Part of the impulse for me in turning their memories into fiction was in tribute to them: my own way of passing their experiences on. Reading these extraordinary diaries of Edie Appleton, I have something of the same feeling I had then, sitting among those brave men – a feeling of extraordinary privilege to be listening to such stories at first hand.

In the following pages, whether she is dealing with the daily horrors and atrocities that faced her as a nursing sister, or the joys she was able to snatch for herself, away from the devastation and carnage, Edie is frank and straightforward. The authenticity of her voice and of what she writes about is something that cannot be replicated. Her vivid recall of detail is meticulous and yet nothing is superfluous: a bomb that lands so close to the hospital and makes the air 'so thick with red dust ... that we could not see out of our windows.' Her own emotions are kept movingly in check, but not out of view: 'we tried to become used to the five-minutely explosions of big shells close to us, but it was difficult and my knees did shake.'

There are heart-breaking moments, like her insistence on giving the dying and wounded soldiers a 'clean handker-chief'. She says, 'I don't know why, but they love to have it.' One soldier tells her that she is 'like a mother to him' and we can clearly see why: it is in just such small, thoughtful ges-tures – like a mother sending a child off to school with a straightened jacket, combed hair, clean handkerchief – that we see her great skill and tact in caring and comforting.

What shines through is her good humour, her determina-tion to get on with the job, to make the best of circumstances. And this includes finding moments of sanity in which to appreciate the countryside – a rest in 'a beautiful wood just outside Hazebrouck, with a picnic tea', or swimming in the sea on a sultry morning, 'the sea absolutely clear with waves smooth-topped and lumpy'; or, even, luxuriating in the bath-rooms and bedrooms of what had once been a posh seaside hotel, turned into a makeshift hospital.

She shows us the reality of dealing with horrors, the 'over-work' and the 'undersleep', which inevitably sometimes leads to hysteria. One poor sister, who is confronted by a mortuary corporal's dismay at not being able to differentiate dead officers from the other ranks, because, (unbelievably) he explains, it made a difference how they were each to be buried: 'Men is 'ammered – officers is screwed.' The sister, Edie tells us, 'went hysterical and laughed and laughed. The more she told herself it was tragic and not funny, the funnier it all looked.'

There are any number of such insightful observations on any page you care to choose. What is remarkable is that in the midst of the most appalling conditions, Edie had the presence of mind, the strength and the courage, to record these things for herself. It is a further miracle that these diaries have survived and, thanks in large part to the care and generosity of her relations, that we find ourselves in the privileged position to be able to re-live her experiences for ourselves in our own time.

Michael Morpurgo

Introduction

The Great War diaries of Edith Appleton paint an exceptionally vivid picture of daily life just behind the lines, in the makeshift clearing stations and hospitals which received wounded and dying men straight from the Front. Simultaneously, they chart the transformation of the northern French towns, villages and landscapes which the conflict irrevocably changed over the course of those four bloodstained years.

Edith (known as 'Edie' or 'E') served in France and Belgium throughout the war. Following the Armistice, she continued to work first on an ambulance train, transporting casualties and repatriating prisoners of war, and then on the staff of the Matron-in-Chief in Boulogne, until her demobilisation in December 1919. A conscientious diarist, it is likely that she wrote her detailed and engaging journals right through from her enrolment as a military nurse in 1914 until her permanent return home. She seemed to manage to create for herself a brief pause in which to chronicle the events going on around her during even the busiest times at the height of great battles. However, the first volume we have begins in April 1915 (frustratingly, on a page numbered 112), almost seven months after her departure from England. There are other missing sections as well, most significantly an entire journal charting her life between November 1916 and June 1918.

Despite this long gap, the 400 mainly handwritten pages of Edie's diaries make a valuable and moving contribution to the literature of the Great War. For Edie was not just an intelligent observer, but a compassionate and nuanced writer, with a gift for thumbnail characterisation, a quick wit and a sharp eye for the telling detail. Acutely aware of the significance of the events she witnessed from the sidelines – the first gas attacks, the ebb and flow of casualties as the great battles waxed and waned – she never deviates from a frank and competent account of what she witnessed. The horrific wounds, the amputations, the seemingly endless procession of agonising deaths. She calmly reports the effects of gas and shellshock – neither of which had been seen before – and the extreme youth of most of those who died. Nothing is spared, nothing is embroidered and Edie never takes refuge in sentiment. Indeed her unflinching account is perhaps especially surprising as the diaries were addressed to her mother Eliza, whom Edie might have been expected to protect from the most graphic details.

And yet what lifts the diaries from an almost unendurable catalogue of horrors is Edie's ability to switch from this grinding ghastliness to a genuinely joyous, exuberant appreciation of the natural beauty around her. She was a robust walker, and a lover of rugged coastlines, and whatever the season every spare moment off-duty was used to tramp around the glorious countryside sketching the views, revelling either in summer flowers or wintry storms. Ever practical, even in the direst circumstances she embraces new pastimes – in Poperinghe, famous for its Flanders lace, she takes up lace-making, and for a favoured colleague she even tries her hand at carpentry, creating a large wooden cabinet with movable shelves, which she polished with beeswax and turps to look like old oak.

Edith Appleton was born in Deal in Kent in June 1877 – the eighth of eleven children. Her father Edward was a master mariner and pillar of the Deal community, who later became a Trinity Pilot, assisting ships as they manoeuvred through the dangerous sands and shallows around the Channel coast. It was an intimate and affectionate family, and Edith remained particularly close to her mother Eliza – the diaries are full of warm concern for her comfort and safety and greetings to the rest of her much-loved family.

A family portrait from the 1890s. Edward and Eliza Appleton (seated, centre) with nine of their eleven children. Edie is standing, right, in the back row.
Photograph courtesy of the Appleton family

In 1897, when Edie was 20, her father drowned while attempting to board a cattle steamship at Dungeness, leaving Eliza with a number of children still at home. Three years later, in October 1900, Edie made the journey from Deal to London, where she enrolled to train as a nurse at St Bartholomew's Hospital, close to St Paul's Cathedral. She lived in nurses' digs and worked in the surgical and medical wards, qualifying in 1904. She had achieved a consistently

excellent record, finishing fifth out of her class of twenty-six
students.

By the time Britain joined the war on 4 August 1914, Edie
had spent four years working as a private nurse, a spell as a
health visitor, and the last two years as a District Nurse in
Crediton, Devon. She quickly realised that there would soon
be a pressing need for such experienced civilian nurses to
work at the front line. Within three weeks she had signed
up, and on 16 September travelled to Fort Pitt in Chatham
to join Queen Alexandra's Imperial Military Nursing Service
Reserve (QAIMNSR).

QAIMNS had been established twelve years earlier and
was considered an elite nursing service. Pre-war, QAIMNS
nurses had been required to be well educated, highly qualified, unmarried, between 25 and 35 years old and ladies of
a 'high social status'. With such exacting standards, it was
hardly surprising that at the outbreak of war there were
barely 300 regular members, but as the scale of the casualties soared these restrictions were quickly swept away to
enable more than 10,000 reservists to join.

And so on 9 October a group of nurses, including 37-year-
old Edie, embarked at Southampton and sailed via the port
of Dungeness – where her father had died seventeen years
earlier – to Ostend. In a letter to her mother Edie described
how, after a night crossing in eerie darkness, with a pilot
navigating the ship through the minefields, they had
steamed safely into port and she had woken to the sound of
dogs barking and church bells ringing. The harbour was
packed with British ships and the town was rapidly filling
up with Belgian refugees, soldiers, horses, guns, ambulances, cars, dog-carts and even London buses – already the
German onslaught was taking its toll. Edie was able to go
ashore and fight her way through the crowds to the cathedral where, she told Eliza, she gave thanks for a safe
crossing.

After a further night's voyage in pitch darkness, she arrived in Boulogne ready for her first posting, which would be to No. 10 Stationary Hospital at St Omer. By the following February Edie was addressing letters home from further up the line, from No. 3 Casualty Clearing Station (CCS) at Hazebrouck. CCSs were mobile treatment stations, usually set up in huts or under canvas near established rail routes to receive the casualties from the Front. If local digs could not be found quickly, nurses could find themselves billeted in tents or ticket offices. When under fire a CCS could pack up and move at top speed, and sometimes they were forced to move every few days.

By April, No. 3 CCS had moved right behind the front lines to Poperinghe near Ypres – which is where Edie's diary opens. The unit had found shelter in two convents and a seminary, but within a few pages Edie is describing how the station suffered three successive days of continuous shelling and bombing. The medical staff struggled to cope with the flood of civilian as well as military casualties as the shells rained down. 'The air was so thick with red dust, bits and smoke,' reported Edie with her customary sangfroid, having been up all night in the operating theatre, 'that it was difficult for us to go on as usual'. The CCS was quickly evacuated, and Edie and the other nurses returned to the relative safety of St Omer until it could be re-established in Bailleul.

In the first year of the war conditions in the CCSs were often very basic and equipment inadequate. A stream of men – some already dead – would be carried on stretchers from motor ambulances and deposited at the CCS. The injured, all suffering from shock, usually had infected wounds and at first there was nothing with which to sterilise new dressings. Frequently rows of stretchers with scarcely space to stand between them would lie on bare floors, a brown blanket the soldiers' only protection against the bitter winter. There were few bedsteads, trolleys or dressing tables. Only the most severe cases were operated on, and evacuations to the base hospitals took place every day by ambulance train before a new intake of casualties was admitted. As Edie herself writes, on occasion the nurses worked twenty-hour days to get the rudimentary work done.

Understandably, the authorities selected the nurses to work in these hellish conditions with care. The nurses had to be in good physical health, to have completed at least six months in the country, living in active service conditions, and to have an excellent previous record. With the unrelenting pressure of dealing with up to 2,000 beds with a skeleton staff, often with unrelieved shelling all around them, the women needed to remain mentally strong, and it was decided that, ideally, they would not spend more than three months at the Front before returning to base for a further six months of relative respite.

Things deteriorated further for the nurses during the Second Battle of Ypres, with the appearance of a new and terrifying enemy – gas. On 5 May, a week or so after the first gas attacks of the war, Edie reported in her diary that the wards were 'full of gas-poisoning victims. They are fearfully sad to see. The slight ones look rather like pneumonia, and the bad ones are terrible – the poor things are blue and gasping, lungs full of fluid, and not able to cough it up.' For nurses like Edie, watching helplessly as so many men died in agony was almost unbearable.

By the end of 1915 Edie found herself on the Normandy coast at Étretat, between Le Havre and Fécamp. She was stationed at General Hospital No. 1, one of several hospitals on the casualty evacuation chain. She remained posted there for more than a year, and while she found the work absorbing and the scenery exquisite – the rocky coastline reminded her of home – she remained anxious to be posted back to the Front. On 18 November, shortly after her last entry for 1916, the five-month slaughter of the Battle of the Somme finally ended. It had cost the British more than half a million casualties.

There are, sadly, no diaries for the nineteen-month stretch between November 1916 and June 1918, but we know that Edie continued to work at hospitals and clearing stations throughout this period. America joined the war in April 1917, and the first US troops began arriving in France on 26 June, shortly before the Third Battle of Ypres. We know from the meticulous and highly detailed diary of the indomitable Dame Maud McCarthy, Matron-in-Chief of the British Expeditionary Force, that in June 1917 Edie had temporary charge of 45 Casualty Clearing Station in Achiet-le-Grand, seven miles south of Arras, from which the Germans withdrew (after devastating the area) in March. In an entry dated 17 June, when Dame Maud was officially meant to be off duty with appendicitis, she wrote: 'Received letter from Sister Appleton . . . to say the hospital had been quite busy and shells had been falling very near. The hospital cook and a patient had been wounded. The patients and staff had had to go to dugouts.' At some point in 1917 Edie received the Royal Red Cross (First Class), a highly prized decoration which was awarded to nurses almost invariably for 'exceptional devotion and competency', and for their sustained efforts over a long period.

With the Third Battle of Ypres raging from July to November 1917, Edie would have been kept busy as British troops pressed from Ypres. The village of Passchendaele was finally taken on 10 November, and Allied losses had totalled more than 250,000 men. Just ten days after that British tanks spearheaded an attack towards the Hindenburg Line which launched the Battle of Cambrai and the attrition continued, punctuated by concerted pushes and offensives by both sides. Reinforced by troops from the now defunct Russian front, Germany launched a major offensive in March 1918, beginning with the Battle of Picardy against the British. Four more attacks followed, starting with the Battle of the Lys in April, near Armentières. United under the leadership of Marshal Foch, the Allies continued to repulse the German offensives at the Battle of the Aisne in late May and the Battle of the Matz in June, which alone cost 35,000 Allied lives.

Edie's diaries resume on 21 June, six days after the end of the Battle of the Matz and shortly before the final 'spring push' which would become the Second Battle of the Marne. By this time Edie was posted to General Hospital No. 3 in Le Tréport, which was based in part of the Trianon Hotel, a newly built and very grand hotel on a cliff top. While the fighting continued the hospital continued to receive a steady stream of casualties, including many German troops – to whom Edie displayed as much compassion as she could muster – but it was becoming increasingly clear that Germany was losing momentum and Edie's optimistic mood grew stronger as she sensed an anticipation of victory among the troops. 'Dare we feel that there is one small chip of Peace?' she wrote as the Bulgarians began to negotiate terms for surrender.

Life in general was improving. 'I sometimes wonder if I realise that I am living in one of France's smartest hotels . . .' she continued, in a rare moment of self-interested gloating. 'Beautifully situated, good rooms, wide corridors, bathrooms galore – I always choose one that looks towards the rising sun and over the harbour and town – it is so quaint and beautiful in the early morning. And all free of charge!' In spite of the work she still finds time to explore the local villages, bathe in a hastily adapted 'swimming gown' and relish the beautiful coastal sunsets. And when, finally, the Armistice arrived on 11 November, Edie comments with her usual crispness: 'Peace! Thank God for that! It feels very queer too – as if your elastic had snapped.'

The work didn't end with the peace, of course, and on 6 December Edie was sent to Boulogne to take temporary charge of an ambulance train just arrived from England to collect hundreds of wounded soldiers and repatriated prisoners of war. The diaries end with the men enjoying a well-earned Christmas feast in a siding outside Calais, seated at a long trestle table made up of the beds from one of the carriages, followed by a whist drive and a makeshift concert.

In late January 1919 Edie joined the office staff of Dame Maud, the Matron-in-Chief, who was based at the Marine Hotel in Boulogne. In her diary, Dame Maud referred to Edie at this point as a nurse who 'has been out since the beginning of the war and who is a woman of considerable experience'. It's likely that Dame Maud had specially selected Edie for a job, and that she also recommended her for an OBE, which was awarded that June. Edie remained in Boulogne until her final demobilisation in December 1919.

On her return to England Edie took a nursing post in London, at Bedford College, a women-only institution based in Regent's Park, which had relatively recently become part of the University of London. Her mother Eliza died in 1922, and the following year Edie and one of her elder sisters bought Buddlebrook, a property with a large fertile garden in the exquisitely pretty village of Brighstone on the Isle of Wight, where she grew fruit and vegetables, kept chickens and even, according to family tradition, a pet trout called Algernon in the brook. Several of the Appleton siblings lived at Buddlebrook, including Fred, who became the vicar of Brook and Mottistone, and the house became a happy and comfortable focus for the extended family.

Edie relaxing at home at Buddlebrook on the Isle of Wight
in the early 1920s, with members of the extended Appleton family.
Edie is on the running board, holding the chicken.
Photograph courtesy of the Appleton family

Edie stayed in touch with Dame Maud, and the year she moved to Buddlebrook she received an invitation to join the Territorial Force Nursing Service. This was the sister organisation of QAIMNS and existed to provide the army with reserve civilian nurses in times of crisis, which Dame Maud had taken over in 1920. Initially, although flattered by the offer, Edie declined. In a regretful letter she wrote: 'Thank you for offering to have me in the Territorials. I am afraid I cannot join, much as I should like to for many things – and should love having you as my chief again. One reason is that I am 46 and the other is that I really mean to give up nursing next year and to make my living at poultry-keeping, etc.' However, Dame Maud persevered and apparently within a few days Edie had changed her mind.

In 1926, at the age of 49, Edie married. Her husband was the stepson of her elder sister Mabel, and at 38 he was eleven years her junior. Known as Jack, Lieutenant-Commander John Bonsor Ledger died of cancer just ten years after their marriage, leaving Edie a widow for the last 22 years of her life. She died on 6 February 1958, at Buddlebrook, at the age of eighty.

Edie's diaries stayed within her family until 2008, when some of her great-nephews and nieces, led by Dick Robinson, began to create a website to celebrate her life and work. Since then www.edithappleton.org.uk has grown out of all recognition, as Dick and his family have uncovered more information and added further documents – including three recently discovered letters, written by Edie to Eliza, that fill in some of the gaps left by the missing first months of the journal. They are indebted to many general readers, scholars, and the descendants of some of the soldiers mentioned in the diaries who have helped them to tease out more extraordinary stories of those extraordinary days. And with this publication, the work goes on.

List of Abbreviations

ADMS	Assistant Director Medical Services
AT	Ambulance Train
CCS	Casualty Clearing Station
CMO	Chief Medical Officer
CO	Company Officer
CSM	Company Sergeant Major
DADMS	Deputy Assistant Director of Medical Services
DCM	Distinguished Conduct Medal
DG	Director General
DI	Dangerously Ill
DMS	Director of Medical Services
DSO	Distinguished Service Order
ICT	Inflammation of Connective Tissue
MO	Medical Officer
MP	Military Police
OC	Officer Commanding
RAMC	Royal Army Medical Corps
RE	Royal Engineers
RFA	Royal Field Artillery
RFC	Royal Flying Corps
RGA	Royal Garrison Artillery
RMLI	Royal Marine Light Infantry
RRC	Royal Red Cross
RTO	Rail Transport Officer
SI	Seriously Ill
SN	Staff Nurse
VAD	Voluntary Aid Detachment

Volume One

answering each other's ravings. One of them tells us he has been killed and does his mother know. Certainly death will be no stranger to him, when he comes in a day or two - or perhaps to-night. 3 ops. - 2 trephines and an arm. A field ambulance at Ypres was shelled last night, 2 orderlies killed, and 10 wounded, some fatally all the patients were transferred to us. So we have been very busy to-day.

6th

2 cases in the theatre, heavy convoy in and out, worked in wards this morning. Gave the little orphans a tea this afternoon. We laid the tables for them. They came in and we came after, and as we entered they struck up "God save the King" in French. Then the eldest girl make us a little speech. Then they fed and we poured out tea for them, then they gave us a little concert, "Vive Angleterre!" Vice la France!" three cheers, all over, very happy - on duty again. Have not been out for 3 days, firstly because of much work, and partly weather, rainy and windy, not good for caps and tempers.

7th

Very busy day, going hard in theatre and wards until nearly 9 this evening. Very tired.

8th

Busy day, but only 1 case in theatre. Men who came in convoy to-day were in a terrible state of nervous collapse, a great many of them having been blown up in their trenches. Went for a walk after tea with Latham.

9th

Heavy convoy, bad cases, I am off for 1 hour, to go back this evening, 2 cases (heads) for theatre. Many of to-day's wounded were shot in the stomach in several cases, the bullet went in in

The first volume of Edie's diaries – the only one which was typed – begins tantalisingly on page 112. Pages 1–111 have never been found.

1915, Near Ypres

April 5

A field ambulance at Ypres was shelled last night – two orderlies killed and ten wounded, some fatally. All the patients were transferred to us, so we have been very busy today.

April 6

We gave the little orphans a tea this afternoon. We laid out the tables, they came in and we followed, and as we entered they struck up 'God Save the King' in French, and the eldest girl made us a little speech. They fed as we poured out tea for them, then they gave us a little concert, '*Vive l'Angleterre!*' and '*Vive la France!*' Three cheers all round, very happy! Now on duty again. Have not been out for three days. First because of much work, but also the weather, which is rainy and windy – not good for caps and tempers.

April 8

Men who came in the convoy today were in a terrible state of nervous collapse, a great many of them having been blown up in their trenches.

April 9

Heavy convoy in with bad cases, but I am off for one hour. I have to go back this evening, we have two cases – head wounds – for theatre. Many of today's wounded were shot in the stomach.

April 14

A Zeppelin was reported as heading this way, but we heard this morning that it has gone south. Off duty this evening, went for a walk and then looked over the college, where we are to move tomorrow.

April 15

There was a tremendously heavy bombardment last night. It only lasted three-quarters of an hour, but it was impossible to sleep through the noise. I stood at my window and watched it all – gun flashes, ground lights and searchlights. It was over by about 12.30. I heard today that it was covering our troops' advance.

April 16

Moved into the college – which is better in some ways, worse in others than the Benedictine place. The theatre is not nearly so good, and I must say, I am rather tired with charring* all odd moments of the day. We heard that the Zeppelin that was sighted two nights ago dropped bombs on Bailleul, near the sisters' quarters – luckily no-one was hurt.

---

* Scrubbing, cleaning, general housework. From 'charwoman': a woman employed to clean other people's houses.

April 17

A Taube* that flew over here early this morning was shot down a little way away. The pilot was killed and the observer taken prisoner. He was walked through the town wearing an Iron Cross. At present there is a big attack being made by our men somewhere near Ypres, and there is much flashing going on. It has been a frightfully busy day again, although only two operations – an amputation and an appendix.

April 18

Sunday. Our men made an attack last night, and we heard the heavy firing that covered their advance – in fact it shook the houses. In three minutes they had taken a trench with 13 prisoners and two officers. The whole work of the night achieved a hill of importance blown up – arms and legs of men flung high and into our own trenches – and six lines of trenches taken, along with 2,000 prisoners. The Germans made a counterattack, and killed and wounded nearly 1,000 of our men, and we have had over 600 through our hospital today, all badly wounded and fearfully collapsed. Some who have been out since August say it is quite the worst time they have had.

We went on duty at 5.30 a.m. and stayed on till 9 p.m., and I missed tea and dinner because we were too busy in the theatre. I came straight to bed and am having dinner from the officers' mess brought up to me. It was a sad day in the theatre and a terribly tiring one, with so many amputations

* The first German mass-produced military plane. At the beginning of the war these basic monoplanes were used for all aerial tasks. However within a few months of Edie's entry they would virtually disappear from front line service as more sophisticated aircraft were introduced, and Taubes were relegated to training novice pilots. 'Taube' remained a generic term for any German aeroplane.

of arms and legs, and insides cut and packed in. Sir Anthony Bowlby* and Doctor Parbury from Sharnbrook each did one operation to give our men a rest.

April 19

We have had more patients in, in two heavy trainloads. Ypres is too dangerous for them to be treated nearby, so we get them brought in a few hours after they are wounded. One, a young officer, had both feet cut off. He was walking in Ypres when a shell struck him. He died soon after.

April 20

A frantic day from 7 a.m. to 10 p.m. – one long rush of badly wounded being admitted, and three trainloads have been evacuated. It is a wicked war. Officers and men come in – many so blown to bits that they just come in to die. Most go straight to the theatre for amputation of limb or limbs, or to have their insides – which have been blown out – replaced, and to be made a little more comfortable for the few hours left to them. The big ward is all agonised groans and pleadings and we feel we don't know where to start on the hundreds of things to be done at once. Ypres is very much ruined and heaps of dead – English, French and Belgian – are lying about in the square and all around the town. We hear the Germans have given up the hope of taking Ypres, so have decided to utterly destroy it.

---

* Sir Anthony Alfred Bowlby (1855–1929) had arrived in France seven months earlier as Consulting Surgeon to the Forces. Later he would rise to become Adviser on Surgery for the whole of the British area, Front and Base. It was Bowlby's insistence that complex surgery could be done at the Front that led to the expansion of a number of Casualty Clearing Stations into fully equipped hospital units. The ability to get seriously wounded men into theatre much faster saved numerous lives and limbs.

April 21

Another frantic day, on duty from 6 a.m. to 9 p.m., first in the surgical ward then in theatre. I don't know how many operations we had – I lost count after 5 o'clock – but they were chiefly amputations. The wounded are coming from Ypres and Hill 60, where wholesale murder seems to be going on. We have had 2,508 through in six days.

April 22

There is bad news tonight. Our trenches are being shelled with poisoned gas bombs – which is forcing us to retire*. If so, where will it stop? As No. 5 casualty clearing station (CCS) is in working order, we have had a much lighter day, but we all feel very tired in mind as well as body. Taubes have been over here twice today – the first one dropped bombs and the second, at dusk, dropped lights, probably showing their people where our guns are. They fired on them but scored no hits. Only three cases in theatre today – two heads and an eye – then two sisters, two Medical Officers (MOs) and five orderlies arrived to help us over the rush, just when it was all over.

April 24

I did not go to bed yesterday – was in the theatre till early this morning. The war is raging terribly and fearfully. Shells! I can think of nothing properly. Wounded have been streaming in all the time and, despite reinforcements, we still have to work night and day to keep pace. It is a terrifying battle.

* This was the first gas attack (chlorine) on the Western Front.

April 28

Under fire from Saturday – the first big shell fell quite close to our hospital and the air was so thick with red dust, bits and smoke that we could not see out of our windows. We had operations on at the time and it was difficult for us to go on as usual. After the first shock, we tried to become used to the five-minutely explosions of big shells close to us, but it was difficult and my knees did shake.

We were so much under fire over the weekend that on Monday night we evacuated all but a few patients who were unfit to move, and we nurses were packed off for St Omer. Just as we were leaving town there were two enormous explosions, but we were not anxious to be sent away and told the authorities that we would rather stay. However, we had no choice, and we could not suppress a sense of gratitude as we were whirled out of the firing line in a car. We arrived at St Omer at 2 a.m., a party of 20 refugees, and were put up for the night in a ward with stretchers and blankets all prepared for us. We did not sleep much though – we were all too newly out of it.

Next morning we were returned to Hazebrouck, where we spent a muddled day, anxiously waiting for news of Poperinghe and our MO. We hear today that the place is still being shelled, and that our unit, No. 3 CCS, is being moved to Bailleul tomorrow, where we are to join it. After a fortnight of working practically night and day, we are having a rest in a beautiful wood just outside Hazebrouck, where we are going to have a picnic tea. It is very restful not to hear the roar of the guns so loud and near, but we know it is going on and our hearts are with the brave Tommies who are 'sticking it' in the trenches.

April 30

We were supposed to rejoin our unit at Bailleul today, but a wire came saying billets were unavailable. Miss Wheatley and one other have gone to see if they can find any, and the rest of us are enjoying a thoroughly idle day. It's a great change from the past rush, when we went to bed at about 1 a.m. and came on duty a few hours later, to work solidly for another 20 hours. We heard from the Roman Catholic padre that we left Pop* just in time. When we left there was a hole in one roof and many windows broken, but soon after the shells started falling right on the building and damaged it badly. Luckily everyone was safely out before the bombardment.

The weather is glorious today, and we took lunch to some delightful woods and lazed, read and wrote there until 3 p.m. We came back to see if there were any fresh orders for us, but there were not, so we had tea and are now all reading or writing again. The house I am staying in is on the road to Ypres, and every night about 50 of the biggest lorries laden with ammunition and goods race past, taking supplies to the batteries and men in the trenches. It is a risky job and they always do it in the dark, because the Germans have a view of the road and shell it all the time. As it is, the road between our lines and Ypres is strewn with dead horses and smashed carts.

May 2

Last night we were billeted in various parts of Bailleul and today we settled our wards. We have one wing of a lunatic asylum, with room for about 500 patients, the first of whom have just arrived, and the night nurses are up to look after them. We are to sleep at the asylum, where our rooms are tiny, with high, barred windows, but mine has a pleasant outlook over the aviation ground. The news was not cheerful

---

* Short for Poperinghe (modern spelling Poperinge), a small Belgian town seven miles west of Ypres, where large number of troops were billeted in camps around the centre. The town became known as Pop to all the British soldiers.

and a big attack has been made today. Let us only hope our men have done well. I was grieved to read of a Zeppelin raid over Bury St Edmunds, and am longing to hear if it upset Mother.

May 5

A very busy day with five cases in theatre and the wards full of gas-poisoning victims. They are fearfully sad to see. The slight ones look rather like pneumonia, and the bad ones are terrible – the poor things are blue and gasping, lungs full of fluid, and not able to cough it up. Today six have died of it in one ward alone. I heard with sorrow that we have lost Hill 60, owing to our men being poisoned by gas. I also heard that we borrowed gas from the French and fired four rounds of it yesterday, but we've not heard the result. There is a good deal of firing tonight … if only we could do really well and make the Germans ask for peace! We had a wounded German in yesterday – a great cruel strong brute. The lunatics in the asylum have been very noisy today, yelling and screaming and stamping about.

May 6

This gas-poisoning is a horrible business. A man told me today that it came like water out of a spout, a greenish-yellow colour, and the men are killed instantly and lie dead in heaps. Only those who have just a small dose of it are able to get away at all, and still many of them die.

May 7

About 12 minor cases in the theatre today, but no big ones. Monsieur le Directeur has made us a great offer – we may use the lunatics' bathroom twice a week, for one hour, which means four of us bathing at one time, as there are four baths in one room. I don't fancy bathing in company, but as I have not sat in water deeper than an inch since last year, the temptation is great. I think four of us will try it tomorrow and see what can be done in the way of screens.

May 8

Three of us went to another part of the asylum at 7 a.m., and had a deep BATH! Up to our necks in water – glorious! A dear old nun came trotting in when I was in my bath and felt to see if the water was the right heat. She thought the bath was too full and pulled the plug by a patent in the floor. I was sitting on the hole where the water runs away and was sucked hard into it!

All our heavy guns have been in action, and there has been a more violent German attack than ever before, north of Ypres, so we are expecting a rush. Heard the *Lusitania*[*] has been torpedoed with 1,500 people on board – I wonder what America will say to that. Latham's[†] cousin, who is in com-

---

[*] On 1 May the luxurious liner had left New York for Liverpool with a secret cargo of munitions for the British war effort. The Germans were probably aware of the contraband, but as the *Lusitania* was the fastest liner afloat at the time, the Allies believed that she could easily outdistance any submarine. However, on the afternoon of 7 May, as the *Lusitania* neared the coast of Ireland, she was hit by a torpedo fired by a German submarine. A second explosion broke the ship apart and within 18 minutes she had disappeared beneath the water. Of the 1,924 people on board, 1,119 perished including 128 neutral Americans.

[†] Miss K. M. Latham, who worked at No. 3 CCS with Edie, then went on to No. 16 General Hospital. In a letter to the League of St Bartholomew Nurses, Miss Latham explains how five nurses, including Edie, joined one of the 'clearing hospitals', as they were initially called, in November 1914. 'It was about 20 miles behind the firing line, and as we were the first sisters to go up so far, except those working on trains, we proudly considered ourselves pioneers. In February we moved across the Belgian frontier to a mean little town which boasted, however, a fine square and three large churches ... We were billeted at first in separate houses, but later most of us moved into a Carmelite Convent. Miss Appleton and I had adjoining cells.'

mand of some Royal Engineers (REs) quite near here, called for her this afternoon in a little one-horse country cart, and took her to cricket then tea and a band. They invited me, but we cannot both get away for the whole afternoon.

May 9

A day of most terrible fighting. They say our casualties are very heavy, but those of the enemy are heavier. Looking out of my window tonight I saw a fearful and wonderful sight – a clear, moonless, starlit night with a strong, cold wind. All along the ridge of hills which forms my horizon there was a continual sparkle and flash of light, and the loud roar of guns and searchlights go on continuously. Got a letter from Mother telling me of the death of three officers and two men of the Buffs[*] that I knew quite well. The one I feel saddest about is Private Ernest Wanstall. He used to clean our boots when he was quite tiny, then grew big enough to take a place as chicken boy to a farmer's wife. He ran away and enlisted in the Royal Marine Light Infantry and came home a week later in his uniform – a funny little object, but the joy of his mother. She grew more and more proud of him as he filled out and was drilled into a fine upright fellow. So he progressed and was always the same nice, shy boy, very devoted to all of us. Now he is shot dead somewhere in France. I hear Italy has declared war. We have had a very busy day – three convoys in and out and a heavy one arriving now. I had to 'assist' with a head operation today, and in the middle Sir Anthony Bowlby and Sir Arbuthnot Lane[†] came in to watch!

---

[*] The East Kent Regiment
[†] Sir William Arbuthnot-Lane (1856–1943) was a brilliant if unorthodox surgeon, who became Head of Surgery for the British Army. Lane pushed forward the early development of specialist plastic surgery for soldiers suffering from severe facial wounds by opening a pioneering centre at Queen Mary's Hospital in Sidcup, which treated more than 5,000 servicemen.

May 11

Excellent news of French progress, I only hope it is true. A beautiful sunset in the west, looking like glory and perfect peace, and in the east, heavy guns, flashlights and dark clouds of war! For the first time I saw one of our aeroplanes being fired at. When it is us firing at their machines, one's only fear is that they *won't* be hit, but when it is us being fired at, it looked as if every shot will hit home.

May 12

Today has been quite the last word in exasperation. The theatre was not busy, but the wards are overfull of very ill men – about 150 all calling out for drinks and mouthwashes. Some 20, not allowed to swallow anything at all, clamoured loudest. Then a heavy convoy of very badly wounded came in and then another, then the theatre again, then more dressings in the ward, then, thank goodness, an evacuation! The poor old things were off on their homeward journey and we were left beaten and worn out. There's frantic fighting going on at Ypres and many badly wounded Cameronians, Horse Guards and Lancers are coming in.

May 14

7 a.m. and the other three have gone for a bath, as we were on duty until past 10 p.m. I prefer not to hurry, so I am not going to go. I strolled in the garden after tea and watched two of our aeroplanes rise, bold and daring from the aerodrome, and fly straight to the German lines. They were fired on at once, but circled round, then flew over again – and were fired at once more. I saw the shells bursting – but happily well below the aeroplanes. I watched the sunset, which was beautiful, rich and golden. At dinner we have the

door open on to the garden, and from the table I get a picture of countryside and sunsets of all colours and shades. The birds are now in full song with thrushes specially noticeable. The country is most interesting and less flat than at Pop.

May 16

The slackest day we have had for a long time, so two of us went for a walk in the country, and sat on a tree stump eating chocolate and biscuits. Views all round very charming and the glass skylights on some of the houses in the towns sparkled like diamonds. An aeroplane flew over us close down over our heads, and the observer waved to us, so we did to him; wish he would give us a lift one day. Light-headedness has done a great kindness to one man in the ward. His head is smashed and he will probably die. He called to me and asked if he might see his wife once more before she went away. He said, 'I saw her and three of the children this morning, but I want to see her again.' I said certainly he might, and he went off to sleep quite contentedly. I remarked to him that it was very happy for him to have seen them, and he said, 'Oh! It was! It was heaven.' He quite believes they were here, poor thing!

One poor youngster was brought in yesterday stone cold – no pulse – perfectly sensible and horribly badly wounded. He loved all that was done for him – his warm, clean clothes, hot bottles, and hot drinks – and pleaded not to be sent away with the others. I promised he shouldn't be. He smiled very sweetly and went happily to sleep, and never woke again in this world. Some deaths are so calm and happy, others just the reverse. We had one poor lad – a Cameron Highlander – with a bullet in his lung, which could not be extracted, and every breath was an agony. For two days he was in such pain every minute that he was not under the influence of morphia. He died an agonised death, struggling for each breath, and with almost his last gasp he said, 'I'm glad my mother can't see me – it would drive her mad.'

A young officer, shot in the stomach, died the other day. He was in for two days and very cheery, thinking he would soon be home in England. When he found he was not getting better, his one desire was for his mother. He said, 'Do send for her, I can't hold out much longer.' They all die brave.

May 17

We had a convoy in at 10 a.m. and then driblets all day. I was on duty in No. 2 Ward most of the morning, then had one case in the theatre – a young officer with both legs very badly wounded and bones broken. Three Zeppelins passed over this afternoon – one was going very slowly and looked as if it had been hit. Our aeroplanes were up and after them, and signalled to the next aerodrome to do the same. I only hope they were brought down.

May 19

Ypres is dead, a silent town of broken and burnt houses and destroyed streets. The padre told me that unburied bodies lie all about the place in a scene of utter desolation. An occasional shell comes over, otherwise all is finished. We have had a very quiet day and only admitted a few sick, but now, at 10 p.m., wounded are coming in. A man who was brought in three days ago shot in the spine has been dying by inches – nay, sixteenths of inches – ever since, and is not dead yet. His brain and abdominal muscles are the only unparalysed parts of him now.

May 20

Two convoys came in during the night, so the ward was full when we went on duty. Slack since midday, so off in the afternoon and went for country walk with Latham. Sat in hot sun and read the paper and my *Omar Khayyam**. It was lovely, lots of birds singing, aeroplanes flying about, buttercups and daisies full out. The aeroplanes look like great live birds, they squat on the ground, then rise, and soar high and skim about, then in a few moments dive to earth again and settle, then off again. It only takes them a few moments to reach the German lines – they see what they want to, and home again, then off to spy out something else. The spine man died this evening, and his brain was the last thing to lose its senses. I have never known a more sad and slow death. The poor man was talking to me up to an hour before he died.

May 21

We still have in about a dozen abdominals, some getting better but some dear, cheerful, brave things, dying slowly. Whenever I have a very ill patient – generally abdominal – I always give him a clean handkerchief. I don't know why, but they love to have it. I gave a handkerchief to one today and he said he hoped he would not be sent on from here, as I was like a mother to him. We went for a walk in the rain this morning towards where our big gun, 'Grandmama' is hidden – spitting fire like a fury at the Germans.

---

* Edie was probably reading Edward FitzGerald's Victorian translation of around 100 poems by the eleventh-century Persian scholar, which became known as *The Rubaiyat of Omar Khayyam*.

May 24

Colonel Bewley came to tea, and told us that Bailleul is to be shelled in three days' time. I felt very frightened, but tried to make myself realise that God is over all and can stop it, or keep us safe – or do just what He likes. Only 13 patients in until this evening, but all very trying and fidgety.

May 25

We had quite the busiest night imaginable. The Germans poisoned hundreds of our men yesterday and our hospital was filled, emptied and overfilled again. There were men lying on stretchers in the garden, in the grass, and even in the patch known as the duck pond. The cases inside were

'There were men lying on stretchers in the garden . . .' British casualties of the gas attack on Hill 60 near Ypres, here receiving treatment at No. 8 Casualty Clearing Station, Bailleul.
Photograph © IWM Q114867

very bad indeed and died like poor flies all night. We evacuated at 2 a.m. and promptly filled to such an extent that I
had 163 in a ward supposed to take 60, as well as 16 very bad
officer cases – and only three ward sisters available. One
dying boy was saying, 'I cannot, cannot, cannot.' 'Ye canna
what?' asked O'Neill, the Irish orderly. 'I cannot … pray,'
repeated the boy. 'Ah thry …' persuaded O'Neill, 'twill
make ye barra.' Quite true – I heard it all.

May 26

Overnight found the ward full of wounds to be changed and
dressed, and *all* demanding drinks every five minutes. We
evacuated 150 at 2.30 a.m. and at 4 a.m. filled and overfilled
again with badly wounded, so had the double dose of changing and dressing. Two Taubes and a Zeppelin passed over us
last night – and we think the Zep must have dropped an
incendiary bomb about two miles behind the trees, where
we saw a huge flare of fire in the sky.

Came off duty at 8.30 and found a colonel with a little cart,
waiting to take us for a drive. We went all round by Locre and
Reninghelst and saw countless columns – Royal Garrison
Artillery, Royal Field Artillery, Royal Horse Artillery – all
going to the front. The men found us rather an unusual sight
and stared and saluted, and some went so far as to cheer.

May 28

An awful accident happened near here yesterday afternoon,
one of our own hand grenades factories blew up by accident,
more than 1,000 civilians and some Tommies were killed
and we had in the wounded. One died in the night, they
were horribly badly wounded. We heard the explosion at
5 p.m. and hopped out of bed to see what we could, and saw
a huge column of grey smoke, solid and high in the air. Small

convoys came in throughout the night. Feel the news in general is very depressing, we don't seem to be gaining anything at all, but we must take what comes to us after doing our best. Another ship lost in the Dardanelles too!* Wish the war was over and we had won.

May 29

In the asylum, we are on top of a high hill, overlooking pretty countryside, and I have spent the last hour standing

Many buildings were adapted as makeshift hospital wards. This photograph was taken by Edie's great friend and colleague Kate Maxey. The location is not certain but is probably the upper floor of the Casino in Wimereux, where Kate was posted in 1915.

Photograph courtesy of the Maxey family

---

* Probably a reference to HMS *Majestic*, which had been torpedoed the previous day by German submarine U-21, just two days after the same submarine had destroyed HMS *Triumph*. It would be another eight months before the end of the catastrophic Gallipoli campaign, which cost the lives of over 130,000 men.

on a table in my bunk, looking at the night. The full moon is facing this way, slowly setting in a sky brilliant with stars and softened by a few light clouds. The land all looks black – hills and trees standing silhouetted clear against the sky. The horizon is alive with rockets shooting up, guns firing, and the star shells – that show up where the trenches are – soaring up and floating gracefully down. I can distinctly hear rifle-fire cracking in the distance, but inside the asylum there's just the peaceful slumber of the officers' orderly. There are only two sick officers and they are all right, so I shall not wake him up. Peace reigns.

July 25

Just back from ten perfect days' leave and feeling disinclined for work. The Roman Catholic padre stole a chair and table and was so proud of them he took everyone to see how comfortable his tent was. While he was away asking one sister to come, some MO slid in, slung the chair up to the roof and hid the table, so when the padre found they had vanished, he started throwing stones at the only MO in sight. Meanwhile the real culprit sneaked in and filled his boots with water. The poor padre was nearly winded with so much exertion, but ran off and filled everything he could find in the MOs' tent with water. Taubes have been over and round us all day. One was brought down at Pop and the two German officers taken to No. 10 CCS. Our craft have been in hot pursuit, one returned tonight with 25 shrapnel holes in it. I have got charge of the Acute Surgical Ward – so have had quite a busy day. Four cases for op, one death and a fairish number of admissions.

July 27

Three Zeps were reported over Ypres, which was heavily shelled tonight, and we saw shells bursting over one of our own machines, which was struggling to get back owing to a 50-mile-an-hour wind. I do not like the big ward as much as being all over the place – but there is a rumour that we are to be moved to Arras.

July 29

Took in only 15 – some bad and three for op. One is a very sad case, a man with his leg pulped so much that it had to be amputated. He was suffering badly from shock and nothing seemed to touch him. This evening I gave him some strong coffee and he just roused enough to say he must go home to his family then, 'Will you pray for me and my wife and boy?' Poor fellow, I suppose he has a glimmer of a chance. I hear from home that Mrs Chambers' son Robert has volunteered for listening-post duty and is now officer in charge of his brigade. Good boy – he is doing well and I do hope may be kept safe. I expect his mother is anxious about him.

July 30

The man who had his leg off is still alive and a shade better, but he does not yet know he has lost his leg. Another has had a bullet taken out – in the ward. It went in between the ribs, slid round and was taken out of the wall of the stomach.

July 31

Rudely awakened at 6 a.m. by shots being fired at a Taube right over us. It is a loathsome way of being called – it feels as if the place is being shelled. Had a half-day off, having evacuated two of my six cases, so I called for Miss Congleton and took tea to Mont Noir and sat in a lonely spot overlooking Ypres. She had got the Royal Red Cross for the Neuve

Chapelle business* and was telling me about it. The whole
staff, orderlies and all, were worn out, the Mortuary Corporal
included, and one afternoon he had come to Miss C and asked
her to help him 'sort them out'. When she got there he threw
off blanket after blanket from the poor dead things. They had
been brought down in such numbers that some of the labels
had come off. He said, 'Did you ever see 'im before? Did you
ever see 'im?' His main job was to sort out the Roman Catholics
from the Church of England, so that each padre might bury
his own. Then he found a fresh difficulty – one man, who he
thought was an officer, had nothing to mark him as such. 'And
'ow am I to bury 'im? As a' officer – or man?' Sister said, 'Surely
they all get buried the same?' 'No, they don't,' said the bewil-
dered corporal. 'Men is 'ammered – officers is screwed.' Poor
sister, who was worn out as well as everyone else, suddenly
went hysterical and laughed and laughed. The more she told
herself it was tragic and not funny, the funnier it all looked –
and the little white-faced corporal, his hair on end, just gazed
helplessly at her. That is such a true picture of overwork and
undersleep. Taubes over us all morning, off and on. Someone
said they were taking the range of the aerodrome. I hope not.

August 2

They've evidently got our range all right, and a Jack Johnson†
was fired into our night orderlies' tent this morning. It made

---

* The Royal Red Cross is a decoration, established in 1883, for exceptional service in military nursing. It can be awarded for devotion and competency over an
extended period or for one exceptional act of bravery. Edie would later receive the
RRC herself. The Battle of Neuve Chapelle, to which she refers here, occurred on
10 March 1915, and was a second attempt to retake the village of Neuve Chapelle
from its German occupiers. Although successful, the casualties were very high –
11,200 Allied troops were killed, wounded or missing, out of a total of 40,000 men
engaged in the action.
† A low-velocity shell which created a cloud of dense black smoke, it was named
after the black US boxer who was nicknamed 'The Big Smoke'.

a huge hole about 30 feet deep and the orderlies were blown many feet away. It killed four of our best men and wounded two. It was so close to the hospital that orders came to evacuate all patients at once, and we got them out by about 3 p.m. All but Miss Denton and I went, but as mine was the heavy ward, I couldn't even get away to pack until nearly three o'clock, and finally went at six.

We have been made most comfortable and welcome in St Omer, and tonight I am lying with the cool night air blowing over me. There are about 70 little tents and a big mess tent along with a sitting room tent and cookhouse. After we had Jack Johnsons sent amongst us, an old Jesuit priest was very good to us. He told us that if it was our lot to die, it would be an honourable death, and gave us a very humble little prayer to use.

August 3

Rain and wind all day – and chilly under canvas. Heard our asylum hospital is in flames – if so, let's hope the MOs and lunatics got away first. Went over the hospital – a fine place well run. It is an old monastery and the monks are still in part of it.

August 4

After lunch four of us walked to a charming old country home with a huge garden, which belongs to a convent and is used as a place of retreat. It is a large, old-fashioned, beautifully kept place – floors all scrubbed and sanded. The caretaker and his wife and daughter live there, splendid people, typically French, merry and light-hearted. They showed us over the garden which was beautiful, so unspoilt and natural. We had tea in the kitchen, first bread, butter and jam, then coffee and two sorts of liqueur. In the evening we went to a concert given by the orderlies and one MO. Quite good. Tonight I am going to sleep with my head outside – the sky is so beautiful, and the planets, stars and moonlight are all so glorious.

August 5

The Quartermaster and Staff Sergeant Riley came from Bailleul bringing our letters and the news that all is calm there. But bombs were dropped on Hazebrouck, so the other two CCSs at Bailleul are not keeping patients – they just dress them and send them on.

August 6

Have done nothing exciting, picnicked today behind Sir John French's house in some woods and saw him coming back from his ride, looking fat and well but very white-haired.

August 7

Walked to town and saw the damage done in the Rue St Bertin by the bombs, then went to tea with the old caretaker.

August 8

If there are no more shells after the weather clears, we shall go back to Bailleul. We had a fearfully windy night – and I like tents best in weather that is not windy.

August 9

We are to go back to Bailleul tomorrow. Today has been the last word in heat. We were stifled inside our tents and roasted outside them. Went to town alone and made straight for the cathedral and sat there to cool down – body and soul. The drone of the women praying in the soldiers' chapel always does that for me. Then went to the public gardens – a blaze of bright colours and grass. Saw some very rare kind of plant called *cactus echeveria*. Wandered round the wild, wooded part and enjoyed watching the swans swimming about.

August 10

We came back to Bailleul by ambulance via Cassel, and saw the huge damage done by one shell. We are back in the same building, and are supposed to take in tomorrow after unpacking and fixing our rooms. Walked to town to tea with Miss Congleton, then took flowers to our orderlies' graves. Had scratch supper, after which Middleton and I walked along the Ypres Road and watched the firing. The gun flashes were very striking tonight among the black storm clouds. A Taube came over the town and two of our machines chased it off, but did not hit it.

August 11

Things were slack so went to No. 8 CCS and took a lesson in lace-making. While there a Taube flew right over the town and two of our machines went after it. We could hear them firing their guns at each other and watched the fight till they were both out of sight. Wonder very much how it ended.

August 12

The guns have been going all day, and we are taking in. Generals Plumer* and Porter and a few others called and seemed to like the place.

---

* General Herbert Plumer, 1st Viscount Plumer (1857–1932) was Commander of the British Second Army. Affectionately known as 'Old Plum' or 'Daddy Plumer' by his men, he is generally agreed to be one of the most impressive generals of the war.

August 13

Last night was remarkable for two terrific explosions which woke us at 2 a.m. and frightened us out of our wits. People have various theories of what they were – Zep bombs, mines being exploded or our own guns a field or two away. The whole building trembled and rattled with the vibration. Have been feeling thoroughly nervy all day, silly fool that I am.

August 14

Evacuated nearly all patients, so had half day off duty and spent it at Mont des Cats with Miss Congleton. Delightful sunny day with splendid views all over Pop, Ypres, Vlamertinghe*. A Roman Catholic padre left his binoculars with us, so we had a wonderful clear view beyond La Bassée, and the colours of the sky at sunset were glorious. As it got dark we saw them sending up coloured rockets from the aerodrome, and there were four flares burning to guide a late-coming aeroplane home. I suppose it arrived safely, as the fires were all put out quite soon. Shells were bursting over our trenches south of Ypres. The picture was vivid, and the huge volume of smoke and muck shot up into the air gave a suggestion of what was happening to our Tommies. All the time the khaki-coloured ambulances were creeping to and fro, bringing the wounded in. We saw one of our Trappist monks walking about looking quite happy, dressed in white serge robes with a brown girdle. It seems they may speak to people in wartime – but I don't think they talk to women.

* The modern spelling is Vlamertinge.

August 15

We had four Belgians among our wounded, their families were in Liège with the Germans there, and they had not heard from them for ten months. However, they seem very confident that the war will end this winter.

August 18

This place is a marvel at rumours. The latest is that one of our big caterpillar guns is being fixed a field away from us, and that we shall have to move as the firing will break our windows. Next, an officer in the ward told me that we sisters of No. 3 were nearer the firing line than any others – and it wasn't right that we were 'in the field'! There is a huge gun firing now – it simply rattles this place and we hear the whizz and whirr of the shells. Took in half a wardful, dressed and evacuated them, then immediately got more badly wounded in.

August 19

A very busy day – and no evacuation. Guns and rifle-fire sound very near – and the flashes very bright. A big gun has just been taken past on a cart, being shifted to a fresh position under cover of darkness.

August 20

Went to tea at No. 8 and met Captains Ormrod and Phillips. They suggest a whist drive and say they will take us to see the shells bursting after.

August 21

Took in about 114 – not many after the 2,804 we have had, but most in my ward are bad and seven very bad. Some, I am afraid, will die. All leave is stopped.

August 23

Yesterday was the clearest day on record through the war, and the men in our observation balloon discovered three German batteries. An officer in the ward says they have got the range of 15 batteries, which they will shell when we make an attack. We hear that a good many German men-of-war have been sunk. Good luck to them.

August 24

Six of us went to a concert in the town this evening, given by the 12th Division, and enjoyed it very much. An officer and one man came in from the trenches to sing, then went back. Some of the men were music-hall professionals in peace-time. There were no lights in the concert hall – so they borrowed motor- and bicycle-lamps and two Tommies behind screens shone lights on the performers. The hall was packed with officers and men and there were 12 of us sisters – so luckily only one song was at all risky.

August 26

Very busy morning – two men are dying and many, many dressings to do. Day *intensely* hot and hazy. Our Sister-in-Charge does not approve of us taking part in the sisters' egg-and-spoon race at the inter-clearing-station sports on Saturday, so we watched the sisters at No. 8 practising for it instead.

August 27

Only admitted 15 or 16, but three were dying and one was screaming with pain. All had bad wounds which took a long time to dress and some had to be dressed twice because they bled so. One of the dying was shot clean through the middle of the forehead – his brains were pouring out and he had fits at intervals of no more than ten minutes all day. Another, a Canadian, had been doing some cavalry drill and two horses charged each other, killing one man and concussing and breaking the back of my patient. I think he will die tonight. The third was shot through the stomach and is sick and in agony all the time.

August 28

We had a lad of 18 in with a fractured skull this morning, and two hours later his brother came to see him. I was certain it would be an elder brother, but to my utter amazement a small, unbroken-voiced, blue-eyed creature of about 15 came in. I asked him how old he was, and he said – standing at salute – '18 ... regimentally.' A poor little creature not much older was brought in dying from a stomach wound – he only lived one and a half hours. He asked me to write to his father and say it was all right – he didn't mind going. Then he said, 'I have done my bit, but I didn't think I should die so young.'

The hospital sports were held in the fields at No. 8 this afternoon. No. 2 won with a score of 32. No. 8 was second with 21, and we of No. 3, badly last, with four – and it serves us right. The Sister-in-Charge objected (old fool) to us joining in – she thought it 'unladylike'. In fact she was terrified of displeasing Miss McCarthy*. The officers of No. 8 did the entertaining and did it well and Miss Congleton, Thompson, Captain Toms, Captain Stirling and I had a gay tea party in our corner of the tent.

August 29

Only two patients in my ward now. Church at 7 a.m., and the padre's voice was hoarse from shouting at the sports. Major Ray took the service. He wishes in future to be called 'The Rather Rev' – he thinks he had better not have 'Very Rev' yet. The war is making a big noise tonight. Much rifle-fire and our own guns sound so near we can hear the shells travelling through the air.

August 30

A new book for my journal arrived with Mother's love, so I had better start it – and trust to luck the copying in of stray, loose notes I have made before.

August 31

Major Ray was telling me that one night when he was with a regiment, there was nothing much doing – only snipers,

---

* Dame Emma Maud McCarthy (1859–1949) was by this point Matron-in-Chief to the British Expeditionary Force in France and Flanders, stretching from the north coast to the Mediterranean, and was responsible for the nursing of hundreds of thousands of wounded men. Popular with the nurses, the troops and the medical hierarchy, the much-decorated matron was a supremely gifted organiser and communicator. Edie and Dame Maud clearly had great respect for each other and maintained a wartime correspondence. In her diary McCarthy refers to Edie as 'a woman of considerable experience' and after the Armistice Edie joined her staff in Boulogne, where she stayed from February 1919 until her demobilisation that December. In 1923 Dame Maud persuaded an initially reluctant Edie to join the Territorial Army Nursing Service.

sniping on both sides. At last a voice from the German trenches said, 'For God's sake stop it and let's go to sleep. If you won't fire – we won't.' So they all stopped and went to sleep. I understand all the trenches are named – there's Harley Street, Brompton Road, Piccadilly ... They are ordered to name them that way. I heard they have been shelling in St-Jans-Cappel today – so I am glad we did *not* take our off-duty walk there. There is a baseball match at No. 8 today, which I hope to dodge. I would rather learn lace-making than watch rounders. So had my lace lesson in Bailleul and found it most interesting – but a little bewildering.

September 1

Captain Shepherd came to tea, he is Aide de Camp to the general commanding 8th Division. He and the General were both nearly killed yesterday as they were up at the trenches when a German mine blew up. While there they saw one of our aeroplanes brought down in the German lines – both airmen killed. I stayed to dinner at No. 8 – and had a very black walk back with no light at all from Heaven above or Earth beneath to show up the irregularities and holes in the road. I was terrified of a man whom I heard but could not see, who was keeping pace with me, whether I went fast or slow. At last he struck a match and I saw it was one of our own airmen, and I gratefully walked the rest of the way with him.

September 3

Three sisters got their marching orders today – Tully and Coulter for No. 8 General Hospital, Rouen, and Charles-worth for No. 3 General Hospital at Le Tréport. Very sorry they are going. I have been here months longer than they have, but am very glad it is not I being moved. I came off duty at two o'clock to take Miss Tully's place on night duty. So far we have taken in two officers, three stretchered men and two cars of 'sitters'. We may get a heavy convoy later of 'sick' after all this rain, and 'wounded' after the firing. There was a heavy bombardment by our guns this afternoon and evening – easily 40 shots a minute – bang – whirr – whizz – bang – whizz – so loud, and for such a long time. This place simply rattled with it. The Germans have been shelling our trenches too – shells looked to be bursting right in them this evening. The Royal Naval Division have charge of observation balloons and the men sometimes stay up for 20 hours at a time. When it is windy the balloons lurch and wobble horribly and make them very seasick.

There is a man in the ward who is going back to duty tomorrow. He may be well as far as his wound is concerned, but he is very nervy. He shouts out in his sleep, and thinks this place is surrounded by Germans. The three who are leaving at 8 o'clock this morning had a joy-ride to Pop yesterday – they say the big church is a good deal knocked about, and one in three houses is smashed, but there are still a few shops open and people about.

4.15: Dawn is breaking and there is another big bombardment going on. I have been watching the flashes as they dart up and there is a constant thunder of bangs and whirr of shells. The guns are big and close, and the brickwork of this building shivers when they fire.

September 4

Saw five sisters off to the base yesterday – three from here and two from No. 8. There are only four of us now until our three new ones arrive. Had a lace-making lesson yesterday morning and brought my pillow back in the pouring rain –

no joke. I have been making lace in my spare time tonight
and had to unpick three times, but I think it is all right
now.

September 5

A very quiet night on the ward – there are three dying, but
the rest are getting better. The guns have been very loud
again tonight. Since we have had big ones round us, we have
had torrents of rain, perhaps the firing causes it. When they
started at six o'clock last night I was asleep and woke with
a tremendous jerk. I thought my own door had banged, but
it was only the guns.

September 6

Got up at 6 p.m. and went for a walk with Miss Congleton –
am paying for it now by being abnormally sleepy. Miss
Clements, who has arrived to replace Charlesworth, thinks
I ought not to have been at a clearing station so long, as 'it
doesn't give other people a chance'.

Went shopping with Miss Congleton yesterday morning
and bought fruit and flowers in a charming old garden. We
had to wait for some of the things, so we sat on a round white
stone which we thought was the well-cover, admiring the
sunshine and the beauty of the sky, until we became aware
of a horrid smell and realised we were sitting on an open
cesspool! I saw a gaudy and pathetic sight in the town – the
funeral procession of a child. First came the acolytes carrying a mace and incense, then a priest and three children, one
carrying a huge cross and the other two on each side holding
ribbons that streamed from it. Behind that was the coffin,
borne on the shoulders of four little boys, still in shorts and
socks, about ten years old. The coffin was covered with a
blue satin pall, and on it stood three metal crowns. Then

came a long line of women and children – but no men.
Perhaps they are all away at the war.

September 9

Went for a lovely walk yesterday morning through the fields
towards Neuve Église. In the far distance somebody's guns
were booming, but nearer, a regimental drum and fife band
was practising. Close round me the birds were singing and
the hops smelled strong. I enjoyed it until I was so sleepy
that I had to march in time to the music to get myself
moving to come back.

September 12

A busy night with some quite badly wounded people in. I
learnt another stitch in lace-making – a half-stitch – and
made about six inches of lace in the night as the only means
of keeping myself awake between spells working in the
wards. I have had a letter from Miss Coulter. She and Tully
are loathing being at Rouen at a general hospital, but we
must all be prepared to take our turn at everything.

I am now sitting in a field by a garden of ripe hops – the
day is perfect. I wish the war were over. Our heavy guns are
making a great noise pummelling away, and a German aeroplane is being fired at. Earlier I saw three small French boys
who pleased me very much. The biggest one was drilling the
other two and giving all his commands in English. The two
drilled as correctly as any full-blown soldier – it was quaint
to hear the two small objects ordered to 'form fours', 'right
wheel', 'quick march', 'on guard', 'as you were' ... Some
Tommies were watching them and were delighted.

It is not surprising that some of these people are spies.
Walking through their horrid slums, these dirty, badly nour-
ished creatures stare at us as if to say, '*You*, in your clean

clothes! What have *we* got?' I fancy a good dinner means more to them than who wins the war. They would live equally miserably under the government of any nation.

September 13

Very quiet night, so chiefly washed stockings and made lace to keep awake. We watched an exciting air duel between a German and an English aeroplane. The German aviator was hit – not by a shell, but by the Maxim[*] of the aeroplane who was duelling with him, which was one from our own squadron, piloted by Captain Miles. He had to tilt his aeroplane right over on its side to work its Maxim and had to shoot straight upwards to hit the enemy. When it was hit it fell like a stone and landed at Steenwerck in a Canadian camp. The German officers fired their Maxim on the Canadians to give themselves time to start off before being taken prisoner and killed one Canadian. The rest were so infuriated they fired two volleys and killed both Germans. One was very smart, wearing all sorts of decorations including the Iron Cross. Our airmen are sorry they were shot – they think the Germans will make it an excuse for shooting our airmen when they are brought down in German territory.

September 14

I have been watching five nuns and three orderlies washing soldiers' shirts in a huge tub in the courtyard of the convent at No. 8. The men were working the washing machines and mangle and they were all chatting happily together – until a

---

[*] The first automatic machine-gun was invented in the US by Hiram S. Maxim in 1884 – a water-cooled barrel fed by a fabric belt. He demonstrated it to the British, who did not immediately take it up, but the Germans did, producing their *Maschinengewehr*. Eventually the British Vickers machine-gun was based on his model.

bell rang. Then the men stopped talking, one nun said prayers and the other four asked the Virgin to hear them at the end of each sentence. Then they went on with their washing. It was quite picturesque – the garden is old-fashioned and rather suited the nuns with their clogs and quaint headgear. We hear that a big push is to be made this month and we three hospitals are putting up 50 marquees each to be prepared for a rush.

September 16

There has been tremendously heavy firing tonight. It only lasted half an hour, but made such a noise and rattled the place so much that some of the sisters got up to see if it was the Germans coming. They must have been tight asleep to think that, because we could hear the whizz of the shells *after* the explosion.

September 17

The town is to be closed from the 20th – no civilians to enter or leave it, and no market to be held – to allow for the passage of troops. Perhaps after all I am lucky to get my night-duty spell done now, as I expect next month will be much busier than this. I wonder what we are going to do – let's hope it will be a successful push.

September 20

Miss McCarthy came yesterday and told Miss Denton she was going to move me soon as I had been here a very long time. I wish she would mind her own business and let me mind mine. An aeroplane has just shot up in pursuit of a German one – the anti-aircraft guns are shooting at it too. Captain Bell Irvine had a nasty accident yesterday, his aircraft engine went wrong and he fell crashing to earth. Luckily he is a splendid pilot and saved himself all injury except a scratch, and his machine can be repaired.

I made about two inches of lace tonight but was kept rather busy with a dotty pneumonia case. He has rather a down on me because he says he only came in to see how I was getting along, but I have kept him all this time. All the same, I'll be sorry to leave this unit and wonder where I will go next ... Rouen or Boulogne, I suppose.

Dame Maud McCarthy, Matron-in-Chief of QAIMNS, looking every inch the formidable woman she must have been.
Photograph: Olive Edis © IWM Q7991

September 22

The town is now closed and hundreds and hundreds of troops are passing through on their way up – it is a sickening and heart-rending sight! These long columns of fine, healthy, cheery men march so gaily to the music of drum and fife bands – but they must know that a great many will not come back and a great many more will be spoilt, with heads smashed, or short of a limb.

I had a lace lesson this morning and was much interested in stories a little girl was telling me of when the Germans were here. A great many of the inhabitants were disloyal and cheered, '*Vive les Allemands*' when the Germans marched in. So I have made up my mind never to buy a farthing's worth again at a shop I used to deal at. At Méteren*, about two miles away, a little boy ran in to tell his mother the Germans were here, then went out again to look at them. When the mother came out they jeered at her and asked her where her boy was. She said she didn't know – and they uncovered a hole in the side of the road and showed her the child, lying with his throat cut†. Then they cut hers and put her beside him. The inhabitants of Lille were made to nurse the German wounded, and three girls who were there said that one day three German, three English and two French wounded were brought to their house. The officer said the Germans were very ill and must be well cared for – then he took the French and English into the garden and shot them – and buried them *before* they were quite dead.

I hear there is to be a bombardment at dawn. I shall soon know, as it is only two hours to dawn now. There was

---

* The modern spelling is Meteren, with no accent.
† There were many lurid stories of German atrocities in Belgium and France, encouraged by the British for propaganda purposes. Research after the war tended to disprove these, notably Arthur Ponsonby's 1928 *Falsehood in Wartime*.

a big bang at ten tonight that they say was one of our own big guns – it rattled this place so much that I made a special visit to see if it had frightened any of the very ill patients.

Dawn is showing in the east and great booms are coming from that part of the horse-shoe of guns that surround us – and everything indoors that will rattle is rattling at each fresh boom. As dawn lights up more of the sky more guns will begin, but at present their flash would give away their position too badly. I can hear rifle-fire in the distance when I am at the window … I wonder where those poor creatures are – the hundreds of young ones, unbaptised with fire, who went up yesterday. Braveness and good luck to them now.

I heard that not far away, several men had been billeted on a farm, and every night men on picket duty were shot by a sharpshooter. They could not find out where the sniper hid himself until one day they caught him red-handed. Lo and behold, it was their host. He farmed and talked to them during the day, then crept out with his rifle and sniped at them at night. So like them!

September 23

I don't think we have ever had such a continuous rumble and thump of guns as tonight, sounding like an angry woman banging at an iron door. Now, at 4.30 a.m., the nearer ones are waking up and joining in. The windows and doors have kept up a gentle rattle all night, which has been uneventful except for one mental patient, who has been like a religious maniac all night, deploring his evil ways and declaring he is doomed. An officer told me today that our whole line was ready for the big push – they were only waiting for orders giving them the date and time.

September 24

Two poor things were brought in tonight with smashed heads – one already dead, the other dying. The guns are quieter but still going most of the time – early yesterday morning they were going at the rate of 62 a minute or more for three-quarters of an hour. No lace tonight, as have a horrid bad headache.

September 25

Tonight has been quite a revelation of what war can be like. All the guns in the horse-shoe shape round us have been going without ceasing, and it has been a panorama of vivid flashes from the guns and the huge bursts of fire where shells

Artillery fire lighting up the night sky. This was taken during the bombardment of Beaumont Hamel at the Somme, but the night-time bombardments that Edie witnessed while she was with No. 3 CCS would have looked very similar.
Photograph: Ernest Brooks © IWM Q751

are bursting – then rumble, thud, rumble, roar – throughout the night. Walking past the windows is like going past a fence with chinks, where the sun glints into your eyes a few times every second. There is a huge fire blazing just behind the trees about a mile off and it is quite the biggest bombardment I have seen. I shall be surprised if we do not fill up after it. We are quiet so far, but No. 8 are taking in. In the intervals of watching the bombardment I am making lace and writing.

September 26

Our army made a push*, and we acted as overflow for the stations that serve the Second Army. All the hospitals here were soon filled.

September 27

The news on the whole is good – we seem to have advanced a little, and taken a great many prisoners, and the French have done splendidly. The wounded are not nearly as bad as those we had from Hill 60, but perhaps the worst have gone to Merville, Sillars and places down south. Went for a walk this morning to Méteren, where the graves are of the Warwicks who were killed there†. They are pathetic little cemeteries, situated in turnip and potato fields or in people's gardens.

September 28

News is excellent – we and the French have advanced all along the line, by five kilometres in some places, so our

---

* The Battle of Loos, 25 September to 14 October 1915.
† Eleven men of the Royal Warwickshire Regiment were killed in an attempt to retake the village of Méteren (just 3 km west of Bailleul) from German occupation in October 1914, and were buried in the local cemetery.

casualties were not in vain this time. We still have one
young officer who was too ill to travel yesterday – he's
suffering from a lung wound and badly from shock. He
cannot sleep, even with the help of morphine, and keeps
on muttering, 'The men were in such horrid shapes',
'Little bits and big bits of men', 'Get the men in – they
will all be killed', and so he rambles on. His mind has
never left the battlefield, and he does not look much like
getting over it. However, youth and a strong body can
stand a good deal.

September 30

No evacuation today, so we have the same 'family' as last
night. The man with most of his insides outside who was so
very ill died during the day, and tonight another, who was
shot in the lungs is dying, I am afraid. A funny old daddy
who was kicked in the stomach by a horse is also very sorry
for himself – but I think he is doing quite well. It has been
raining on and off for 48 hours and it is like walking about in
a duck-pond – gumboots, mackintosh coat and skirt are
needed. I made lace at No. 8 this morning and left my pillow
there as it was too rainy to carry it back.

A man in the ward told me what an abject picture some
Germans made who were giving themselves up – they were
trembling like leaves, shambling along, some with hands up,
and all more or less wounded, ragged and hungry. The news
tonight is quite the best we have had – three divisions, cavalry and all of the French have broken through the German
lines at the Champagne District and have got them on the
run – long may they stay so! The French have taken the
three front lines of trenches at Souchez, and we and the
Russians have also done well.

October 1

Last night was a busy one, we did not evacuate until 11 p.m., then two men were very, very ill, and one died. Was glad to come off night duty. Spent my first half day in the town at No. 8, where I sewed, lunched, then came back. Had an hour's gramophone and then to bed with some deadly illness – a chill, I think.

October 5

The guns have been very noisy all day, with shells bursting about five miles off. We hear they are shelling the road, trying to get our troops moving up. One poor wretch came in with a self-inflicted wound, and has been taken to a hospital for those unhappy men who must await their trial. He's such a highly-strung, nervous youth, one can only feel very sad indeed for him. One wonders how one would have borne oneself in his circumstances . . . I have been to No. 8 tonight and find poor Miss Coulter is really ill, she has some horrible form of neuralgia that comes on in agonising attacks every half hour or so. After what she has been through the last eight months, I don't wonder at any sort of breakdown.

October 6

Off duty from noon to 5 p.m., so lunched at No. 8, made some lace and had tea there. A Taube was brought down quite near here a few days ago – wish I had seen it! A silly fool of an orderly watched the whole thing and never told a soul. We have rather a trying Canadian patient who wants to know his temperature and the drugs used in his medicine all the time. If he were not so ill and badly wounded I would feel irritated by him.

October 7

We have taken in around a hundred – chiefly Canadians. Two poor men had wounded spines; one is dead and the other dying. It's cold and damp with little sunshine, and I was so grateful to receive a parcel from home of warm clothes and pyjamas.

October 8

I was dressing a man who had been shot all over the place, including his left eye. I told him I was afraid the eye was done for. He simply said, 'Oh, well, I shan't have to shut it for shooting next time.' There is a charming variety of little carts in this town, from the size of an ordinary goat chaise up to a big donkey cart. They're drawn by one, two, three, four or five dogs of any kind, and sometimes there's an old man or woman perched on it, driving.

October 10

I am staying late on duty to help with the first night convoy. I wish it would hurry up and come, as I want to go to bed. One poor man who came in this morning, shot right through the head, is trying hard to die, but it's taking a long time. We wouldn't allow an animal to remain alive in the condition this poor fellow is in. He can scarcely breathe for all the brain matter that is oozing down his throat, his whole head is in a hopeless state and he makes a terrible noise all the time.

October 13

I met Colonel Christie over tea at No. 8, and he told us about when they had their headquarters at Ypres in a dugout. The Germans knew they were there somewhere and were always trying to locate it to shell it. The shells fell closer and closer and at last they shook the dugout so violently that all the acetylene lamps went out*. They dared not use paraffin in case of a shell coming right in. He said the language was appalling! The officers would be reading or writing, then every few minutes were left in total darkness. Theirs was an old dugout that had been made by the French early in the war and had become very thin on top, so it was not at all bombproof. They wondered which would be better – to remain old-looking and unsafe and hope not to be hit – or to have loads of earth put over them, which would have made them safer but more noticeable. They chose to take their chance with the old grass-grown roof, and were only hit by small shells twice.

October 14

Another sister went this morning, and Latham hurried in to say goodbye – she has orders for No. 8 Station, Wimereux. So all my old friends are going and I expect I shall be sent *toute suite*. I did not go to bed until 4.15 this morning as we had a bad abdominal op in the theatre until 2.30, then I helped with the convoy in from Kemmel. Our men attacked the German trenches to discover their strength – they found only a few, but quite enough to wound hundreds of our men with their Maxims and rifles.

October 16

We had a rather busier 'taking-in' day with some serious abdominals who were operated on and are now doing badly. But if the intestine is like a badly damaged inner tube of a

---

* Also known as carbide lamps, the simple apparatus burned acetylene gas, the product of a reaction between calcium carbide and water.

bicycle, with tears and holes all along it, the operation gives them their only chance of survival, albeit only a slender one. Major Ray took fifteen inches out of one man, and four during each of two further operations.

October 17

Went to town in the evening with Lawton and Constable, to the Canadian service at the theatre. We were just in time for the last hymn, 'Abide With Me'. It sounded fine played by their brass band, and they played on for about an hour after the service – all sorts of things, but chiefly patriotic music. About five weeks ago some of the Canadian Battalion thought they would like some music and set to work to form a band. They collected £60 among themselves and sent to England for instruments, and now have a good band going. The theatre is a huge hall with a stage, all hung round with flags, and it was rather a war-like looking place last night, packed with officers and men in all stages of cleanness and dirtiness, including some who were in the middle of a march. The sides were lined with rifles, axes and all the equipment brought in by those who were on the march. The audience loved the music and for the most part looked cheerful. There were only six women – two of us, three sisters from No. 2 and one from No. 8 – but we get used to being very much in the minority. The music was most refreshing, and I only wished the poor fellows who lay dying in our hospital could have heard it too.

On the way home we met a battalion coming in from the trenches for a rest – a ragged, sandy-looking crew, but very happy, singing and cheering as they marched along to the music of a drum and fife band. There were streams and streams, chiefly infantry, but some officers on horses. They looked picturesque in the moonlight, filing up the quaint narrow street, clanking their boots on these hated stones.

They were cheering for anything and nothing – they cheered when they passed us – and the little band, away at the head of the line could hardly be heard for the noise they made.

The big gun that was sitting at our gate for some time is now in position not far off and has started coughing, so this place rattles and shakes worse than ever. It is really difficult to sleep through, although it is amazing how one gets used to it.

October 18

Went with Hutchinson, Lawton and Constable to Mont Noir to get autumn leaves. Glorious it all looked, with its hundreds of soft shades and tints, the sun setting and a blue haze over all – really beautiful. I had a large lunch of steak and carrots, then we found the two from No. 8 had to be on duty again at five, so we had tea at 3.30 of boiled eggs, anchovy and sardine sandwiches, plum bread and butter and tea. So I don't want my dinner tonight – at least I wish I didn't, as it would be more refined.

October 20

A very young officer, about eighteen, came in yesterday with his poor head cracked like a nut, he died this morning. Later I received a letter from Mrs Chambers at home, telling me of Robert's death from wounds and severe concussion. He was a dear boy and I am terribly sad about it. As I was crossing the aerodrome, coming back from dinner, a sentry called 'Halt!' in such a sharp tone that I halted and stood still looking for him, but the moonlight was not good enough to show him up. I coughed in a treble voice and went slowly on. I don't think he was challenging me, but I had no fancy to be shot.

We have three men suffering from shock. One is stone

deaf, the second is not deaf but dumb and has a nervous tremor, while the third sits with the expression of a thoughtful monkey and keeps saying, 'I remember playing football – but after that . . .' I think what happened after that was that the shell broke up his football pitch and buried him. We have eight cases left over from the convoy – five very bad. One, who has had his right arm and foot and left hand forefinger amputated for gas gangrene, is now mad from septic poisoning. There's another abdominal who is dying slowly, one more who I think will die, and two head cases – both mad as hatters.

October 21

We had the two head cases trephined* in the theatre, but I am afraid the poor things haven't much chance. There were two explosions this afternoon – very loud and very near. We thought they were shells, but someone said they were our own people, experimenting. Miss Hutchinson and I went to a concert given by the Canadians in aid of British prisoners in Germany. The concert was excellent and they raised £60 in proceeds. The 'Minstrel troop' were very cleverly dressed in hospital 'blues' – jackets blue-side out and trousers white side out, with a flaming red bow at their necks. There were many staff officers there, along with the Earl of Cassillis, Sir John Stewart and Canon Scott.

October 24

We had a very young officer admitted this evening, very badly torn and wounded in a painful part of his anatomy, and

---

* A trephine is a surgical instrument with a cylindrical blade, used for drilling holes in the skull. Trephining, or trepanning, is a procedure that has been used for millennia to relieve pressure on the brain.

heavily under morphia. The man in No. 2 Ward who had 15 inches of gut taken away is dying – he is quite mad, poor fellow, and looks terrible. Major Ray came to tea and he'd been in Pop today. He says the place is deserted, but people still live in a few of the houses, although the place is shelled every day. I believe the man who was Mayor there in our day has been taken as a spy.

October 25

We should have been taking in today, but after getting only a few ambulance-loads we were stopped – instead No. 2 was taking in. This afternoon I heard why – the King is coming on Wednesday and will be taken to No. 2 as it is the senior casualty clearance station here and they want to have plenty of patients in when he comes.

October 26

It's been a glorious day, sparklingly clear with simply wonderful views. Went to town to buy vegetables for the mess and drove in in a motor lorry. At one point I noticed that every single person was looking up at the sky, and soon could stand it no longer. I got down just in time to see a Taube hit and then fall – in our own lines. The observer was killed and the pilot wounded in the head – they said he looked a mere boy, just 17 or 18. I was on duty in the ward from two o'clock to six, so made lace there for about an hour and a half, then took my lace pillow to town and had a lesson. The little girl was full of news and told me that King George had been to Bailleul today and visited the hospital. It was being kept a dead secret, so how these people get to know everything is marvellous.

October 27

We saw the King today*, quite close up, on his way to No. 2 Hospital. The whole procession had outriders, consisting of a car with two staff officers and three motor bicycles, all flying red flags, then four cars with officers in the first and the King and General Plumer in the second. Four of us sisters, four MOs and some officers of the Royal Flying Corps stood at our gates to salute the King as he passed – he looked very grave and saluted us. The road was uncommonly like a river with mud and we were splashed from head to foot, but it was nice to see him so close.

October 28

Today has chiefly been remarkable for it having rained heavily without stopping a single minute, all last night, today and tonight. Paddled into town, took a lace lesson and waded back with my lace pillow under the large German umbrella. Captain Hey came from 9 Field Ambulance at Vlamertinghe and says there are only about three buildings left there now. Last week he was going up to Ypres with two ambulances to fetch wounded, and just outside the town a shell burst close to them. It killed the driver on one side of him, wounded the padre (who was going up to bury the dead) so badly that he died a few hours later, and wounded all three men on the second car. He was the only one unhurt and it shook his nerves rather. It is so cold tonight, I could not face my bath. One inch of water covers one such a little way up and the rest shivers, so here I am in bed 'all unwashen'.

* Before he changed his German name from Saxe-Coburg-Gotha to Windsor to underline his Englishness in July 1917, George V emphasised his support for the British troops by making several visits to the Western Front.

October 29

Our two abdominals died in the night. One was Lord George Sanger's son[*] – such a charming man and so grateful for all that was done for him. I am afraid the man wounded in the chest will die too, he is terribly ill. I took my lace pillow and sat beside him working this afternoon – he liked it very much and hated me to move, even to get things for him. At three, I made him a feeder of tea with brandy in, he said it was *very* good and wanted me to have some of it, but I refused. He pressed and insisted, and was making himself breathless over it, so I did drink some from the back of the feeder, which pleased him. He is a very nice man, as most of them are.

A boy who had his leg blown off by one of our own guns is doing well. He told me all about it today – he remembers everything. He was mending a wire in front of the gun when the telephone message came for it to be fired. He did not hear the order 'Fire', and the shell blew his leg off without exploding, then went on and burst in the German trenches. He said, 'We aren't in action all day, only when the German infantry give any trouble, then our own infantry telephone back to us with orders to fire on them to quiet them. Each battery has four guns, and each gun has its own division of German trench to attend to, so the infantry telephone and say which part of the German trenches they want shelled, then the gun to be used is ordered, "Eyes front", and fires so many rounds – and if that doesn't quiet them, we go on firing.'

We took in some bad cases – one, a bomb accident, died

---

[*] 'Lord' George Sanger (1825–1911) became famous as the 'English Barnum', a flamboyant animal tamer, conjurer, showman and circus owner. A penchant for dapper dressing rather than any aristocratic connections had earned him the prefix 'Lord'.

as he was being brought in. He was quite a wealthy man who had joined as a private, and the sad part is that it was one of our own bombs. There were four badly smashed heads and now the chest man we had in three days ago is dying a slow and very painful death. I was writing a letter for the abdominal boy to his fiancée and he wanted to know if he could say he would soon be better. I told him what I thought and he said, 'Never mind, I must just trust to God. He will take care of me.' These dying men are so tired and don't seem to mind dying if only it will rest them. They are splendid people. I heard a rumour today that the King was injured while he was in the town*. The story goes that when he was reviewing troops, they cheered and startled his horse, which threw him and rolled on him. I hope it is not true.

October 31

I have a pouring, horrible cold and have had it for days. I think it is from getting hot in the wards and then going over in the rain and mud to meals – also the stone floors are not the warmest things to stand on in the theatre. I think I will skip dinner and go early to my bed. The big gun near us was trying to get the range of a crossroads at Messines yesterday. I think it must have got it because, although it is cloudy and misty today, it has still been firing. Now for my bed. There goes that old gun again – 'Lizzie' – I wonder what damage is happening at the other end of the shots.

November 1

It's All Saints' Day and it's been pouring all day without ceasing. There was a service held in the Soldiers' Cemetery

* During this visit, George V fell from his horse and broke his pelvis.

this afternoon for all our Tommies who were lying there. It was quite impressive. They had made a mound, nicely done with paths round and flowers, and a flagstaff in the middle, flying the Union Jack and tricolour flag at half-mast. Four chaplains took the service and the Earl of Cassilis and several staff officers gathered round the flagstaff. Then, all along the paths by the graves, were lines and lines of Tommies, and in another patch, officers and sisters (nine from the three hospitals). We sang two hymns – 'For All the Saints Who from Their Labours Rest' and 'Oh God, Our Help in Ages Past' – then some prayers and a splendid short address from the chaplain. It was not one to make the Tommies weep – as they so easily do. He simply said we had come 'to rejoice over the loyalty and devotion of the men who had died, not to mourn over their death', and he felt sure if they could have had it otherwise they wouldn't. It was quite true that 'we faintly struggle – they in glory shine'. After the sermon we sang 'Through the Night of Doubt and Sorrow', then after the blessing, 'God Save the King'. It was a simple little service, but I don't think one could forget it. The whole crowd of us stood singing in the pouring rain and thick mud, with the guns booming away to eastward of us and these pathetic graves, each marked by a simple wooden cross. Just outside in the ordinary town cemetery, crowds of French civilians stood watching.

November 2

We saw some reinforcements going up yesterday with some very tired, hobbly old men among them. I so wished they could have been taken out of it and sent back. Went to town this afternoon to shop for the mess. Two cauliflowers, 2lb sausage (none for me thank you!), 1lb tomatoes, 1lb grapes, a huge bundle of leeks, ointment envelopes and so on – and I was going to carry it all back in the pouring rain. Mr

Stragnel, a Royal Flying Corps officer, kindly settled it by lending me his car to do my shopping in, and we picked him up on the way back.

One charming man I was writing a letter for tonight told me he could not write very well as his education hadn't been good. His father was killed when he was a one-year-old and his mother died from the shock. He was passed from farm to farm until he was seven, when he ran away and joined a circus – then his good days began. Before that he was sometimes short of food and had only a little shirt and breeches to wear, no shoes or socks. His brother was through here a month ago with one eye shot out. German shells have been bursting very audibly today and our guns are taking their turn tonight. A Canadian who died this morning was so worried all day – he said he had to go on 'sentry' that night and did not feel well enough. After much careful explanation, I got him to understand that he was not to go on duty, but that he was going to his mother (dead) and he was delighted. He was quite off his head, poor man.

November 3

Miss Middleton and I went for a walk this afternoon and found the roads so deep in mud that we tried coming back via a different way, through St-Jans-Cappel. To our dismay the roads were worse – so bad that we had to give up and simply walk through deep mud. Our feet were entirely submerged as we put them down. We met a man and asked if we had better go back or keep on. He said, 'Go on, it's shorter, but you haven't come to the worst bit yet.' The worst bit was where a lorry had quite broken up the road and it was just a pond, but by that time we didn't care and waded through it. The traffic was constant – lorries, cars and motor bicycles – and each vehicle sent a wave of filthy mud right up to our heads.

We have four sad cases that we can't evacuate, and perhaps the saddest of all is a man with a bullet wound through his big toe. It's self-inflicted, which is why he is being detained on suspicion. Perhaps when shells are bursting all round them they feel they must do something to save themselves for the wife and children at home, and in a moment of madness shoot themselves. He has told three different tales of how it happened, the last one to his wife. 'Dear wife, I hope this finds you and the children quite well. I am slightly wounded, so don't send any more letters and parcels until I am back in the trenches. I think I shall be all right again soon. I was cleaning my rifle and, it being greasy, when another man pushed me it went off. Your loving husband, William.' His first tale was that it was done by shrapnel, then that a shell made him jump, so that his own rifle went off. Poor thing, he has my sympathy.

November 6

I am writing this beside a poor little abdominal boy. He is quite off his head today and when he does rouse up and talk, he asks me if he is being punished that he has all this pain to bear. I have tried hard to make him understand that he has done splendidly and it is an honour to be wounded as he has been. We evacuated 36 from this ward – three to heaven and one to a place where the less fortunate ones go, who are marked 'self-inflicted'.

November 7

My little abdominal boy died quite peacefully at midnight. It's been a quiet day, so went to 7 o'clock service, but not the parade.

November 9

A *very* busy day, with many in-takings, and evacuations by train – and through death. The 15 who stayed are extremely ill. In a day's work I walk miles, very quickly, being bombarded right and left with requests for water, for morphia, to be lifted up, turned over and so on, when all the time I am trying to get the routine work done.

November 10

A very busy day and much lifting of very heavy men. I'm afraid the poor dears don't know how heavy they are, or they would not ask to be lifted up so often. One of our aerodrome machines had a nasty accident today. As it came down, the wind blew it into some high trees, where one wing got caught and the engine and men fell to the ground. Luckily the officers on board were not killed, but both were concussed, and one had a dislocated shoulder and broken rib.

November 12

Today is the first time since I joined the unit that I have not been in theatre or a heavy surgical ward, and I just don't know what to make of it. Am quite pleased to have a light ward for a time, but should like to go back to Ward 2 again.

November 13

This afternoon General Porter and Colonel Geddes came to inspect the place. They want a rest camp for a regiment and think of borrowing us until something else can be arranged. Fancy being a rest camp! General Porter says we are losing 1,000 men a week – all for the want of resting them. Tonight the Bishop of Khartoum* held a confirmation in the Chapel of No. 2. Eight of our orderlies were confirmed and he gave them a very good, simple little address.

November 14

Today was chiefly remarkable for a concert, held to get some money for the Fund for British Prisoners in Germany. Mr Gregory and Mr Howe took us to it in a funny old motor that had been under fire fairly often and was not improved thereby. The 13th Battalion Canadian Scottish pipers played in the interval – ten minutes without a break. It was a glorious noise of bagpipes and drums, and they brought with them their regimental mascot – a goat wearing a handsome silver collar. While they were making that deafening noise, it walked calmly among them, sniffing them and eating little bits of dust. The first half was the Canadian Minstrels, then after the interval 'The Casualties' did the rest. They were excellent – a troop consisting chiefly of orderlies got up by Captain McKenzie at No. 2 Casualty Clearing Station. At the end we sang the 'Marseillaise' then 'God Save the King'. As soon as the first chord for our National Anthem was struck, every man in the place stiffened and stood to attention and we all sang it with great gusto.

One dear old officer on the ward is very charming. He told me last night it was such a long time since he had talked to a woman, and today the poor old thing wept and said 'God bless you' as he left. I suppose it was his long abstinence

* Swansea-born Llewellyn Henry Gwynne (1863–1957) was consecrated Bishop of Khartoum in 1908, but returned to Europe at the outbreak of war to become an army chaplain. In 1915 he became Deputy Chaplain-General of the army in France.

from talking to our kind that upset him. We evacuated all six officers in the ward and took in two more, who stayed. They belonged to our aerodrome and had had a nasty accident. Their machine did not rise and would have rammed into the fence full force, but the pilot had the presence of mind to steer towards our gateway. The wings smashed into the gateposts and were broken up. One man was badly shaken and the other had a nasty scalp wound.

November 16

Have received orders to proceed on arrival of relief to General Hospital No. 1, Étretat. Constable and Bond from No. 8 are going too. A tremendous bombardment is going on tonight and it sounds like continuous heavy thunder. Last night I slept in the officers' ward. There were no patients in and I didn't care a straw if the orderlies came, so I put a screen round bed no. 9 and slept there. Then the orderly officer came in at 11.30 and said he was going to sleep here as it was too cold on the stretcher downstairs. When the night sister tried to put him off he said, 'What are you so fussy about? There's no one here, is there?' and buzzed his torch up the ward. She, little fool, said, 'Oh no', so *he* slept in bed no. 2. He was quite a long way off – but I lay stiff as a mackerel until I heard him snore before I dared move. I was up at six o'clock and away before anyone was any the wiser.

November 18

We left Bailleul at 8.08 and got to Boulogne in time for lunch. I can't remember all the places we came through – Wimereux, Le Tréport, Le Touquet, Abbeville, Étaples (swarming with hospitals in huts, houses, hotels and under canvas). Lady Gifford's place, that she has lent to tired

nurses, looks lovely – all wild sandhills. When we got to
Abancourt we decided to go no further and put up at this
'*buffet*'. It's very comfortable – a room each with a *ripping* bed
and two mattresses, which is lovely after having none.
Madame made us an excellent omelette this morning – the
rolls and butter were good too. The whole life at the inn
reminded me of *The Scarlet Pimpernel*. All the time French
officers and soldiers were in and out, sitting down and banging on the tables until they were waited on. Some were
dressed in most glorious uniforms and fur coats and the
suave French people were serving everyone so attentively
and politely. There is a thick white fog this morning and the
snow that has been falling the last four days is still
unthawed. We are going through pretty bracken-covered
woodland and ploughed fields white with snow.

November 20

I called on Miss Clements, the Matron of No. 8, in her
office and had a little chat – then she invited me to spend
the night there instead of putting up at a hotel. So, after
taking the others to town and fixing them up at the Hotel
Dieppe, I returned and was made welcome by Gascoigne –
an old 'Bartsite'* whom I only knew by name before. Tully,
Coulter, Matthews and I dined with Matron then had a tea
party in Tully's hut. I went to bed at 10.30 in the sick sisters' ward, and was much entertained and amused there. A
VAD took care of us and warmed my bed (my first bed
apart from Abancourt for over a year). At 6 a.m. she brought
me tea and filled my bath – a proper big one. It seems that
sisters can be just as exacting, fussy old patients as anyone
else!

I walked in to Rouen to see the cathedral which is

---

* A graduate or employee of St Bartholomew's Hospital.

beautiful, especially the little chapel behind the altar. I saw the place to advantage, standing at the western end and looking up the long aisle and chancel, where a dear old priest in magnificent robes was conducting a service. The organ was playing some soft chant, and there were little choirboys in their scarlet, with the sun shining on them from the side windows – it was really beautiful.

Volume Two

went to the Cathedral for a short time alone – I enjoyed it
It is no use for me to try to describe Rouen Cathedral, it is too great
a task, but it is beautiful, specially the little chapel behind the Altar.
I saw the place to advantage – Standing at the Western end
& looking up the long aisle & chancel. where a dear
old priest in magnificent robes was conducting a
service; the organ was playing some soft chant –
& the little choir boys – in their scarlet & all with the sun
shining on them from the side windows – was really beautiful.
Etretat. We arrived here at lunch time y^r day. & were kindly
welcomed – The place is charming – cold – wild. high cliffs
rocky shores – sandhills like home – the inevitable Casino
& multitudes of Hotels. where the Casino patrons live during
the season. Found two people I knew – an old Nottingham
Childrens Hosp. nurse. & one of our batmen who
was my patient at N.O. last winter.
28th. Never spent such a calm week – for a long
time – not much work to do – have slept well
eaten well – & walked a good deal.
Our Padre is going up the line tomorrow to Bailleul or Bethune or
somewhere – lucky devil – wish I were.
29th 4 lrs to C.S. 4 to England. Off for half day –
could not do much as it was pouring with rain – & I have

Late 1915

November 21

Étretat is charming – cold and wild with high cliffs, rocky shores and sand-hills like home. There is the inevitable casino, and multitudes of hotels where the casino patrons live during the season.

November 28

I haven't spent such a calm week for a long time. There's not much work to do and I have slept and eaten well, and walked a good deal. Our padre is going up the line tomorrow to Bailleul or Béthune – lucky devil – I wish I were too.

November 29

The VADs are a source of great interest to me, they are a splendid bunch. They may be roughly divided into four sorts: 'Stalkers', 'Crawlers', the irresponsible 'Butterflyers' and the sturdy 'Pushers'. At the moment I am thinking of a 'Butterfly' who is on night duty in these wards and says with a light-hearted laugh – 'It's rippin' nursin' the men – great fun. When I was in the officers' ward I did housework all the time – great fun – but there the men are really ill – great fun.' When I show her how to do anything

fresh, she twitches to get at it and says, 'Oh do let me try –
I'd love to do that – simply love to.' She is an aristocratic
little person, most dainty and well groomed, and the
thought of her doing scrubbing and dusting all day makes
me smile.

The 'Stalkers' are nice girls, very lordly with high-
pitched, crackly voices. They look rather alarmed at some of
the jobs they have to do, but they do them well and with
good grace. By 'Crawlers' I mean the little people with their
hair done up at the back, who think they are unworthy to do
anything at all. They have an expression that says, 'Stand on
me if you like. I should be pleased to be your doormat.'
There is little to say about the sturdy 'Pusher' ones. They
are not remarkable for anything, but are quite reliable, very
strong and never forget – and they are always ready to do
every bit of work.

There is a charming boy upstairs who is just 18. He
enlisted when he was just over 15 as a drummer boy. He has
been in France since the beginning of the war and was a
bugler all through the retreat from Mons. He has been
wounded five times, shot through the chest and the stomach once, and in the arms and legs many times. He has a
bad toothache tonight and says it is worse than all his
wounds. He tells the most thrilling stories of the Uhlans[*] –
and what dread of them he had. They are great strong fellows and they carry long bamboos with bayonets at the
end – and they just dig them into the enemy without turning a hair.

---

[*] At the outbreak of war the German Army had 26 regiments of these mounted cavalrymen, who wielded 10-foot lances of steel (not bamboo) that were sharpened at
both ends to provide a double-ended weapon.

December 6

I have had cracking neuralgia, which evidently means to spend the rest of the winter with me, and it is making me loathe the place and everything else. I would ten thousand times rather be busy and have no headache. There is a legend about this place, that many years ago a poor suffering woman and her child went to a mill and asked the miller for help. He refused and she turned away cursing him. Next morning his mill was dry, and the whole stream was found pouring down the beach into the sea. Whether this is true or not, I don't know, but the stream here pours in full force down the beach and tumbles into the sea. The women of the place make good use of it, and it is a quaint sight to see them every day, spade under one arm, bundling a heavy wheelbarrow of wet clothes down to the beach to rinse the things they've washed and boiled at home. They dig deep holes in the beach which become their wash tubs, and a river of water runs swiftly through them so it is always perfectly clean.

Overlooking the beach at Étretat: Edie describes how the local women used the fresh water seeping out through the rocks on the shore to wash their sheets, which can be seen here laid out on the beach to dry.
Photograph courtesy of Brian Dunlop

December 7

A true story of Étretat is that an Indian prince once came here to visit his father. The father died and the son said his body must be cremated that night, according to his religion, and asked the Town Prefect's permission to have it done. He would not give his own consent – but telegraphed the Chief Prefect in Paris and asked his permission. He said, 'If I get no reply, ceremony will take place this evening.' No reply came, so the ceremony was performed on the beach. Half-way through, the body fell off and had to be lifted on to the pile of logs again, using poles. Next morning a telegram was brought to the Prefect. 'On no account allow ceremony.' The Prefect's office had closed at its usual early hour, and the message had been there all night. Still, no evil consequence happened. The patch of beach where the body was burnt is just opposite the Roches Hotel, where my ward is. One of the sisters wants us to get up a play for the men for Christmas! I told her I would help if needed – but oh help, I really can't see me acting! Perhaps they will find enough people without me.

December 9

Lena Ashwell's* concert party came and gave us a good selection of songs. All the voices were good and there was a clever conjurer, but to me the cream of the whole thing was the 'cello – the girl was very musical and she seemed to forget all about us, and she played beautifully. I bought a

---

* Lena Margaret Pocock (1872–1957) was a leading actress who had appeared on the London stage with Ellen Terry and Sir Henry Irving. Also a theatre manager, earlier in 1915 she had become the first person to put together companies of entertainers to travel around France and perform to the troops, often close to the front line. Her concerts contained not just music but excerpts from Shakespeare and poetry, which apparently went down very well with the troops.

cheap umbrella, and at last my longed-for mac has arrived –
so now it may go on raining if it likes.

December 11

There has been a big explosion at a munitions factory outside Le Havre, and I am afraid a great many women have
been injured. Some of our orderlies were sent to help and
eight sisters – of whom I was one – had orders to stand by.
We packed our bags and went on with our ordinary work, but
in the end we were not needed. Today is Sunday and I went
to the early service as usual – and found myself the entire
congregation. Up at No. 3, five of us supported our padre at
the early service every Sunday, but here out of about 50 no-
one seems to go.

December 16

Great excitement prevails over Christmas preparations, and
each ward is secretly doing its utmost to outshine the rest. My
men have made some lovely paper flowers and chains, and
the orderlies have stolen quite a lot of greenery – I hope they
can steal more before the 25th. Meanwhile, we have had to
be like yeast in the dough, making every one rise, with plan-
ning what we will do on Christmas Day. We think of joining
forces with the other 'Roches' floors and having games for the
men, then a short act by three of mine, a clog-dance by
another – and the other floors will raise some talent too.

December 17

The men have been very busy making decorations and now
we have yards and yards of red, white and blue paper-chains.
Also roses, purple and white irises, poinsettias and lots of
greenery ready to put up – all made of paper.

December 19

Had a half day off, so went with Wood and Burnett to Bénouville for tea. It was a pretty walk and a charming place.
The sky was wonderful, first clear and intensely blue like
Switzerland, making an excellent background for the hills
and fir trees, then the sunset and afterglow were really too
beautiful not to stand and watch, changing from gold to red,
then to purple and green, then to slate.

December 21

Very busy finding civilian clothes for three men who are getting up a little sketch for Christmas, and I have also started
thinking of feeding arrangements. News has come of a
convoy arriving during the night. If it does come we shall be
called, so I shall put my light out and get some sleep first if
possible. It's been a fearfully rough day, and one door
slammed so hard it broke a panel right out.

December 22

A convoy of 300-odd came in at midday, with 41 to me. With
settling them in and seeing about decorating there was no
time off, but it was great fun doing the decorations with 70
men in various states of health helping – only a few were
confined to bed. We have decorated in red, white and blue
as far as possible and one wall has a huge Union Jack.
Opposite that, two crossed French flags. On a third wall – or
at least the archway – a big red twill drape with 'Merry
Christmas' on it, and ornaments done in white wool to look
like snow. Our artist Wynn has painted some Christmas pictures which we've put on the walls and framed in 'snow' and
ivy. The ceiling is draped with red, white and blue streamers and ivy, and they are all very proud of their work.

December 24

It's been a very busy day – 72 patients take quite a lot of keeping pace with, added to all the Christmas preparations. I gave a little tea party and invited two of the MOs to help us fill stockings, so now we have these ready for distribution by the night nurse, and we have large stores of cake, dessert, crackers, mince-pies ... so I hope they will be happy. We sisters had our Christmas dinner tonight, which was quite a success. It made rather a pretty scene, with the big room and tables daintily decorated with flowers and ribbons, and a present in each place with the owner's name on. In orders today I learned that I am to receive sister's pay – and wear stripes!*

December 25

Happy Christmas all! Went to early service, then to the ward to do dressings, but gave NO medicines all day. After the MO's visit we gave each of them a hot mince-pie and a glass of claret. At midday they had their huge feed in the big hall, all together, then all hands cleared the decks and got ready for our concert – which the Company Officer (CO) told us to postpone, so we called it a 'dress rehearsal' and carried on.

At five they had tea, each landing feeding its own men. It was a big job feeding my 70-odd – and they did all eat. They looked rather pretty, sitting under the decorations in their blue clothes and the caps from their crackers. We iced two of the cakes and lit fancy candles on them, then after tea they

---

* QAIMNS sisters wore two red stripes on their lower sleeve to signify rank, and these were stitched to the dress material

settled down to a sing-song among themselves. The CO
came and told them a few Irish stories and I joined Matron's
party to go to dinner at the officers' mess. I did not want to,
as I was very tired, but I enjoyed it very much, all the same.
We had a good dinner with claret, champagne and port.
Then there were toasts to King George – for which we all
rose in our places – to us, the sisters – for which the men
rose – and after drinking the toast they sang 'For They Are
Jolly Good Fellows'. After dinner some of the others joined
us and we had games and music round the Christmas tree
and finally went home around midnight.

Patients and staff together worked to decorate the wards and make
them festive for Christmas. This is from the combined English and
Canadian hospital at Le Tréport, where Edie was posted in 1918.
Photograph courtesy of Jean-Luc Dron

December 27

Tonight there was a concert at the casino, which was quite
good. Captain Johnson – one of our MOs who is a New
Zealander – trained a gang of orderlies to do a Maori *Haka*

dance, all with their faces made up ... I expect the orderlies felt a bit shy about it. There was a hospital sketch too, taking off everyone – Colonel, Major, the MOs, us, the orderlies – which was much enjoyed.

December 29

We of the Roches were 'at home' for tea to a crowd – Matron, the CO, Captain Martyn, Captain Davidson, Mr Chaplin and Major Franklin – and then we gave a concert, which was got up by some of my patients and was not at all bad, then some of the sisters kindly sang for us.

December 30

Most of the sisters have gone to the pantomime at Le Havre, and I am staying on for one of them – so am going to have breakfast in bed tomorrow morning. The old car that takes them generally breaks down, so goodness knows what time they will come back. We have a man in who was in the attack on Hulluch where Robert Chambers was killed. He knew Robert and told me lots of war stories. After an attack, the stretcher-bearers were all tired out, having been carrying the slightly wounded through the trenches throughout daylight, and then bringing the seriously wounded in over the open ground under cover of darkness. A corporal of the Black Watch crawled in with a wound which had bled a lot – he'd been shot clean through the thick of the leg, and was faint from loss of blood. While he was being bandaged up, he heard some moaning from between our own and the enemy's lines, and recognised the voices of some of his men. He shouted to them and they answered, saying they were hung up in barbed wire. Nothing would keep the corporal back and he flew out and brought in five of his own men, one at a time. Once he leant against the parapet and said, 'If only I had some of my own boys here, they would help me. I hear the voice of another of mine – I must get him in,' and in spite of his condition, he went out and brought the man in. There were men in the trench who would have liked to help him, but they hadn't the pluck. There was a perfect hail of bullets round him all the time, but luckily he was not hit. The snipers were trying to get the gunners who were working a Maxim about five yards from the trench. What a gruesome noise there must have been!

1916, January 1

Happy New Year to all! About 50 of us, including the MOs and sick officers, gave a children's party last night. We had musical chairs, bumps and all sorts of tricks. In one game everyone had the name of a well-known person pinned on their back and had to guess who they were by asking questions, such as 'Am I still alive?', 'Do I write books?' and so on, until they guessed right. Then they had a new name pinned on. When the bell rang the one who had guessed correctly most times won the prize. It was a little pig, and an Irish girl won it.

January 2

Went to church tonight and early this morning too, but our padre is not a success – he has no brain, poor dear. He prays and reads and preaches on one doleful note. Tonight he took as his text 'Spare me, that I may brighten up' – which everyone thought he should apply to himself. When he was at our New Year's party, he was seen absent-mindedly sitting directly under the mistletoe. When, by people's glances, he noticed it, he was too shy to move away at once, so did it by edging off, inch by inch, and then making a bolt for it.

*

I hear that four of our orderlies are wanted higher up the line and that they are to be replaced by ward maids – and I do not look forward to the change. There are rumours that I am to go on night duty, but I don't want to. Captain Martyn has been promoted to Company Officer in place of Major Franklin, who has been made Deputy Assistant Director Medical Services (DADMS) to the Third Army. Miss Rentzsch has just come to my room to tell me my name is mentioned in Despatches!

January 4

I have had the day off, and much enjoyed it. Breakfast in bed (always a joy), then got up at about ten, bathed and went for a long walk alone to the lighthouse, then home by the Le Havre Road. It is a wonderful walk for scenery, with the most beautiful little peeps of sea, over the 'downs' in the cliffs. The hills are all colours and shades of purple, mauve, blue, green, brown, red, with dashes of bright yellow gorse, while the sea and sky were both a cold blueish, greenish grey. The sea was smooth, and the sky covered with rough clouds. I missed dinner, so had two pieces of Lil's *most excellent* plum pudding instead, then took my lace pillow into the sick sisters' room and made lace and had tea.

January 5

Have only 29 patients on my floor, so it's slack at present. I thanked Miss McCarthy for sending me to such a nice place, and she said she thought people who had been a long time at the front needed it. Miss McC was much pleased with the hospital and went off in a very good temper.

January 9

Three very charming VADs asked me to go on a little
jaunt with them in what they call the 'bus', which is really
quite a good Ford car. We went for a glorious two-and-a-
half-hour spin through pretty villages and country to
Harfleur and saw the damage done by the explosion at the
bomb factory last month. The church was a good deal
broken too, and the windows of nearby houses smashed. At
some place, dead in the country, we passed an old French
château with a moat around it, very old quaint towers and
lovely grounds. We stopped just to gaze at it for a little
while.

We halted at a place called Gonneville-la-Mallet at a
famous old inn, which had old French china on the outside
walls – plates, dishes, mugs, jugs – all stuck on with cement
or mortar. The lunch was intensely interesting, too. In the
kitchen there is a wonderful array of highly polished brass
and copper, and upstairs is quite a museum of curios of the
war. In the dining hall are many panels, beautifully painted
by different artists who have spent holidays at the inn.
Each was asked to paint a panel while he was there, and
they are shaped like a church door – some fastened to the
wall and some just standing there. Well worth a visit. I hear
there is a man about who tries to get into the sisters'
quarters, and now they have a guard outside the house. I
hope I shan't meet him on my next round. The streets are
very dark, but they are cold too, so perhaps he won't be
there.

January 12

I have moved into a quieter bedroom in the annexe of Hotel
Blanquet. It was very dirty, so I spent the morning helping
to clean it, then bathed and went to bed. Tonight a man told

me about the battle of Loos*. They had a short, fierce battle of two hours and had the Germans fairly on the run, and if our reinforcements had been there, we should have kept them going. We had six corps of cavalry – two English, one Indian and three French – all ready to gallop straight on and into Lille, but our infantrymen were too dead beat to follow them up. Reinforcements were nowhere to be found for all the telephoning, and the German observation balloon reported that we were short of infantry. The Germans were ordered to make a counterattack – which they did with great effect.

British troops advance to the attack through a cloud of
poison gas as viewed from the trench which they have just left: a
remarkable snapshot taken by a soldier of the London Rifle Brigade
on the opening day of the Battle of Loos, 25 September 1915.
Photograph: The London Rifle Brigade Collection © IWM HU63277B

* The British had suffered devastating losses three months earlier during the nearly three-week battle to retain the town of Loos, an action that was continually hampered by a shortage of ammunition and terrible weather.

The man telling me this was at Ypres while that fierce battle for Calais was in process*. Stationed high up in a wood, he could see the whole battle. The British line was very thin – almost broken – and the Germans seethed! They goose-stepped up the Menin Road by the thousand. Sir Douglas Haig† saved the situation – he brought up machine-guns and Maxims from everywhere and men from wherever he could get them. He had the guns placed in a close-formation line, and when the Germans got near enough, they fired – each gun delivering about 600 shots a minute – mowing them down again and again. They lost frightfully heavily – and of course did not break through. There is supposed to be a big attack at Hulluch tonight with bombs, trench-mortars and so on. Good luck to the attackers. I hear that No. 3 CCS is leaving Bailleul! Why was I ever moved? The orderlies have had fur coats served out to them – so perhaps they are for Serbia.

January 14

Colonel Moore is in the Honours List and five matrons and 36 sisters have got RRC. I'm sorry Miss Denne has not got one too. Being 'night super' is not all sweetness. When an orderly gets drunk, it's 'Send for the night super'. I gave my advice that, as the ward is slack, I'd let him sleep it off – and blow him up in the morning. Then the Ward Master came along, found him drunk and sleeping and wanted to run him straight in to the guardroom, but first came to ask the 'night super'. Three different people had three different opinions –

---

* The First Battle of Ypres, 19 October to 22 November 1914, not the Second Battle of Ypres which began a few days after the first entry we have from Edie's diary, in April 1915.
† Field Marshal Douglas Haig, 1st Earl Haig (1861–1928) commanded the British Expeditionary Force from December 1915 to the end of the war.

and strong ones – as to what ought to be done, but all ended up saying, 'But of course, you are night super – you must decide.' So I did, and pretty quickly too, being sick of them all. Went for lovely walk to Bénouville with Raper and Scott, then home to bed in decent time. There was a Lena Ashwell concert, but I told them on pain of death not to call me for it.

January 15

The nights are very lovely now, rough and moon-shiny and the stars big. I never knew so little of the war anywhere as in this quiet corner in Étretat.

January 17

A quiet night, the only excitement being when a man in for something quite different suddenly found both legs paralysed. The MO can't understand it and thinks he may be hysterical, but I don't agree. Yesterday I skipped my walk and bath and all such wholesome things, and went straight to bed and slept all day. It was glorious – only I wanted to go on sleeping when they called me. One poor little VAD was pathetically sleepy and very funny. Her ideas of night duty when she is sleepy are worth hearing – but she is a clever little wretch and has a sketchbook in which she has caricatured VADs in all circumstances. Tonight is freezing cold, with blue moonlight and very calm. The reflection of the moon in the sea was so beautiful, I made the sisters come and look at it. The sight of the cliffs in the moonlight is past description.

January 18

The night staff have got into the habit of inviting me to supper, and last night I supped with Thomas over in the officers' mess. Tonight I am invited to the casino to partake of crab, then apricots and cream. Perhaps tomorrow will be the Roches, but I am very content with my own headquarters at La Plage, where I feed with one VAD.

January 19

The Moon, Sirius and Castor and Pollux, and Capella and Auriga and Deneb all look lovely beyond description shining brightly on a cold night. The man who suddenly became paralysed the other night has lost all use up to the hips now. One of my patients, poor old Berrel, died at 4 p.m. today.

January 20

Four of the night people hired 'the bus' and went to Fécamp yesterday morning – but not I. I don't like being late! They had a glorious drive through pretty country and saw all over the French Hospital and the Benedictine convent, where the world-famed liqueur is made, and the famous old abbey. I would like to go there some day.

I talk to the men most nights and hear all sorts of interesting stories about when they have been at close quarters with the Germans. Once when they were billeted on a farm at Kemmel, they were worried every night by a hidden sniper, and they hunted but could not find him. One day their major told the farmer he wanted hay for the horses – the farmer was most unwilling to give it, but at last told them to take it from the hayloft. The men went up and began dragging the hay down from the highest stack of it, and the farmer came and told them very sharply not to take from there. But he was too late and they had pulled it down – and left exposed a trapdoor that led into a big pigeon cote – and sitting in the pigeon cote, surrounded by empty beer bottles, sat the sniper – a German, in full German uniform. They shot him.

Another time they – the 5th Dragoon Guards – were in a
ditch at the side of the road, and the Germans were in the
one on the other side. He said it was most exciting. They
would see the muzzle and barrel of a rifle, stealthily pushed
up and levelled down towards their ditch, then slowly the
spike of a German helmet would appear – and then it was
the moment of their lives for the one who shot first and true.

At one place, where the village was being taken alter-
nately by us and the Germans, our police found two spies,
inn-keepers who had been most jovial with the men, and
gave them beer and took no money. They were German soldiers in disguise, and when they were taken to be shot,
marched and right wheeled in a most soldier-like way. Their
inn was looted and all the furniture – chests of drawers,
counters, tables – was taken out to make a barricade across
the road. In the same village another spy was discovered by
one of our pilots, who said he had seen signalling from the
air. All inhabitants had been cleared out by then except for
one old bed-ridden man, who had been a cripple for years,
and the old woman who looked after him. But the airman
was so certain of what he had seen that he asked to see the
invalid. When they got there, he recognised it as the house
he'd seen the signals coming from, and went in. He said he
had a fancy that the invalid could beat him in a race for life
and flung back the bedclothes to find the man fully dressed
in uniform. They shot him – and her too.

January 26

Had my night off all right, and enjoyed it very much. Went
straight to bed, then was called at 1 o'clock by my little land-
lady who brought me the daintiest little lunch imaginable –
grilled steak done with parsley, potatoes nicely browned, and
apple jelly and cider to drink, followed by *café noir*. The car
came at 2 p.m., and several of us went in to Fécamp. The

scenery was beautiful and we passed some buildings and
ruins of great interest – an old French château and, in
Fécamp, some old overgrown ruins of the house of the
Dukes of Normandy. We went to the abbey, which was
being heavily draped for a mourning service for all the men
of Fécamp who have died through the war. The abbey is a
fine old place – chiefly Gothic I think – with some good old
carving and beautiful windows.

We went on to the Benedictine convent, part of which is
being used as a French military hospital. The rest is where
the Benedictine liqueur is made – the only place in the
world – and they send to every part of the globe, except to
our enemies just now. We were shown all over and it was
most interesting. In peacetime they had 400 workmen but
now many of them have gone to the war and their places are
taken by women and little girls. The men wear blue caps
and long blue smocks, the women have overalls and a belt
with 'Benedictine' worked on it round their waists. It is an
enormous concern, they make 18,000 bottles every day. First
we went through many huge halls of casks of the finished
stuff – the casks vary in size, the biggest holding 36,000 litres
each, the ends of them more than six feet in diameter. Then
we went to where pure alcohol was being distilled and the
syrup made – huge plants of machinery all about, vast
wheels joined to little ones by wide leather straps – and the
noise!

The syrup was boiling in huge copper pans about three
feet deep and five across the top. Next we went to where it
was being bottled. Two women tended a filling machine,
which fills about 18 at a time. They had to go as fast as they
could, taking away then replacing an empty bottle. Then
they handed on to two more who washed, and handed on to
two more, who worked the automatic corking machine and
handed on to two more who loaded up on trolleys. The
bottles were taken to the next department where two

unloaded and stood the bottles on the end of a long table with girls down both sides of it. The first ones cut the corks and held wet parchment over, while the next ones wired it and cut it off. The next people trimmed and stuck on labels and the next soldered metal ribbon round the neck and down the side. The next sealed the top, dipping into hot wax and sealing it, the next sealed the metal ribbon down on the side and the next wrapped them up in paper. The next stuck another Benedictine label over the join in the paper, the next loaded on to a trolley and took it to the packing room where three men were at work. There were stacks of cases there, and they have divisions made to keep the bottles from touching each other. Each case holds about two dozen bottles, and in less than two minutes the first man fixes the bits of wood, throws in the bottles, the next layer of wood and so on, and passes it to the next man to nail the box down – and he passes on to the next man to pack. There was a huge wall with names of the places they have to send things to, and there are some most unheard-of places amongst them.

After that we had tea and came home by the long coastal route. From one point we had a good view of Étretat, and apparently in February, crowds of people come from all around to watch the sun set behind the cliffs. It sinks down right in the cleft and looks very quaint[*].

January 27

Talking to a patient tonight, I found he was at No. 10 Stationary Hospital as a patient when I was there. He remembers a Prussian guard being brought in and recognised as the man who had been killing our wounded Black

---

[*] The rock arch at Étretat was a justly celebrated landmark, and was the subject of several well-known paintings by Monet.

Watch – and was tried and shot for it. Serve him right. The government is docking our sisters' lodging, fuel and light allowances – in all £57 15 shillings a year. The men are not giving up anything.

January 29

Officers are having a soirée tonight and about 20 sisters have gone, but only three from my staff. We learned that No. 14 Stationary Hospital has been burnt down and poor old Miss Congleton is Assistant Matron there! I expect she has taken it badly as she is so highly strung and has had a hard time through this war.

Jaunary 30

Nurses are the most inconsiderate wretches under the sun, they tramp about, slam doors, pull plugs to distraction, then the orphans are let loose to kick tins and play, then the paper man blows his horn, toot tooting and yelling, '*Petit Parisien*' . . . Now, at 1.30 a.m., I feel I shall bust if I don't say what is *truly* unkind – that the VAD who sits in this room will drive me to drink. She talks tracts, gives tracts and is bulging with saintly and innocent holiness to the point where I could shriek.

Went for a walk *toute seule*, in a thick, white, wet mist, then at the top of the hills I suddenly found myself in hot, bright sunshine – birds singing, blue sky, and below me, nothing but fluffy whiteness, that I felt I could jump on to like a feather bed. After a time that cleared and the day was perfect. Sea dead calm, the fishing boats looked so pretty, painted bright colours and with red sails, going out in a long line, one behind the other and making a vivid reflection in the sea. I received a letter from Miss Congleton. She says the fire was awful – too awful to write about – but no-one was hurt. They are now nursing the enterics in the compound of wooden huts. My VAD has just threatened me with reading something aloud from the *Church Times*. I can't stand it – I must make my round early. Poor little VAD. It was horrid of me to feel irritated by her – she is such a good conscientious little soul.

Edie illustrated her diaries with sketches of scenes which caught her eye, amongst them the boats of the local fishermen – a reminder of everyday life in the midst of war. The diving duck is a nice touch with its 'going . . . going . . . gone'.

At 11 o'clock a sick officer lurched into the Plage and asked 'Plege ca'nyou te' me where the shickossifers' hoshpital is?' There was nothing for it but to take my lord by the arm, and gently lead him there, along two streets and up a short hill. I did not carry a light as I did not want anyone to see me arm in arm with the poor chap, who was distinctly the worse for wear.

January 31

Went for walk along the shore and found a secret passage running under the cliff towards inland. I went along it for some distance and then came back. To bed early. News of convoy coming in today at 11 o'clock, so we shall probably be much busier tomorrow. I see by today's paper that bombs have been dropped on Paris, causing loss of life and material damage. That will annoy the French, so I should not be surprised if they did something big in the way of reprisals.

February 1

The convoy came, but there were no very serious cases – only about five on the seriously ill list. Miss Garrett has got influenza, and everyone seems to be getting it now. Went for a walk alone and was much alarmed by hearing heavyish firing, and I came in expecting to hear that a German submarine was at work off our shore. To my joy, found it was gun practice at Le Havre. I hear that Paris has been attacked again – the Germans really are asking for it!

February 4

Not a quiet night, the wind has blown a gale and roof tiles and chimneys have been flying and doors banging. Craig, our new batman, was put here to sleep as he had a temperature and felt sick, but he rose up in his sleep and walked – as is his habit when ill – and wandered off back to the quarters. The orderly and I chased after him in double-quick time, and as I didn't know where the men slept I had to hunt every coal shed and stable until I found their billet, in a loft over stores. After much anxious and fruitless searching, I found him fast asleep on his own bed. He seems much better this morning, so his night run in the rain has evidently done him good. I have taken great care of myself the last two days as have been feeling a bit influenza-ish. Been for a brisk, short walk every morning, had a good hot mustard bath over in the quarters, then rushed like a lunatic back to the annexe to my bed – and straight in between the blankets.

February 5

All wards seem to be settling down, but one young officer is suffering badly from nerves. He is so restless in his sleep, and calls out, 'Let 'em have it – turn on the gas – give it them – now – more – more – get your bayonets to them, the swine.' Then he wakes up in a heavy sweat, fearfully disappointed to find no Boche to gas and kill.

February 6

I have put my exasperating little VAD in a ward where there are two staff nurses – she is very happy there and I have someone older, more a woman of the world, in La Plage . . . so that's an improvement.

February 9

Roughest night I have known – heavy hail storms and a full gale. I could not breathe, or walk against it, and was just blown hard against the walls of the houses. However, I quite enjoyed it when I did manage to fight along sideways. We have all been writing strong protests against having our allowances cut off, but don't know if anything will come of it. Have just had a glorious deep bath, then a glass of Bengers Food* (with brandy) and am going to bed.

I have bought an old Normandy paste piece – a St Esprit jewel pendant – for 150 francs on a walk with Thomas. Later, we saw some beautiful little terrier pups at the canteen. Their mother cannot be bothered to feed them, so we bought the corporal a baby's feeding bottle for them.

---

* A wheat-flour based white powder mixed with hot milk to make a creamy, vanilla-flavoured drink. It was a popular compound to give to children and invalids.

February 11

Have been told to take over No. 3 Casino tomorrow morning. Mair, Gibbens and Johnstone have gone to Le Havre, and Craig has to go this afternoon, so they will be a very tired family tonight.

February 13

Have taken my Ritchie-Thompson Ward to Casino 3 and 4. A convoy of 399 arrived at 6 a.m., and one ward is quite full, but the other not, as it was in quarantine after a case of scarlet fever – so I was not as busy as most people. Have felt *very* ill all day – always do when changing from night to day duty. Hope for better things tomorrow.

February 15

There is a big gale blowing and shutters, glass, and tin keep crashing down from somewhere and hurrying towards the north-east. This house is rocking and shaking and gritty stuff falls constantly. I am wondering if it is the mortar, and the bricks will come next. Bang! Another shutter – there won't be many left on the Blanquet Hotel in town! More glass – this is the biggest blow I have ever sat through. Only wish I dared open my shutters – which I had to put gumboots and a mackintosh on to shut – to look at the sea. It sounds like high tide and a tremendous gale. We have heavy zinc tins for refuse outside our quarters, and I *think* they have all made off. My room has French doors for windows, and one large pane was blown out in a recent gale, and now with my shutters closed, the wind is blowing through with such force that the curtain is just a streak, straight across the ceiling.

Edie never lost her sense of humour. The wind was often extremely
strong at Étretat, and the risk of having one's skirts blown
over one's head was a frequent hazard.

February 16

The enemy scored one today – they have made a big attack
near Ypres and taken 600 yards of trenches. It's a tremendously rough day and the place is strewn with broken glass,
slate and woodwork. The natives say it is the same every
year – which is why the entire place is battened up and
closed during the months of winter. Our English patients
who left this morning are held up at Le Havre as it is too
rough for the hospital ship to go.

February 17

Am dead beat with the weather – a gale has been blowing for
days without ceasing one minute, and the tremendous noise
of sea and wind all day and all night is really very tiring. Our

English patients are still held up, waiting for the sea to calm down.

February 20

The convoy arrived at 7.15 – not a bad time – and it's not a heavy one. One poor young fellow, only 24, died after four hours from deadly gas gangrene, and another had his leg off at once to save the same thing happening. He is such a nice man, with a wife and six children – I so hope he will do well. One man tells me that the Station Master and our driver at Pop have been shot as spies. Good luck! The more the better – the place is riddled with spy vermin.

February 22

This is a morning to be alive! Everything covered in snow, and the impatient cold sea is beating itself into white foam at my very feet. Cliffs and rocks all cold and clear.

February 23

The view from my window this morning is beautiful. Boats, rocks, boathouses, beach – all thick with snow. Raper and I went to the woods yesterday and picked primroses and catkins and were caught in two snowstorms. My poor old amputation man told me about his wounding yesterday. He is a gunner and he and his mate had had a busy day dragging their guns over a ploughed field to a fresh pit. They had finished firing and were waiting to be relieved when the enemy started shelling. It was too violent a bombardment for the reliefs to come up, so he and his mate stayed by their gun. A shell came right in to them, blowing his mate to bits and wounding his own knee, but never touched the gun. The shock of seeing his mate in bits made him a little light-headed and the only thing he could think of to do was to get someone to help his mate. He cut off all his equipment and dragged himself to some stretcher-bearers in a trench 50 yards off, and implored them to go and save his mate. Of course when they knew he was dead they didn't go. They put our man on a stretcher and trotted him off to the nearest dressing station. If he had stayed in his gun pit, he would probably have bled to death.

February 26

It was not a big convoy yesterday – only about 300 – but as we were fairly full before, it gave us a very busy day. Poor beggars, they were cold! Three in the morning is a chilly time to arrive, and Étretat was well under snow and becoming more so. Today is the same, everything is thick in white snow, only little edges of shelter round each boat showing brown beach. Cliffs, huts, houses, boats, breakwaters – all are thickly covered and looking very beautiful and unsuggestive of war, but the nights are cold and I could not get warm enough to sleep for such a long time. The night is silent here, not even a clock strikes, so perhaps the time seemed longer than it really was. The sentries change at 2 a.m. and I didn't hear them! All leave is stopped, so it looks like work ahead. *Alors*! We can only do our best.

February 29

The mail-boat has not been allowed to cross lately as the Channel is thick with mines and submarines. Six vessels have been sunk in the last few days and, sad to say, lives lost. This morning it happens to be a little less icy, and there is no sign of snow about. Everything, including the sea, is lead colour, and all looks calm ... more snow perhaps. No. 3 Ward is light, and No. 4, although they have only 18 patients, is a back-breaking one to work in, as they are always so very heavy.

March 3

We are really busy with convoys in and out constantly, and we are very much under our complement of sisters – about 20 short, VADs the same, and 40 orderlies short. Went for a short walk last night – first for a long time – delightful!

March 4

I have a good old-fashioned cold – so went straight to bed, where Madame brought me Bengers with brandy in.

March 5

All things have conspired to make the day seem long. Convoy, cold and horrid headache – but oh joy, it did end and I found home letters awaiting me!

March 7

Slept through the first bell but woke at the second – to find my room aglow with a beautiful pink light. The outside world was a foot deep under snow. Telephone wires look like those fluffy bell pulls, about three inches round in snow, and all glittering in the early morning sunshine. Truly beautiful and unwarlike. Now I must quickly dress or I shall be late for breakfast, but by tonight if the snow thaws I may forget what the morning was like, as there is plenty every day to drive out all thoughts but patients, wards lists ... and convoys.

March 8

We have a big convoy to get off to England, and another arriving – supposedly at 10 a.m., so we shall not be slack – but the difference here is that we have about 12 hours' notice of a convoy coming, and up the line they just tumbled in at all hours of the day and night. My heart is very sore for one poor boy, Kerr, and for his mother. We have had him ten days, and he is no better and is in a state to die at any moment. I have been writing to his mother and telling her so, and she is evidently a refined old lady. She wrote back to say she is 'so glad to hear Charlie is with us – the rest and good food will do him good.' Have my letters not reached her? Or won't she understand that the boy is dying? I think he must have been gassed as he is purple, in the way of gas patients. This is Ash Wednesday and I ought to be at the 6.45 service, but some horrid crank always takes me in Lent. I miss more services and eat more nice things and *smoke* more than any time of the year. Étretat is really beautiful now. Yesterday's snow thawed a little in the sunshine, but is still deep and frozen again with the night's frost. My western horizon is just tinged with pale pink, which suits the soft clouds and pale blue sea to distraction and the cliffs are a picture, all snow-covered and rugged. If only I could sketch, I would make the most lovely little pictures in this diary.

March 9

I was to have been called at 2 a.m. to help with a heavy convoy, so went to bed and to sleep at 9 p.m. – and the next thing I knew it was quarter past six and broad daylight, and no one had called me. Here I sit in my night attire at 7 a.m., trusting it is all right, that the convoy has been held up somewhere and we are to go to second breakfast as usual.

Yesterday was a delightful day of calm between the

storms, and today my pneumonia boy benefited from the quiet – perhaps the creature has a chance after all. I feel he must get better, if only for his mother, poor thing. She wrote to me again and said she was heartbroken – however, it was no good for me to pretend he was not dangerously ill. He was – and still is. Our Matron, Miss E. M. Denne, had sudden orders to go to Le Havre to relieve Miss Steen who has been invalided home. She was sorry to go, and we to lose her, although it is a great promotion. She will be Principal Matron of Le Havre district soon.

March 10

Very big day, as a convoy arrived at 7.40 – 590 men, chiefly sick and only about 30 badly wounded. The greater part were such things as trench-foot. Poor Kerr is worse and I am sure that boy has been gassed and will die. I shouldn't be surprised to find his cot empty when I go on duty. His poor mother – how will she take it?

March 12

Too much sadness to write about, besides being dead beat. My poor little boy, Kerr, died today. He had been in 15 days, suffering from gas, pneumonia, bronchitis – and has been extremely and dangerously ill all the time, but only the day before yesterday he realised that he was not going to get well. I am glad to say we never left him night or day, and he was fond of us all. He kept whispering all sorts of messages for home and his fiancée – then he would call, 'Sister,' and when I bent down to hear, 'I do love you. When I'm gone, will you kiss me?' All the time heads would be popping in making demands, 'The sergeant wants to know if you can lend him a couple of men to . . .' But in spite of all, I did kiss the boy – first for his mother and then for myself – which pleased him.

Then he whispered, 'But you still will, when I'm gone …'
The night before he asked me what dying would be like, and
said it seemed so unsatisfactory. He felt too young to die, and
him not even wounded, but just with bronchitis. Then
another time he said, 'They wouldn't let me go sick. Every
time they said it was rheumatism and would wear off, and
marching with full pack and dodging the shells was dreadful.'
Thank goodness, what I told him dying would be like happened exactly – a clear gift of Providence. I told him it would
be that, little by little, his breathing would get easier, he
would feel tired and want to go to sleep, and then he would
just sleep, with no morphia. That is exactly what happened,
without a struggle. He was quite conscious up to 20 minutes
before he died. I just asked him now and then if he knew I
was still with him. He said, 'Yes,' so I asked, '… and you're
quite happy, aren't you?' He distinctly said, 'Yes, quite.' Then
the last and very trying part was to walk along to the other
end of the village beside the poor dead thing, to see him
decently put in the mortuary, all with hundreds of French
eyes turned 'full on'. Our own people always clear out of the
way when they see a mortuary case coming.

March 13

Yesterday was a difficult day to be 'Sister'. We sent 13 to
England and are getting a new convoy in today, and this is
really the only time I have for my own writing. Every day is
busy, and at night I am too tired.

March 14

6.30 a.m. – a bugle has just gone, which means an ambulance
train is coming in, and I expect we shall be called for early
breakfast. We have much to be thankful for that many
patients went to England the day before yesterday, and the

convoy did not arrive yesterday, as three more sisters went down with measles, making our staff about 26 under number. The rest of us have been spread out to the best advantage, but it has meant precious hard work, and no off-duty time. Imagine my joy when I was in Constable's room, telling her she must report her rash out of fairness to other people – to see eight beautiful, fully-trained sisters arriving at the quarters . . . all in the pink of health! Dear things – we nearly fell on their necks with joy. They have just come home from a slack time in Egypt, so ought to be good for work now. As always happens, everything in the way of relief comes at once. My three heavy cases died and the convoy did not come . . . and eight new sisters did. Sergeant Middleton died the same day as Kerr so they were buried together, and we had a glorious sunny afternoon for it. The third was an abdominal, poor creature. He came in in an agony and remained like that until he died – having been operated on and all things possible done. The post-mortem exam showed it was typhoid.

March 15

We were all called for early breakfast and got on duty just before the convoy arrived. There were only 300-odd but we filled right up in No. 3, then five fractures went into No. 4. Three are on the Seriously Ill (SI) list, but I think there are good hopes for all of them. Sam Murphy has both legs broken and his left eye shot out, Burke has one leg badly broken – and Moules has gas gangrene in his shoulder and is badly wounded. It is a great relief having these eight new sisters and I was able to give three of my people off-duty time.

March 17

The orderlies of this unit are chiefly Irish and we shall have a glorious time with them today – Saint Patrick's Day. They started by marching down to parade WITH A BAND! And such a band! Whistles and drums playing Irish airs – and at 2 p.m. there is to be a football match, England v Ireland. After that we will draw a veil!

The sea is angry about something this morning – I can't imagine what. There is no wind at all – maybe because the fishing boats are late in getting off. When the fishermen heard our Irish band it was too much for them and they ran to see what the excitement was all about. They are chasing round now and it won't be long before they're away. The fishermen live a very sporting life, they race to get off in the morning and race back in the afternoon. First boat ashore sells its fish first. There is a salesman who goes from boat to boat as the fish are unloaded, and sells the haul by auction. It takes the men about two minutes to arrange the fish – all the cod together, sole, plaice, dogfish, crabs – all separated. Then the salesman, and crowds of women with baskets follow on and hold the sale. It is most entertaining to watch. Before the war they used to throw dogfish away – but now they get tenpence each for them.

I have a half day today, so at sisters' breakfast we fermented a plan. Allen, Wilson, Maxey* and I would hire the old Ford and go to Caudebec en Caux. The morning was wet with fine rain falling, but there was always that small chance it would improve. Wilson had been in the theatre all morning and did not come to either lunch sitting – so the other three of us flew along, hoofed her out to get some food, cleaned the place and instruments for her and all were ready to start

---

* One of Edie's closest friends working alongside her in France was Sister Kate Maxey whom she mentions many times in her diary. They were together at Étretat for most of 1916 and may have been later than this but sadly the diaries are missing from the period of mid-November 1916 to June 1918. Edie and Kate shared many off-duty hours together going for walks, collecting flowers for the wards and some more exotic adventures. In September 2011 members of the Maxey family contacted Edie's great nephew, Dick Robinson, and shared wonderful photographs taken by Kate in 1916.

punctually. The car rolled up at 2 p.m. sharp and off we went. The rain cleared after we had gone a few miles – the sun shone brightly and all went 'merry as a marriage bell'.

The scenery was glorious, the first part through pretty country lanes carpeted with primroses (I threatened to get out at every fresh patch, but was not allowed to), and then through little old villages, all interesting – Criquetot, Bolbec ... Then through a long and wonderful stretch of country overlooking the Seine. The lights and shades on the river and country on the right, and high cliffs on the left, overgrown with beautiful vegetation, gave us much to contemplate, and we drove slowly and silently through it all. At one place, nestled in the cliffs, we saw a homestead, well kept with an aviary of rare birds, peacocks and creatures whose names I don't know, who squawked and strutted about, and looked very pretty.

The next village, Lillebonne, was *very* old and particularly interesting for its Roman ruins. We drove slowly all round the place and then on through equally pretty scenery in Caudebec en Caux. The Seine is navigable here and we saw six quite big steamers on their way to Paris. It is a very favourite place of English visitors in the summer, and our driver told us the winter population was 2,000 – but in summer 6,000. We put up at the Hotel de la Marine, ordered an omelette and toast for tea, then looked about the place – cathedral, shops and the town itself – all very interesting. Some of the streets are very narrow, and one is a canal, very pretty with its old houses on either side. We went back and lingered over our tea – the view was so pretty across the Seine to the dim hills beyond. We loaded up at ten to six and returned via Yvetot.

A few miles out, the engine stopped dead. The other three sat tight, but as I had to get down, being in front, I stayed down and went for a ramble in the woods. After tinkering about for some time, our man discovered that we had run out of petrol, so back to C en C we went, ran downhill with no engine working, bought up all of one man's petrol, then on to another village. Bought all we wanted and then started back again and had a fair run home – first in twilight then in bright moon- and starlight.

The football match ended in a win for us – England 2 – Ireland 1. Patients who were able were allowed to attend the match and 12 Irish men in their hospital blues, their faces blacked and in gay turbans, got up a wonderful band of whistles and drums and led them off. Such a procession of the maimed, the sick, the halt, the blind and men in wheelchairs you never saw. One of my VADs has been moved to another ward, as two more folk – a sister and a VAD – have gone sick. So we are understaffed again. However, we won't cry out till we are hurt.

March 18

We sent many patients to England yesterday and are now reduced to four in 3 and five in 4. Being so empty, I turned everyone on to work and had every bed and every scrap of everything put out in the parade. I got the whole place cleaned from top to toe, and it looks lovely now. We made lunch for them at 11 o'clock, and called a halt for refreshment. They seemed to love their job better than slacking about – they are good creatures, both the orderlies and patients.

March 20

Miss Denne, the Assistant Director Medical Services and a couple of civilian lady visitors came round yesterday. My No. 4 ward is for 'fractures of the lower extremity', and one visitor, after I had shown her round, remarked that they all seemed to have broken legs in that ward ... I suppose she didn't realise what lower extremities are. But she was a charming woman and so nice with the men. Maxey, Truslove and I had a half day, so we walked to Bénouville in the rain

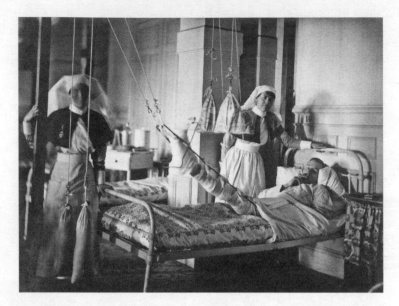

'My No. 4 ward is for fractures of the lower extremity . . .' The nurse on the left wears the solid red cape of the regular QAIMNS, and two red stripes denote that she is a sister rather than a staff nurse. She is Daisy Martin, who went on to be Matron-in-Chief of the service between the wars. On the right is a staff nurse of QAIMNS Reserve – her cape is grey with red facings, with the 'reserve' badge on the right lapel.

Photograph © IWM Q008011

and picked primroses that were hanging from the banks in yellow tufts. At Bénouville, we peeped into the church and found service in progress – so went to the café for tea of bloaters*, boiled eggs, toast and tea. After tea the woman showed us her old china and pewter. Such a nice little woman – her husband is away at the war and she was busy making herself a coat out of an old one of his. She turned the stuff and piped it with black velvet and made a strap for the waist and sleeves – very smart.

---

* Lightly smoked whole herring

March 23

The day before yesterday I went for a walk to the woods –
and lost my pen-case with pen and nail-cleaner inside. Now
I am reduced to one of the old fashioned dip-in-each-time
variety, so if I am off today I shall go and look for it. The
man 'Moules' in my ward with the shoulder injury had
another operation yesterday. They found pus in the joint
and a good deal of necrosed bone – poor man, he has a
painful time between him and recovery, I'm afraid. In No.
4 we took in only three fractures, but filled up to relieve
other wards. One, an old man of 59, such a dear old thing,
has both legs badly wounded and may have to lose one. Off
in evening, so walked to woods to look for my pen-case –
but did not find it.

March 24

I heard that *35* new sisters are arriving today from a hospital
in Egypt that has been closed. They will only be here for the
time being and will be sent where they are wanted – but we
could do with 12 ourselves. Wonder if leave will be restored
on the strength of that ...

March 25

Lady Day. The 35 did not come yesterday, although every
preparation was made for them. The sitting room has been
gutted of furniture and 20 camp-beds made up – the
remaining 15 are in bedrooms, but, thank goodness, not
mine. At night we got a message to say only ten were
coming and they didn't turn up either, so perhaps this
morning we shall hear it is all a hoax. We had built such cas-
tles in air! Learned I am leaving Casino 3 and 4 today and
going to Roche D.

March 26

A day of quick change as I handed over Casino 3 and 4 to Ritchie and took over Roche D three hours later, and was sent off to be ready for night duty. Thomas (who is a Nottingham Children's Hospital friend of mine), was taken ill, but was sensible and Colonel Gray was called in to examine her. When he said she must be operated on at once, she trusted him to do it. It would be too truly awful to be operated on by a man you know well and are working with. She had a 2-pound cyst removed from her inside. She is so far doing well, and a good patient. I am now doing night duty for her. Today is the Annunciation of the Blessed Virgin Mary and the Roman Catholics had a great time with a wonderful procession all round the town. There are two tiresome little VADs in the room next to mine, coughing their heads off – I never did like coughs, so I have filled them up with glycerine and lemon, and given them hot milk, but still they bark.

March 27

My patient, Thomas, is very good and doing well, but sleeps very badly. She likes to lie there with me in the room and the light out, so I spend a good many hours sitting and doing nothing more than thinking – can't even make lace to pass the time. The ten sisters arrived yesterday – they are supposed to be a new unit, but cannot find a place to settle. Among them is Hindle, an old Bart's contemporary of mine. I wonder if they will let us go on leave now – it's the same old motto: 'wait and see'*.

* This is a reference to Prime Minister Henry Asquith's catchphrase. French matches, notoriously difficult to light, were called 'Asquiths' by the troops because they had to wait and see if they lit.

Several of Edie's colleagues had been her contemporaries at St
Bartholomew's Hospital, or had also trained there. This portrait
photograph from the early 1900s shows Edie as a Barts probationer.
Photograph courtesy of the Appleton family

March 28

Thomas has not had a good day, but seems inclined to sleep
tonight. There is a terrific storm in progress with shutters
being blown down, and the windows have just blown open,
in spite of the shutters being fastened. I have just been to
the kitchen for my supper and there are at least 12 cats –
mangy, starved-looking creatures – stealing what they can
find to eat. One would think this was the only place in Étretat where there was food. I think 11 of them are for
destruction today. One very mangy one was half in the

stockpot, eating meat off a bone. I think I will be off soup
for a bit. There has been a local tragedy. The hairdresser's
maid stole off to the woods at 1 a.m. yesterday and some
children, up early this morning picking flowers, saw her
staggering back and a little later found the body of a new-
born baby – still warm. The girl has been taken to prison,
poor thing.

March 29

A tremendous gale is still blowing and more shutters are
down. It is quite the thing in Étretat, apparently – the winds
don't come gently. Went for a lovely long walk to some
woods to find daffodils. Found carpets of primroses, but no
daffs.

March 30

Thomas is still doing well. I had a letter from home tonight
telling me Basil Blogg has been killed – how terrible for
poor Mrs Blogg – let us hope her other two sons will keep
safe. Went for a lovely walk alone this morning for miles
along the Canteen Road in beautiful hilly country – some
parts thickly wooded, some smothered in primroses and
daffodils. The air was sweet with their scent – larks singing
and the colouring of the whole sky and country wonderful.
It would have been a perfect feast for an impressionist!
How some of the sisters can spend their half days going
to Le Havre, I don't know. The car we have is an awful
old thing, and yesterday they got back at 11 p.m. instead
of 6.30 because the car had broken down on the way
home. They were stranded until another car came by and
towed them in – they used blankets knotted together for
a tow-rope.

March 31

My patient, Thomas, has slept all night with me sitting in a
chair. I am looking after a sick VAD too, and have been into
her room twice – both times the door has made a disastrous
noise but she has not stirred. Maxey and I went for a glorious walk to the woods and brought back a big basket full of
daffodils, primroses, blue and white violets and anemones.
Children would think they were in fairyland!

April 1

A perfect day – hotter than many summer days. I took a
piece of cake, a cigarette and a book of poetry (in case I
fancied any of them) and went to the prettiest spot in the
woods I love. It was an hour's quick walk to get there, but
once settled on a carefully selected spot where I shouldn't
crush the daffs and primroses, I just basked in the hot sunshine. I fancied all three things – cake, then cigarette
(about the fifth since November) and book – then I lis-
tened to the hum of insects and the songs of birds, and
revelled in the sun and flowers until I was nearly asleep.
There were no human beings near, but millions of live
things all busy with their own lives and taking not the
smallest interest in me.

We have such a charming cook for our mess, he has fits and
is very small! I asked him for a fried potato to take to eat
before I went to bed, and as he turned round to say 'yes', he
pulled the whole tin of gravy for both lunches off the stove
on to the floor – about a gallon wasted. I was terribly sorry
and told him I would keep out of his way at meal times, so
last night he said, 'Aren't you coming no more for a snack
before you go to bed?' and I said 'No'. Then tonight, when
I went to get my tray of food for the night, I found he'd

made a wonderful fancy cake for me. He was a pastry cook in peacetime!

April 2

I am looking after a sick VAD tonight – an elderly woman who has travelled and read and lived. She has come from No. 10 Rouen and has been working in the German ward, because she speaks German. One of the men told her that they were giving themselves up to the English in big numbers in some places, but that the English wouldn't take them, and sent them back to their own lines – where they would be shot for desertion. Another German told her that before Christmas the Kaiser called up a number of men, but was not able to get nearly the number he wanted, thank goodness. Perhaps they are running short at last.

The four o'clock guard has just changed, which means that about two minutes before changing time, two sleepy Frenchmen stagger out of the house which is open for the men on duty. Two come up from their billets to take over, and when the late guard are well away, the fresh ones go into the house and to sleep! The little dog calls them if, by unusual chance, anyone should pass – then if he barks loud enough to rouse them, one comes out and curses him and goes in again.

April 3

I think there must have been some spirit influence at work this morning that made me do a thing I hate doing, quite against my own will, but which ended up giving me great pleasure. I started for a country walk as usual, but then suddenly found myself making straight for the station to meet the ambulance train. There I found that the two sisters off the train were old friends of mine – one was one of the four from St Bart's that

I started the campaign with, and I was with another one at Chatham. We had a great talk about old times from St Bart's onwards. Back then I had given my camera up for lost, but Paterson has sent it to her own home to be kept for me! I brought them both up to meet Matron, then out to coffee. I showed them over the hospital and bits of Étretat, then back to their train. Miss Rentzsch donned red cuffs today, denoting the rank of Matron. I have begun to feel like a perpetual night nurse to the sick sisters as I have another one to look after tonight with an abscess in her ear. I know it is a most painful thing, but she was a bit hysterical about it. I gave her aspirin and a good tot of whisky after treating the ear, and the last I heard of her was heavy snoring ... whisky is good stuff.

It is now 3 a.m. and I have just been promenading on the verandah, which is the shape and size of a ship's bridge. It was pitch dark except for stars, and the sea beating at my very feet made it seem like being on the captain's bridge at sea – and I wished I were.

April 5

These blessed submarines are a nuisance! Le Havre harbour is closed again, and the two who went on leave yesterday are still there. This may affect all our leaves. Thomas is doing well so far and her stitches were taken out today. The monotony of the night was relieved at 3 a.m. by the coming of the night super to say that the staff nurse in Casino 5 – a fearfully heavy surgical ward – had fainted badly, so we decided to tell Matron and have her brought along here where I could keep an eye on her. She is fixed now with hot bottles and soda and *sal volatile**, and the night super will be coming back in a few minutes to take a friendly plate of porridge with me.

* Smelling salts

April 6

Felt tired for some reason and went to bed early. No sign of coming off night duty yet, and have done 12 nights now. Every morning at daybreak the crows amuse me very much. They come up in battalions of about 1,000 over the cliff on the left – and they drill, exercise and squawk for about half an hour, then fly off again to their various feeding grounds. They do everything exactly as one bird – swing round together, ascend, alight. There was great consternation in the dovecote tonight because the Church of England padre has called to see me *two days* in succession – but if they had only known, it was only to talk about the chapel arrangements and to get some photos of graves for relatives of two of my men who died.

April 9

Hired the bootmaker's car and started off at 10 a.m. for Le Havre. We did some shopping and lunched, then went to the galleries, where our car was to meet us. Come 1 p.m., no car – 1.30 . . . no car. At 2 p.m. the bootmaker bustled up in a heated condition to say the car had broken down and would not be repaired for three days. No cars to hire, no ambulances, and no train to Étretat until 4.30 p.m., so we went to HQ and saw the ADMS, who told us a car was coming from Étretat to meet the mail-boat and collect Smith, who was returning from leave. At 3 o'clock the car arrives and at 3.15 up strolled Smith, who had been lunching since 1 p.m. in the Garden Tea Rooms.

I had little more than one hour's sleep before night duty, so made up my mind to get some sleep in the night, but Fate said 'No'. McBride, the night super, was off with a throat problem, and I had to take her job – and am doing it again tonight. Matron said she knew I ought to be off night duty, and would take me off soon. I said I was pleased to fill a gap, but had a horrible feeling of being caught in a web of night duty, as if I never should get out. I have done seven weeks this year already.

April 10

Night chiefly remarkable for having lost a sick officer. He was out at lock-up time and could be found nowhere. We reported it to the Chief Medical Officer, the Major-in-Charge and the Ward Master, but no one could find him. Finally he turned up at 12.30, having lost his way in the country. Enjoyed my day off very much, although it poured all day. I turned out everything and repacked (a sure sign of a move, they say). In the afternoon I had Hilda Hindle and Constable in to play cards, and we had a cosy tea in the kitchen with toast and boiled eggs, and honey and cake.

April 13

Matron got orders yesterday to take duty on the *Asturias*[*] – I don't fancy she will care for a seagoing job – and there are no allowances on board ship!

April 14

All leave is stopped as ten Australians – or should I say 'Austr-I-lians' – arrived. It's Palm Sunday, so went to the early and 11 o'clock services – a good sermon and the church was full.

[*] HMHS *Asturias* was built in 1907 for the Royal Mail Steam Packet Company but was requisitioned by the Admiralty in 1914 and converted to a hospital ship able to accommodate 900 patients. In 1917 she was torpedoed by a submarine. The attack blew off the stern, killing 35 crew, but the hulk was kept as a floating ammunition store in Plymouth until the end of the war.

April 17

We heard a rumour last night of heavy fighting at La Bassée and Verdun – then that we had taken La Bassée. I am afraid the casualties will be terribly sad, whatever happened. Yesterday an airship and a torpedo-destroyer were up and down, to and fro, round and round, like a couple of terriers after a rat. The airship sighted the quarry – a German submarine – and the steamer blew it up, crew and all complete.

April 18

Maxey, Constable and I had a half day, so we walked to Bénouville and dug up a basketful of primrose roots – then went to the inn for our usual boiled eggs and bread-and-butter tea. Then to the cemetery where we tidied up nine graves, took away all the dead flowers and planted the primroses. Those of Colonel Thackery, Captain Hammond, and Kerr and Sawden came under my special care. If everybody does a few we may have them all tidy for Easter – the cemetery is very beautifully kept.

April 19

We saw Thomas off to England overnight in our ambulance as one of four stretcher cases, along with an officer and two Tommies. She stood the journey well, but when we got there the boat was not in – so we left her in charge of a sister, screened off in a corner of the officers' hut. The padre went to see some officers off, so we all rattled home together in one ambulance. At about midnight some New Zealanders hailed our car and asked if we were going anywhere in particular – a nice thing to ask at that time! They wanted a hurt man taken somewhere, so we took him in, then sprinted for Étretat at top speed – so fast that the pipes inside the car burnt holes in our rugs.

April 22

Miserable wet weather for Easter Day – but I have a slight idea of leave starting soon. I went to the 7 o'clock service and all three early ones were packed with patients, us and men of the unit. Morning service at the big church was very well attended, and the evening service was packed out. The church looked very pretty, and Mr Parry Evans gave a good, sensible sermon (short), and one that appealed to the men. I did not go in the evening – instead went for a walk with Wilson, and landed at the church after the congregation had left. I played the organ and she sang – great joy! It is a dear little instrument. We of La Plage clubbed together and gave our 100 men fruit salad and whipped cream for tea, and they all enjoyed it very much indeed – much better than the sticky cakes one buys here. Besides, I have finished with the woman at the cake shop, she would not sell cake cheaper than two francs each for things no bigger round than a breakfast cup for our men at Christmas – so I didn't buy them there, and have spent not a penny in her shop since.

April 25

We have been called for early breakfast – a convoy came in about an hour ago, and they called some people to go and help receive it. I started scratching my head yesterday, to think about equipping the new theatre that is to be in my charge, along with the two hernia wards. I ended up giving the dispenser a list a yard long of things to get ready for me. I have had my staff nurse changed three times since I took on this job – it would be quite useful to know which one is to be the right one. There's a rumour of leave starting, which does not excite me because in the next breath it will probably be stopped again.

Volume Three

1916.

May. 8th. Back from leave. Mrs Wilton Smith. R.R.C. run Pop. Matron is now in charge. Poor old Barclay Smith (with us at no 3) died a week ago, of septic endocarditis. Enjoyed my leave in the bosom of my family very much – am in C of La Plage again – & frantically busy. Have handed of Sisters & Orderlies – operations every day C – is full of operated on patients, & part of D. which makes the washings & bed makings alone – a stiff job. however. ——
3 Sisters have joined the Asturias – & like it. 2 have gone to Calais & do not. Off duty yesterday afternoon – planted plants on the men's graves. lovely day – this morning very rough & stormy. Coming back in the boat – I was standing at the very end of the deck looking forward – there were many officers sitting behind us also looking forward – when a sudden gust of wind blew my dress & coat up over my head – so that I looked like a grey tulip with a couple of flame & black stalks – you know my flannels – It was a terrible business getting out of it all. We saw three torpedoed vessels – as we were going in to Havre. Did not get in till 11.30 a.m. 9th One month from today & I shall be 39 – oh 'orrors 'ow old I am –

Summer 1916

May 8

Back from leave, having enjoyed my time in the bosom of my family very much. Coming back on the boat I stood looking forward at the very end of the deck, where there were many officers sitting behind me, also looking forward, when a sudden gust of wind blew my dress and coat up over my head, so that I looked like a grey tulip with my legs a couple of flame and black stalks. It was a terrible business getting out of it all.

Miss Wilton Smith, RRC, our Pop Matron, is now in charge. Poor old Barclay Smith (with us at No. 3) died a week ago of septic endocarditis. I am in C and D wards, La Plage, again and frantically busy as we are short-handed of sisters and orderlies and there are operations every day. C and part of D are full of operated-on patients – which makes the washings and bed-makings alone a stiff job. However, three sisters have joined the *Asturias* and like it, while two have gone to Calais – and do not. Was off duty yesterday afternoon and put plants on the men's graves. It was a lovely day, but this morning was very rough and stormy.

May 9

One month from today I shall be 39 – oh 'orrors 'ow old I am! Yesterday was the busiest day imaginable – six evacuated and six admitted, five operated on, and six transferred, carried in blankets to the upper storey to leave the beds on my lower floor for the newly operated-on ones. We have 47 bed-patients to do every mortal thing for and only two orderlies, one nurse and me to do it all. However, we worked hard and fast, got done, and all had off-duty time. It is no use waiting for a less busy time to give off-duty, because at that rate we should not have any.

May 11

A calm morning, so the fishing fleet were off and about six mine-sweepers out. They did a funny thing just now, and I must ask somebody who knows about it. They were going along in a line of three, far apart, when suddenly the one furthest away disappeared and all I could see was a thimble-shape of what looked like spray. I wonder if it could be an exploding mine. I watched closely, and now can see all three sweepers proceeding as usual. They are going so slowly that I should not have thought they could set off a mine, but I don't know what else it could have been.

Yesterday was busy, but not quite as busy, and our new matron is altering things for the better in La Plage. The theatre is on the ground floor, and hitherto patients have been carried from there to the third or fourth floors, which is bad for them and fearful work for the orderlies. Yesterday she came in and stopped it and had them put – with the major's consent – into beds on the same floor as the theatre, which throws some of the acute nursing on to the sisters there. I hope in time we shall amalgamate so that the whole staff run the whole place.

In the afternoon went to a concert given by a troupe of Army Signals Command (ASC) and ordnance men from Le

Havre, calling themselves 'The Red Dominoes'. They were beautifully dressed in black sateen with red trimmings and the local photographer arrived during their turn and took a photograph. It must have been rather quaint to see the smart troupe out on the Casino parade with rows and rows of many-coloured quilted beds with patients in, and a group of 'up' patients as an audience, with a few French people and us thrown in.

I was talking to a patient last night who has been out here since the beginning of the war. He told me the same stories of the German cruelties as many others have done, of how he would go through villages and see old, bearded men pinned to their own doors on lances and swords, babies lying about naked and maimed, dying and dead, women with their hands or arms cut off. It's all horrible and perhaps best left untold ...

May 12

I heard that the mine-sweepers found what they were looking for. At about 5 o'clock yesterday afternoon we saw three mine-sweepers, a torpedo destroyer and a funny thing like a small terrace of China junks in the tow of a tug, going past. Three hours later we heard they had found a submarine between here and Fécamp, and were going to repair it for the French to use. Bond left yesterday to get married. She had a very tame send-off, but no one knew she was going until nearly 7 o'clock. Good luck to her! Maxey and I were too tired for a long walk last night, so we went to the grounds of a house owned by a French doctor who has an English wife. He is on military duty somewhere, and she and the children are away, but she has given permission for her caretaker to give us flowers and for us to walk in her grounds. It's about a 50-acre property – part park and part woodland – with many lovely gardens. There's even a tennis court and

Kate Maxey was one of Edie's closest friends among her nursing
colleagues. A sister in the Territorial Force Nursing Services
(note the stripes on her sleeves), this photograph shows three
of her four medals: from left to right, the Royal Red Cross,
the Military Medal and the 1914 Star.
Photograph courtesy of the Maxey family

pond. I should like to meet her and thank her. We loved it
there! Just for an hour I tried to pretend to myself that there
was no war and that it was my own place – and I had this
poor tired nurse, Maxey, staying with me for a rest.

May 13

Maxey and I took a half day off and planned a 'business
and pleasure' tea picnic. We started off at 3 o'clock with tea

and punch for pleasure, and stockings to darn for business. We decided to go to my favourite wood, far from everywhere. Before we got there a few clouds had rolled up and a spot or two of rain fell, but in spite of that we spread out our macs and settled ourselves to tea. Before we had got to the end of the hard-boiled egg stage, the fun began. A gust or two of wind and then an inky sky and a downpour. We crept into the bushes, but in a few minutes that was worse than outside, so we packed our goods and walked fast to the nearest shelter, where we found a Frenchwoman and her daughter.

We were under the eaves of a thatched roof, and our foothold was the side of a cement gutter. It was very steep and every time our feet slipped we were in a swift-running river. The old Frenchwoman soon gave up trying, and simply stood in the water. They had walked out from Étretat to drive home with the old father in his tip-cart. Maxey and I soon moved on and found good shelter in a shed with a couple of wagons in. We settled ourselves on one and resumed our tea, but we were absolutely drenched to the skin from top to toe. My big coat must have weighed about 20 lbs and Maxey's waterproof evidently leaked. The next excitement was a sharp thunderstorm and very vivid lightning, which drove mother, father and daughter, wagon and horse in beside us. We shared what was left of the food and enjoyed a merry time for about 15 minutes, when the force of rain abated a bit. We joined the driving party and rode home in state, much to everyone's amusement. The old Frenchwoman was simply weak with laughter all the way.

May 14

Miss Rentzsch has joined the *Asturias* as Assistant Matron, and some of our sisters went to Le Havre with her to see

Allen, Mason and Leedam. They appear to be in the lap of
luxury, in beautiful wards, with a large and well-furnished
cabin each and plenty of stewards, stewardesses and boys
in brass buttons to wait on them. They are all looking
well and rested. There is talk of them taking out-of-action
Australians home – lucky people! Fancy going to Australia!
It's a very windy day and the little orphans love it. When
they are walking out in a crocodile they throw their caps
up in the air and the wind blows them far away – and they
have to chase them – which annoys their keepers very
much.

May 16

Had an unexpected half day yesterday, and Miss Smith
wanted me to go to Le Havre with her – to do the talking!
She must think my French has improved! We went by the
2 o'clock ambulance and got in just over an hour later. We
did our shopping, then the ambulance picked us up and took
us to No. 2 General Hospital. I met some sisters I had
known up the line, and Miss Smith met some she had
worked with in Egypt, so we had a gay tea party. That part
of No. 2 General is the station and station hotel, and from
the window of their mess room you can see where the train
comes in just below – so close that if you spat it would hit
the train. Just to one side the hospital ships and leave boats
come in. This is just where the Seine ends and you see the
opposite bank of it in the dim distance – it must be very
interesting to live there.

May 17

There's been a mild flutter abroad among us and the
orderlies over the forthcoming inspection by the Director
General (DG) and Matron-in-Chief some day this week.

I suppose we shall have to be at our cleanest, which does not appeal to me much. I'm not naturally good at having the place smart. I took time off between two and five as it was too hot to do much, and Maxey and I went to the beach and watched the fishing boats come in, followed by the fish auction. Then half a dozen orderlies entertained us by diving from a boat and swimming. We repaired to my room for tea and did mending for the rest of the afternoon.

Last night was a joy! The moon was well up in the east and Venus the same distance in the west. The sea was like a millpond and everything flooded in moonshine as Venus made a shining path across the sea. I should like to have stayed out instead of having to go to bed.

May 18

I was off duty yesterday evening, so went with Matron to call on the chauffeur VADs – they have a glorious house and garden. Their unit consists of 17 persons – 14 chauffeurs, a cook, housekeeper and housemaid. I was talking to the housemaid – she's such a nice, well-educated girl, and I admire her very much. I think she sometimes wishes she were doing more than housework for the war, but I argued with her that it was a necessary job, and that personally I admired the people who took the 'out-of-sight' jobs, or quietly carried on with necessary peacetime work. They have asked us to tea on Monday. I took Matron to the garden of the lovely house that we are allowed to visit. We roamed all over the place and found no one there, but later Maxey and I found the gardener, and he gave us each a double armful of flowers for the wards.

May 19

Last night I heard Major Segundo yelling under our windows at 9 p.m. for someone to go round to the lady chauffeurs with him to see the sick one. I lay low, as I was in bed. He only seemed to know two of our names, but as my light was out I didn't answer. We had a convoy of 300-odd in yesterday, brought in by the No. 1 Train, and my old chum Paterson came up to see me. She is not looking at all well and dislikes life on the trains, but I always feel I should quite like it for a bit. Some of the men are very badly wounded, and now in one ward there is a poor youngster with both legs broken, both arms wounded, one eye shot out and the other badly damaged. He is on the DI list, then there are three others in the same ward on the SI list – one with his whole buttock muscle blown off – and many are really very bad indeed. Last night I went for a stroll in the gloaming with Miss Atkinson, who is the New Zealand VAD, about 56. The poor thing is being sent to England after having had an outbreak of nasty boils, and she is terribly sorry to go.

May 20

We were all on duty in the afternoon in accordance with Matron's wishes that we should be at our posts if the great ones came to inspect. We sent the VADs off on condition that they kept their weather eyes open and came back at the first sign of Miss McCarthy. I was off in the evening and had my new dress fitted – it is becoming quite a pastime with me and they have fitted it four times already. Afterwards I took Matron on one of my favourite walks along the Rouen Road, up through the woods and home by the Fécamp Road. The wild flowers are such a joy and we found Solomon's Seal*

---

* A lily-like flower with medicinal properties.

and all sorts of lovely things, and I brought some back for the church. Matron and I had a good talk over the old days at Pop and Bailleul and about the present. She is a very good and enterprising matron and tries to make life pleasant for her staff – but at the same time is most particular that rules should be kept.

The sea is dead calm at low tide, and the sunshine is making an edge of sparkling diamonds round the rocks. Fishing boats are under full sail far out, and the sky is a pinky, ripe-melon colour. If I am to take night duty again this year, I should like to do it in June and be up to watch the sunset and sunrise every day.

May 21

We were inspected yesterday by the DG and he seemed to like the place all right. Miss McC and Princess Victoria* are supposed to be coming today. Truslove and Collings played a horrible trick on me last night. I tried on Wood's bathing gown with a view to having Madame make me one like it. I had to search high and low for the old thing and was flying upstairs four at a time when I suddenly found myself under a spout of hot and cold water, and they gave me a real drenching!

---

* Edie is actually referring to Princess Helena Victoria, a granddaughter of Queen Victoria who was born in England but when Edie was writing still bore a German title, that of Her Highness Princess Helena Victoria of Schleswig-Holstein. The reference to Schleswig-Holstein would be dropped when George V anglicised all the Royal Family's names in July 1917. In her capacity as founder and president of the YWCA Women's Auxiliary Force, the princess obtained permission from Lord Kitchener to visit British troops in France and arrange entertainments for them.

May 22

Yesterday we were duly inspected by Princess Victoria, Princess Christian's daughter. I hope she is not a spy! Her having a brother with the Germans does put one off her a bit*. However, she seemed to like everything. The VAD chauffeurs lined their convoy of cars up and stood by them in the square, and were the first to be visited. PV shook hands with them all and they made their curtsies to her. The Princess is very smiling etc, but it gives one a feeling of nausea to think she has a brother doing his best for our enemies. Lady Guernsey and two other ladies were with her. Poor little Lady Guernsey is a charming young thing, but she lost her husband at the beginning of the war and has been running a French hospital at Fécamp ever since.

The great excitement of yesterday was on the sea. Two torpedo destroyers, three pairs of trawlers, and a huge submarine elevator were up and down all the afternoon. I do hope they caught something, but have not heard. An airship and hydroplane were busy overhead all the morning, and I think eventually they found something, because at one point two of the trawlers stopped and one blew her whistle in great agitation, then the two torpedo-catchers came to them. However, I didn't see any great explosion.

May 23

Went to tea at the chauffeurs' and afterwards for a walk with the chief chauffeur, Mrs Graham Jones, whose husband is at

---

* Princess Helena Victoria had two elder brothers, Prince Christian, who had served with the British Army, and Prince Albert, who had served with the Prussian Army. During the Great War Prince Albert was excused from service against the British, and spent the war years in Berlin on the staff of the military governor of the city.

Edie's sketches are full of observational detail. This one
shows the search vessels and the submarine elevator she refers
to in the entry for 22 May. To the left is the famous cliff arch
painted several times by Monet.

one of the general hospitals. I found I had many acquain-
tances in common with her, and our tea on the terrace was
cool and delightful, with the weigela looking beautiful. I
have received a letter from an old patient of mine, telling me
he is enjoying a month's convalescence at a castle belonging
to the Duke of Buccleuch in Dumfriesshire. They have the
use of trout streams, tennis, bowls, croquet, and golf, and he
says it is a glorious place. How kind of Lord B to lend it.

May 24

Many happy returns of the day to the Empire!* The Austr-
I-lians went back to their own unit yesterday. They liked
being here and were sorry to go, and we shall miss them too.
Our staff is very fluctuating, and it means we are minus
seven trained people. I am to take over the annexe today,

* 24 May was Empire Day. The date was chosen because it was the birthday of
Queen Victoria, who had died the year before the first Empire Day was celebrated
in 1902.

and am pleased to. It is the one part of the hospital I do not know, but Major Martyn is in charge and he's a nice man to work for. A new job always makes one feel terrified, though.

May 25

Cold, rough choppy sea today and the fishing boats are having a fine pitch and toss. I wonder if the bathers will go in this morning ... We had no mail last night and there are rumours of a six-week blockade of letters in the near future – I don't know what for and hope it will not be necessary. I took over the four annexes yesterday – which means 118 beds. At present have only one VAD, and we are a bit short of staff again.

An old sergeant was telling me about the different sorts of shells the Germans send over. There's one kind called the 'oil can', whose duty it is to upset the nerves of the troops, and is the most feared of all. It looks like an oil drum and explodes with a terrific noise and vibration that is most unnerving, although it is not nearly as dangerous as the others. What the brutes do is send one of them over, and the infantry all run away from it to a dugout, then they send over a big one to destroy the dugout. Infernal inventive demons – may they suffer a martyrdom of conscience and die a slow death.

May 28

A very busy day, as the colonel, who apparently thinks the best way to get more titles is to say 'yes' to everything asked of him by those in authority, said 'yes' he could take another convoy. There was no push to do so as other hospitals were longing for it – but still he said 'yes'. He might have added that, understaffed as we are, the patients here only just get all the attention they need – but as for the care of three or four hundred extra ... I had to be prepared to take 190 instead of 140. But enough of the CO. I loathe him.

May 29

I sat beside my illest man, Maddox, for a great part of the afternoon. He can neither read nor write, but has a good memory. He has been out here from the beginning, all through Mons, the battle of the Aisne, Marne – and was at Ypres while we were at Poperinghe. A slow, funny creature, he said he used not to like fighting, 'but when your blood's up it's alright'. His injury is a kick in the stomach by a horse, which has since been shot for cruelty. I asked him what he meant by a horse being cruel. 'He was terribly cruel – used to run about biting people and knocking down the pickets – but it was a shame to kill him. He was a prize animal and a lovely worker. He didn't mean to hurt me. There were two of us on picket and he owed the other fellow a grudge because he had teased him with a stick, and he came straight for me and dug his foreleg at my stomach. I just said 'Nancy!' and he knew me, and was quiet as a lamb and nosed me and stayed beside me until they came to pick me up. He was terribly sorry for what he had done. Once, when another man was told to harness him and he went gingerly up to throw the harness across him, the horse waited until he was near enough and then picked him up by the back of his shirt and flung him away. They oughtn't to have killed him though – there is a chap in the Warwicks who can manage him. Why couldn't they get him transferred for him to look after while I am away?'

Maddox was at Méteren near Bailleul – and apparently loved it. Our men were charging straight through the village, driving the Germans before them, and as they passed one house my man's mate saw a bayonet being shoved out to kill him, so he turned his own bayonet backwards and dug it in the way the other was coming from, and killed his man. They all went into the house and found a woman fastened to the table to make a screen for them – and behind her was a little child with both arms cut off. When they saw that their blood was up and they killed all six Germans. He also told me about an occasion at Ypres when they had a lovely observation post and were not being shelled. The Germans were bombarding from six different batteries, so our men took careful observation and let them bombard. Next morning our artillery let fly at all the battery positions and gave them a thorough peppering. Next night all was quiet and the lieutenant with them said, 'Boys, you can get a good sleep tonight. I think the Germans have gone to get fresh guns.' Colonel Bairnsfather[*], the artist, was with them, and used to make true pictures of the men, write down what they said, and sent them to a newspaper.

Maddox then told me how one sapper was made up to sergeant. There was a company of REs working with them and the Germans were making a fine big sap[†] – but had not finished it. The sapper dashed down among the Germans, set a fuse and dashed back. It took a number of seconds to go off, so he was well away when it exploded. It went off well and blew up the Germans in their own sap. Meanwhile, the RE captain was sitting at a vantage point, sniping at any odd Germans that tried to escape! When our artillery were shelling the batteries, our infantry cheered as the shells burst. The German infantry heard the cheering and thought something was coming and flew to their dugout, so we put a shell in the dugout and took their trenches. He has suffered the usual hardships of eating nothing but biscuits and bully for so long, with no chance of a wash for a month and the only drinking water from a stream

---

* Actually Captain Bruce Bairnsfather (1888–1959). He was a prominent cartoonist who in 1914 had created the massively popular character of 'Old Bill', an ageing British infantryman with a balaclava and bushy walrus moustache. After the Second Battle of Ypres in 1915 Bairnsfather suffered from shellshock and deafness.
† Saps were short trenches, around 30 yards long, that ran at ninety degrees from front line trenches into no man's land. The heads of these saps were used as listening posts. During an advance, saps could be joined together to make a new front line trench.

where dead bodies were. He swears their captain was a German spy, because when he got angry he spoke so furiously they could not understand him. He says the men will kill him if they get a chance, and that an officer who is hated often gets killed by his own men when they go into action.

May 30

Another gruesome thing Sam Maddox told me was that when they were marching into Ypres they saw a company of Warwicks resting by the roadside, some sitting on the kerbstones, some lying about. They took not the least notice of the passing officer – no salute or acknowledgement. Then the officer went up to them and touched one man's cheek – and white powder fell off. He was stone dead. They had all been killed by gas as they sat or lay. Maddox said it was a horrible sight, some of them were still smiling, and some looked as if they were asleep. Major Martyn is sick of life out here and has written to the CO requesting to be transferred to the home service so that he can have his wife and children with him. It seems so comical, he and the CO mess together and see quite a lot of each other, and yet he has to write such a very formal application and 'begs to have the honour'.

Rules concerning bathing arrived yesterday. 'No mixed bathing will be allowed. The nursing staff will bathe at a given place at the given time – 2.30 p.m. to 3 p.m., when a boat will be in attendance. Bathing before breakfast will only be allowed with a responsible sister in charge.'

May 31

A convoy of about 300 arrived yesterday, which overfilled the hospital, but some will be going on to England by the next boat. Yesterday was the first of three days' *fête* for the Roman Catholic Church, 'First Communion' for the children. They went to church in a long procession, the girls in white and carrying very long candles, the boys in ordinary suits, their left arms tied with white ribbon and wearing white sailor hats. There must have been more than a hundred of them.

The glorious 1st of JUNE

A lovely morning for Ascension Day. Yesterday was blessedly peaceful, and the orderlies odded round and looked up equipment for the monthly inspection. My two VADs and I had time to spoil the patients a little. It must be a ghastly thing to be buried alive, as one of my men was. He knew his company was short-handed and that chances were he would never be found as only a part of his hand was showing above ground. His head was doubled over on to his chest and there was only ventilation enough for him to take slow, short breaths. There was a tremendous weight of sandbags and earth on his shoulders, and he spent the time wishing he had been killed outright by a shell instead of being buried in a mine. When at last they got him out, he fainted and knew no more until he was in hospital. He is a quaint, dreary creature and says he will never be the same again.

We had another of the chauffeuses in for treatment yesterday. She had crushed her hand trying to take a tyre off. She's quite a nice youngster, and it seemed to open her eyes to be in a sister's bunk for a bit. I cleaned her hand up and left it to soak in lotion while I saw to various things. The orderly came up and I did each man's diets with him, then the VADs came to be told what to do regarding treatments and a thousand odd things – then I finished the sore hand and sent her off. She came back in the evening to have it looked at and said, 'I had no idea you had to do such a lot of

Edie captured vivid glimpses of local life, such as this one of the
children of Étretat at their first communion. Her note reads,
'without the veil as they run about the streets for the rest of the day'
and *'a wreath of white flowers round her head'*.

things, you seem to have to see to everything.' I told her that
was the sister's job. I think she had an idea that the chauffeuses were the people who counted and we just kept the
patients amused.

June 2

Yesterday's Ascension Day festivities were held in perfect
weather and the place swarmed with happy trippers of all
classes. They started pouring into the town at an early hour,
some on bicycles, some walking or pushing perambulators
full of babies and food for the day. Later on the carriage folk
rolled up in dogcarts, landaus and motorcars. It was just like
a regatta day at home, all the flags were flying and people
were dressed in their Sunday best. The event of the day was
the annual service to ask a blessing on the sea for the use of
'the fishermen and all save our enemies'.

The first part of the service was held in the church, then
they came down to the sea – a long procession of first the
newly confirmed children in their robes and ties carrying

banners, then the very young orphans, beautifully dressed, the girls in white with white wreaths instead of hats, and the boys in smart little suits of all sorts, from Lord Fauntleroys* to sailors. After them came the choirmen in black cassocks and lacy surplices, the acolytes in scarlet and lace and the priests magnificently robed in handsome lace and yellow silk. Our Roman Catholic padre took the leading part and wore the most wonderful robes – there was something that looked like Brussels lace, almost trailing on the ground. When they got to the shore, the priest and his acolytes and the man bearing the crucifix were pushed out to sea in a little boat and asked for the blessing from there. The priest made the sign of the cross in the sea, using the big crucifix that was carried at the head of the procession – first at one side of the boat, then the other. Then he sprinkled the sea round him with water that had been blessed. For this, to our amazement, he used an old wooden bowl covered with silver paper and an ordinary blacking brush decked the same way.

The rest of the day was *en fête*, and in the afternoon our Scottish Canadian band from Le Havre played in front of the Casino. The bagpipe turns caused great excitement. It was not by any means all unselfishness that made me send both VADs off and the orderlies turn about for the afternoon. I quietly kept house and patients myself – I loathe being in a crowd, and I could see a good deal from the windows, including all the latest Paris fashions.

June 3

Had a half day off yesterday and walked with Matron along the Criquetot Road to a tiny village called Villainville in the

---

* The eponymous hero of Frances Hodgson Burnett's classic children's story was famous for wearing a velvet suit and a ruffled lace collar – a look that became fashionable for middle class children all over Europe in the wake of the novel's success.

Grand Val of the Seine, about 6 kilometres away. It was beautiful all the way, and we walked along a tiny road which formed the bottom of the valley. On both sides of us hills rose high and irregular, covered variously with trees, woodland growth and bracken, and there were foxgloves, bright red clover and multitudes of marguerites. Lazy old cows, tied by one leg, grazed among it, eating all they could of the clover. Occasionally we passed a small farm, or a big house in an exquisite garden, otherwise we saw no sign of human beings. Rhododendrons were at their best and were growing in clumps of mixed colours – heliotrope and bright red all in huge masses – so pretty. We went over the church – just a little old plain one – with seats for 172 people, lit by a few candles, and with little decoration except statues of Saint Antoine, Saint Joseph and Saint Marie – all decked in flowers. There were two beautiful big houses and two small farms, and the place where we had tea – a café, public house and grocer's shop, all combined. The people ought to have lived about 100 years ago, dear simple things!

After much explanation of how to get tea ready for us, the man and wife said they would do their best. We came back 15 minutes later and found one of the bar tables cleaned with a loaf of bread sat on it – no plate – and two eggs, with an egg cup and plate each for us, and that was all. We asked for butter and they seemed delighted we thought we could manage a little butter as well as all the rest. The tea had them quite stumped. The man said '*pardon*', but would we drink it hot or cold? We told him hot, and he quickly brought a big jug of it. They used no milk, but it was most delicious and very hot. Their children, big fair baby things, hung round the door and wondered what strange creatures we could be. The man's brother was coming to see him next morning and he was half laughing and half crying with joy over it. Matron's little dog distinguished himself by nearly killing a chicken – he is just a pup. We rescued it and scolded him, so that tragedy was averted. Walking back I don't wonder that they called the place 'Étretat' – which means 'Hamlet of the Setting Sun'*. Walking towards it along the valley one sees it to great advantage.

June 4

Too terribly sad news of a naval battle in which we appear to have lost very heavily – 18 ships and many men[†].

June 5

News of the sea fight not quite as bad as was rumoured yesterday. It seems we won – but with a terrible loss of life. A sergeant in the ward was opposite the gas attack made by the Germans in April. Soon after the gas was let out, the wind changed so that it was blown back over their own lines. He said it was a sickening sight to see the men lying in heaps. It took four rows of ambulances, night and day to take them away. Rather fitting that it was their men and not ours.

June 7

A horribly short-handed, muddled day, all the time trying to get the place clean. There is more cleaning to do, relative to the number of patients, than anywhere I have ever nursed. In one house there's a huge stone hall to be scrubbed, four

---

* A book called *Étretat, Hamlet of the Setting Sun* written in 1895 by American author, Henry Bacon, was used by Edie as a guide for her walks.
† This was the Battle of Jutland, the largest naval battle of the war, which was fought through the afternoon and night of 31 May and into the morning of 1 June. The Royal Navy suffered more losses than the German High Seas Fleet, but the battle effectively put an end to any German threat in the North Sea.

flights of polished stairs and landings to be kept immaculate, and landings and nine rooms the same – and two kitchens. That is the accommodation for only 28 patients, and the next house is as bad, the third worse, and the fourth worst of all. If only I could have a couple of good-sized marquees and be done with all this housework, we could get on with looking after the patients. A man told me the other day about a doctor in their regiment who drank and took no trouble with his patients – he simply ordered 'Medicine and Duty' for everything. One man who had been terribly neglected died, and the doctor was court-martialled and, said my man, ''e got 'orribly acquitted and was sent 'ome.'

June 8

Lord Kitchener and all on board the *Hampshire* were blown up off the Orkney Isles on Tuesday evening. No survivors. I wonder if there was a spy on board. If so, he succeeded in giving a famous man a glorious death, and many more suffered too. Do the Germans think for one moment that the burden of the war was on poor Kitchener's shoulders? And him aged over 70!*

June 9

A very beautiful morning out to sea, which is green and choppy and the sky very blue with white flecks of cloud. I'm quite content with it for my birthday. Mother has sent me

---

* On 5 June HMS *Hampshire*, with a crew of 650 men, set off from Scapa Flow in the Orkney Islands for Northern Russia, where Kitchener and a number of government officials were due to negotiate the Russian purchase of munitions. A great storm soon forced the *Hampshire*'s escorting ships to turn back, but the *Hampshire* ploughed on until at 8 p.m. when it hit one, or possibly two, mines and sank within 15 minutes. Kitchener's body was never found. He was in fact 65.

what I was going to buy myself – a pair of grey gloves – and
Madge and baby have sent me a champion needle-book
with fine big bobbins and needles that I have great use for,
in carpentry as well as sewing. I got them last night but
saved them to open on my veritable birthday. I finished
making my cabinet yesterday – all but the polishing – and
hope to hand it over to Matron today. I have stained it dark
oak, made from a concoction of Condy's*, methylated spirit
and iodine.

June 10

In the evening Maxey, Constable and I walked to the
English lady's garden and gathered armfuls of lovely flowers
for the wards and graves. I kept some roses and honeysuckle
for my own room and they are a great joy. Matron is much
pleased with her cabinet, and now it is polished with
beeswax and turpentine it does not look unlike old oak.
Here comes the fiend with the bell – I wonder if he will
knock and say, 'Convoy, Sisters please,' which is the polite
way of saying, 'you have to get up for first breakfast'.

June 11

Whitsunday. We had a convoy in yesterday morning and sent
about 300 away to England in the evening. I did not get any
very bad cases in the annexe, but they did in Casino 5. One
poor man had been shot in the head. There was only a tiny,
dry wound the size of a small pea to be seen in the corner of
his eye, but his brain was hit. He did not know who he was
or where he lived, he just babbled incomprehensible words.
Another with a fractured skull and one with a hand blown off
are both on the DI list, along with one poor boy with a bullet

* potassium permanganate, usually used as an antiseptic.

near the heart. It was so near that when they operated, they could not get it out because they dared not go any nearer the heart itself.

June 12

Have closed A, B and C annexes, and have only 16 patients in D. There is great excitement watching the fishing boats get off on a day like this – rough with a full high tide and strong wind. They are shoved off as far as possible then pull themselves through the big shore waves with a rope. Then when they drop that, one man punts at the stern for all he is worth while the other two fix the mast and hoist the sail. Then, quick as lightning, the man ships his oar, and fixes the rudder – then if the wind is kind, off they go. If not, they stand and the sails quiver until they get right with the wind, then it is the finest yacht race you ever saw to see half a dozen of them trying to get round the corner first. A man told me the other day that a whole lot of American ammunition had to be called in and some of the shells did not explode[*]. They found some were filled with sawdust and in many cases only the nose and time-fuse flew over to the enemy while the shell burst on our side.

June 14

Went to Villainville with Maxey. We got a lift in the funniest little cart on our way out. The old man was just a little bit drunk and was very keen to take us to Criquetot where he lived, so he could tell his wife that he was content he now had two English wives. We would have gone if the weather had looked less threatening but it meant two more miles each way. A French officer dashed past in a smart dogcart

[*] This is one of many untrue rumours that circulated during the war.

and stopped and saluted, and I fancy wanted to ask us to change to his cart, but we gave a final sort of bow. We preferred our old drunky. At the place where we had tea, the man's brother had been home on leave from Verdun. Of his section of 180, only five are left. Another man home on leave wrote after he got back to say that while he was away, all the rest of his section fell. So leave saved his life. Once at Verdun they were three days without rations – they must have been done up!

June 15

Yesterday from 6 p.m. we were officially recognised as a 950- instead of 750-bedded hospital. Our share in the annexes amounted to putting 60 mattresses down, with blankets, which gave us a good deal of furniture moving to do. VAD Turner left for good and had an auction sale – she made nearly 50 francs! She sold a variety of things including shampoo powders, a dressing-gown and the mat on the floor – which belonged to the hotel – and a candlestick she did not own. She was a nice girl, but too young for this work.

June 16

Only four well patients to mind instead of 195 in my four homes and one of them will be going out today, so we really are ready for 'the Push' when it comes.

June 18

The air is vibrant with the awe and excitement of the great advance. The well men are being hurried back to duty and the others sent to England, so all along the lines, the hospitals, from base generals to clearing stations, are prepared to receive any number of the poor fellows who must inevitably suffer. We are all waiting, breathless, for Joffre[*] to give the word of command to advance and attack, and that may be any day, or may even have been given. We shall soon know.

The Bishop came to tea yesterday. He is a fine man and earns reverence for what he is touring round to do. He told Major Martyn, who is an old friend, that he was visiting all the chaplains and telling them to pray as they had never prayed before, for success in our 'Grand Push'. He has been told something of which lines it is to be launched on and we should take the tip and pray hard – we may as well ask for the lion's share for our side – which we believe to be the right one.

June 19

I had the day off and thoroughly enjoyed it. Breakfast in bed, church at 11 for a good sermon, then lunch with old Madame – all A1! First a topped-up plate of petit pois with a few new potatoes and shreds of lettuce boiled with them, covered with plenty of fresh butter, then a beautifully dressed salad with all sorts of greenery and a hard-boiled egg, then cheese, cider and coffee. Most enjoyable. After lunch walked to Pierrefiques, a very little old village, and we went over the church. Like many others it was small with only 104 seats and very plain. On the way back we discussed whether or not it was possible to bear another person's mental burden. I said yes, to help them bear it, but Madame was not certain.

---

[*] General Joseph Joffre (1852–1931), the French general best known for his skilful tactical regrouping of the retreating Allies to win the first Battle of the Marne in 1914.

June 21

Busy day as the convoy which was supposed to come at 7 a.m. arrived at 2 p.m. There were two brothers of different regiments, who met in the train coming down – both had been to Gallipoli and were suffering from trench-foot. They were almost weeping for joy when they found themselves both marked 'E' – they deserved it. In all we have already marked 13 for England, which is fine. Kerr, who plays his pipes daily to the great delight of Étretat, was telling me about his work in mining. They often find themselves making saps so close to the German ones that they have to be totally silent. They wear rubber boots and their trolleys have rubber tyres and run on wooden rails. Sometimes they can hear the Germans under them, and when they do, they make a cross sap and let down a shaft into the mine under them. It's all up to who happens to blow up first. We have mined an entire village somewhere up the line where he was, and when the right moment comes will blow it up, Germans and all!

June 23

We hear our bombardment has started, and that our men have been practising open-country fighting for some time. We have heard guns the last day or two, but hardly think they are as far off as our business ones – probably practice going on somewhere. It all looks like the awful push, however. Colonel Douglas, who is on the Staff and knows a good deal, says we are not going to make a push, but that we are intimidating the Germans from taking troops from this front. Personally I think and hope we shall, and have done with it.

June 24

I love the way the men talk about happenings on their own front. A poor bag of bones who is 'done' and waiting for the boat, was telling me about his part of the line. 'Our part by Arras is better, but we must have the Vimy Ridge.' I said, 'Must we – why?' 'Oh, we must have the Vimy Ridge to make things right for the cavalry to go over and get them on the run. They have been sweeping our roads with their guns from the wood – so our artillery have got to blow the wood to pieces.' He talks with great interest about it all, as if there is never a doubt that what we 'must have' done will be done.

June 25

The patients for England have gone and the rest returned to duty, leaving me with 12. The hospitals all along the line are slack, waiting for 'the Push'. Three more sisters were sent up to clearing stations and I wish I had been one – although in my sane moments I know it is selfish and all ought to have a turn. If my chance comes to go again, I shall rejoice, but I am not going to ask to be sent anywhere.

June 26

My chief occupation yesterday was hunting my senior orderly. He is a man who, when he's good he's very, very good – but when he's bad, he's horrid. I cannot let it go on any longer and he will be before the colonel this morning for absenting himself from duty. We have heard distant heavy firing – I wonder if it can be the big business guns, though I hardly think so, as our nearest front is 80 miles off, more's the pity.

June 27

Quiet day. Hospital is getting very empty, but we heard that our 'Push' was to begin yesterday. BATHED for the first time and swam to the raft and dived. Water cold but lovely.

June 28

A youth in the ward had his 21st birthday yesterday and some of the men gave him a party. It was a great success. There were 13 of them but two had to feed early as they were leaving – so only 11 sat down together. They had a real gorge of strawberries and cream and cakes, and were very happy. One dear old vet said he had never seen such a tea – he only wished he could have had a photo of the table! They are such dear, grateful creatures. I heard on good authority that in future VADs are to be paid only £20 a year, with no allowances, and their camp kit is to be handed in when they leave – and a good thing too. I always have felt very strongly on the subject. We trained people hardly smelt money for our three first years, and worked much harder. These people have had money simply pushed at them, with the result that absolutely unsuitable ones have joined for the sake of the pay. Perhaps now each one will do what she is best at.

June 29

June has been a very rough month, bluster and rain nearly all the time. We bathed yesterday afternoon, then I went for a walk alone to Bénouville in the evening, which happened to be calm for an hour or two. It is rough again this morning. A convoy is expected at 6.30 a.m. – something over 300.

June 30

We were all called early yesterday for a convoy of 362, which was chiefly surgical with very few sick, and many terribly badly wounded – some in many different places. One poor fellow died soon after he was brought in. They tell tales of great doings at the front. We have been bombarding hard for five days at the rate of 1,000 shells a battery per day – and how many batteries? Hundreds upon hundreds. The Germans are getting very windy and if we send over a shell or two, or send out a small party to find their strength, they blaze away as if the general attack has begun. Also, they are carrying on with their dirty tricks. Their snipers bandage themselves up and shout for mercy, and when it is shown they start sniping our men – but not twice! I'm afraid they have done their own wounded a bad turn. One old man who had lied about his age to be young enough to enlist, wept like a baby yesterday when I told him he was going to England by the next boat. All he could say was, 'Oh, I have been lucky,' and told me that once, when they had to attack, he dropped as soon as he was over the parapet because his rheumatism was so bad, and an officer hauled him up and pushed him back over it – and neither was hit! He has a wife and ten children to go back to, and has honestly done his bit, so good luck go with him.

July 1

Our English patients left yesterday, leaving the work light – and five sisters arrived from England, two stripes and three staffs. They had been travelling a long time and were very weary. Received a little silver paper-knife from Thomas last night as a memento of her illness, which is very kind of her.

July 2

The last eight days the guns have been firing the whole time. Fine big ones they must be for us to hear them so distinctly, and how the china must be rattling at the clearing stations! The Germans have been giving themselves up and coming across in dazed groups – which is fine. How absolutely glorious if we knock them right out and level them flat, so our infantry and cavalry can have a walkover such as would make good reading in history. Took a half day and went to Gonneville with Matron and Toby. We walked the nine kilometres along the Le Havre Road, then had tea at the famous old inn there. We found a couple of padres having tea, so we all came back in their car, along the valley by Criquetot. There was a wonderful sunset last night, the sea like a millpond, and the reflection on it like molten gold, too bright to look at. As it changed through every colour in the paint box, it became more and more beautiful.

July 3

Our much-longed-for advance has begun after many days of heavy bombardment, and we launched an attack at 7.30 on Saturday morning*. They went over in waves, the second one so many minutes after the first, and so on. Where one man from the first wave was wiped out, so was the second, which gave the Germans time to adjust their machine-guns to receive the rest. After the second wave they began to make headway and had them fairly on the run. We took the front-line trenches for a distance of 25

* The massive Somme Offensive had finally begun on 1 July, and on the first day alone British casualties amounted to almost 60,000 men. By the time the battle petered out in mid-November, there were nearly 1,110,000 casualties in total.

miles and actually took the four front lines, but had to retire to the first because they had the range of the other three and started shelling them. We had a couple of trainloads of wounded down – 1,100 in all, including 153 officers (very dirty), and the London Scottish kilts were a sight to behold. I don't know how many we took in the annexes, I remembered up to 140, then lost count. The first lot were all fed and more or less washed, but not all dressed, when the second lot came at 6 p.m. At 9.30 we sent off 360 from the whole hospital, then at 2 a.m. more were to go – then at 7 p.m. the next train of wounded is expected.

July 4

Wounded! Hundreds upon hundreds on stretchers, being carried, walking – all covered from head to foot in well-caked mud. The rush and buzz of ambulances and motor-buses is the only thing I can remember of yesterday outside my wards. Inside it took us longer than the whole day to anything like cope with the work of changing, feeding and dressing the wounds of our share of them. We had horribly bad wounds in numbers – some crawling with maggots, some stinking and tense with gangrene. One poor lad had both eyes shot through and there they were, all smashed and mixed up with the eyelashes. He was quite calm, and very tired. He said, 'Shall I need an operation? I can't see anything.' Poor boy, he never will. Three men died in the train and two only just reached hospital before they went west too. Three were completely dumb. They say we are serving the division that has acted as a 'draw' to save the other divisions. If any are left, they deserve all honour.

Early casualties from the Somme: some of the first stretcher-borne
wounded reach an advanced dressing station, surrounded
by a crowd of curious onlookers.
Photograph: The Royal Engineers No.1 Printing Company © IWM Q56

July 6

I give up trying to describe it – it beats me. In ordinary times
we get a telegram from Abbeville saying a train with so many
on board has left and is coming to us. Then they stopped
giving numbers – just said 'full train'. Now not even a
telegram comes – but the full trains do. Yesterday, in addition to our 1,300 beds we took over the lounge of a large
restaurant, the orderlies' barracks, the ambulance garage, the
Casino front and part of the officers' mess, and used all
except the garage – which is ready for today. We were not
able to send any on to England, as the boats were full, so if
full trains continue to pour in today we shall have to start on
private people's houses.

I have 41 German prisoners among my lot and I don't

know how many English. I hadn't time to make lists and they just sent in as many as they liked. It is just a case of all houses overfull, and the restaurant lounge and officers' mess belong to me too. Some of the men are terribly wounded – eight have died and more will. One thing to be grateful for – very few officers came down with the last lot. It is wonderful how sufficient work makes one not mind certain things. Unpleasant insect companions are the terror of my life. Many came down with the Tommies, and some have transferred their affections to us. We hadn't a quarter of a second to hunt them, so just forgot all about them until bedtime, which came late. It is a mercy to have had dry weather for the sake of the men we have out in the open. My Germans see very little of me or of my VADs, and some must do without a woman's care and be left chiefly to orderlies – with my pleasure. Some of them are Prussians and very bitter, so they can just get on with their bitterness. Yesterday I had to close the shutters of their room – the French people were treating us like a peep-show.

July 8

It is to be hoped our attacking is doing useful work for the war as we are paying a tall price! Every day now we have trainfuls down – the place is thick and threefold with them. The surgeons are amputating limbs and boring through skulls at the rate of 30 a day – and not a day passes without Death taking his toll. We all get up early and work late and feel a bit 'done' sometimes, which gives us the satisfaction of feeling that now at least we are giving our full strength to the war.

This is the last straw! Yesterday afternoon we were doing dressings as fast as we could and in came Major Martyn, who said, 'If you can find 12 stretcher cases who could sit as

far as Le Havre, get them quick and I can put them on full
cars going now.' I then had to rush like a lunatic through all
the houses to find 12 (and only got eight) who could sit for
one and a half hours. Rigged them up in any clothes, got
them carried to the ambulances as they passed – and now
the batman has just rung the call bell, but he has not
thumped on the door and said, 'Convoy, Sister please.' I am
so thankful. They took one of my orderlies yesterday for up
the line, leaving me one VAD (a good one), and three orderlies for who knows how many patients. One house has 100
in, the other three not so many – but more stretcher cases
are coming in. However, we can only do our best.

July 9

Yesterday was a big scramble – 600 were evacuated from all
parts of the hospital, chiefly to England but also to convalescent camp, and one to Le Havre. We moved all our
stretcher patients and English walking cases, so all had
dressings to be done, all patients had to be fed once or twice
and all had to be got ready – then off or on a stretcher.
Moving these painful people takes it out of one! To get as
many as possible away when there was room on the floor of
a car, I looked round for a stretcher case who could sit for a
short time and shoved him in. I think they would rather be
strapped to the roof than left behind.

July 10

We evacuated all day yesterday and cleared most of the hospital, and I have only eight patients left. Spent the afternoon
in Casino 5, where the cases are too bad to travel – and was
OFF DUTY in the evening. Went to church with Matron
and heard a good sermon. The padre asked me to play the
organ and I said, 'Yes, failing a better.' Thank goodness, the

'better' soon came. The Presbyterian padre plays beautifully and he arrived in the nick of time. It is like old times – and very old they seem – to be sitting up in bed and writing before getting up instead of being as quick as a lunatic from 6 a.m. to midnight.

The sea looks lovely and jumpy and clean and thirst-quenching ... I wonder if anyone, short of a wounded man, really knows what thirst is. Standing at the door of any ward you hear one continuous plea from all sides for water, a drink – anything to drink – and all of us are giving drink as much as we possibly can, as well as doing the other jobs. One man in Annexe 5 died while I was there, and at least three will be the happier when they manage it too – one with his brain out, another his intestines, and a third wounded all over and wildly off his head. Some drink deep, vomit it any-where, then plead for more water. Many men have told me that after our men have attacked, the Germans sweep the ground low with a machine-gun to kill our wounded. I should think that is an act best left to God to reward. He will do it thoroughly.

July 11

We were grateful for a calm day yesterday to let us put our houses in order. The DG, Sir Arthur Sloggett*, and Colonel Black came round, and the DG asked Matron to accept for herself, and to convey to her staff, his thanks for the way the rush of the last week was met and dealt with. It was kind of him to be appreciative.

* Sir Arthur Thomas Sloggett (1857–1929) had been Director-General of Army Medical Services since 1914. While a competent administrator, he was completely ignorant of psychological disorders such as shellshock, describing sufferers as 'lunatics' and in at least one case forcing the closure of a psychiatric unit.

July 12

I have slept late this morning and now have been called with the well-known 'Convoy, Sister please.' Yesterday was a peaceful day and I gardened in our back yard in the morning, then crabbed in the afternoon and caught quite a lot, but gave them to the woman who showed us how. I took my shoes and stockings off and the sea was warm with many vari-coloured anemones, shells and seaweeds, which made the rocks beautiful.

July 13

Yesterday was a very busy day – a convoy in first thing and one sent out in the afternoon to be ready for the next one. I had only 63 of yesterday's convoy – two too ill to go on for a time, and I fear one boy may not get better. He has pneumonia caused by a lump of lead in his left lung and I suppose they will not be able to operate. He is so blue and bad, poor dear. Went for a short walk with Matron along the Fécamp Road last night. She is much distressed that the muzzling order is to be enforced here and Toby has to wear one or die. We made him a soft little one and hope he will get used to it. Yesterday's cases were on the whole not so bad – only about 20 on the DI list. We had 5,000 men through this hospital last week.

July 14

Of my two ill boys, one is still *very* ill – DI – and the other a little better. If only I knew the creature had no bits of shrapnel in his lungs I should be much happier, but am terribly afraid he has. One motor VAD told me things last night that, if true, are horrible. She said sometimes on the way to Le Havre the men on stretchers cried out with the pain caused by jolting, and one man told her that he would rather stay in

France for 20 years than do that journey again. Another started bleeding badly from the jolting – but what is to be done? Our poor MOs have, on the one side, a man fit to travel – then on the other, if he is going to die, they want to get him home to see his people. Also, the DMS and ADMS are sending orders to say, 'Clear all beds any way you can.' Still, there is the fact that the driver VADs are very young, and probably can't help thinking a molehill a mountain.

If I had the time I would collect seaweed in a book – there is one sort I have never seen before. Under water it is a bright blue, but out of water it is just like that valuable old pottery – a sort of blackish brown with a blue glisten on it. We walked across the freshwater stream and found it strong and cold, and the old washerwomen thought we were quite mad, but that we are used to by now, the old villains! We saw how it is our clothes come back in holes – each of them had a bottle of chloride of lime and at the least stain they pour it lavishly on all the same – coarse or fine cloth. In the evening after supper I went for a walk with Matron and Toby – without his muzzle. Later in the evening I made him a new one that is a muzzle, but he can still open his mouth wide in it.

July 15

I watched patients loaded on to the *Asturias*, and meanwhile spoke to some of the sisters whom I knew on her. She is a magnificent boat. The ship's officers were playing tennis on a deck away up in the sky! On the way back we found our way to St Jouin, a charming little seaside place famous for its old hostess – La Belle Ernestine* – and her home, where

---

* Ernestine Aubourg (1841–1918) was a society beauty and hostess famed throughout France in her day, a magnet for the artistic and literary set and the subject of tributes from writers such as Dumas and de Maupassant.

one can get tea. We saw the house we thought it was, but would not go in without asking, it looked so exactly like an old château belonging to some high and mighty family. In its beginning, I feel sure it was. Having made sure, we went in and were introduced to La Belle. She is 75, a tall, fine woman, not very pretty now, but such a dear old thing. After tea she showed us some of her treasures, a letter written to her in Indian by an Indian Prince who lived for some time at Étretat and was an admirer of hers, and some queer Indian gods he had given her. There was a picture of his body being burnt on the shore at Étretat, according to Indian custom, and a little sketch of Queen Elizabeth of Spain*, done while she was staying there. She had several poems written to her many years ago by artists and poets staying there, and she read them to us with great feeling. I couldn't understand all, but most of them eulogised 'her beautiful blue eyes', her figure and her spirit, which was so joyful and so kind, that to demand was to have the thing done. The house is full of valuable old china, pewter, copper and brass, and it would take days to really see it all – and the garden is a dream. Her granddaughter – her daughter's child whose father was a nobleman – was also there, a very pretty aristocratic girl of 18 who spoke English like a well-bred Englishwoman.

We walked home by the valley, through Bruneval, La Poterie-Cap-d'Antifer and Le Tilleul and were home at 8.30 – late for supper. The VAD who drove us was a nice woman, poor dear, she has lost both brothers in this war. The elder was a barrister, doing well in China, and died at No. 2 CCS at Bailleul three months after he joined the army. The younger was in the navy and lost his life in that great battle

---

* Not Elizabeth but Queen Isabella of Spain, deposed in 1869, who lived in exile in France until her death in 1904. She came to Étretat in September 1880.

that our muddle-headed papers at first gave out as a defeat, silly fools. He was on board one of the three plucky little cruisers who rushed like terriers into a pack of mad bulls, full speed all guns blazing away, right in amongst the German fleet and drew all fire on to themselves. It was a splendid act of the utmost bravery, for the sake of our battle squadron coming up behind, and they expected and knew they must all die in the doing of it. Miss Douglas' father retired an admiral and was given a beautiful all-silk admiral's flag at the time. She had been longing for a naval victory for an occasion to hoist it. When the news of this battle came she thought it wasn't a victory, but she heard the truth later and hoisted it on the day of her brother's memorial service. She was very sad about her elder brother's death, because he did not belong to the army, and was her advisor and about all she had. The younger one, she said, had been in the navy since his school days and they always knew he might have to give his life.

July 16

Calm day yesterday. My ill boy is holding his own, but that is all. If there is a bit of lead near his heart, has he a chance? He may even be dead when I next go on duty. Off in the afternoon and had the most delightful bathe I can remember, the sea warm and absolutely clear with waves smooth-topped and lumpy.

July 17

Convoy of 300-odd arrived at 1.30 p.m. None, thank God, DI or SI. Where they all went I don't know, as I only had 34 – 13 stretchers and the rest sitters. They all seemed very comfortable. My poor little chest boy is dying. The lump of lead is in the diaphragm, causing an agony of pain with a poisonous abscess. He has general poisoning from it now and a temperature of 104° all the time. I hope he will still be there this morning, so far as I am concerned – but for him, I wish him well away, where he will only know about happy things. The British cavalry has been in action for the first time since 1914 and we have entered our enemy's third line of defence! Oh happy day, when the blighters start to run!

July 18

My ill boy was surprisingly well yesterday, and yet they say there is humanly speaking no hope at all for him. Perhaps he will have quietly slid out through the night ... I hope he won't mind going. It was one of our MO's 15th wedding anniversary yesterday. He says he is quite pleased with married life and thinks it infinitely preferable to living single, and he advises one to 'take the man if he loves you', as even if you don't love him, it will grow in time. I said I would bear it in mind, but was afraid it had come a little late for me.

July 19

I hardly dare write it down, but my dying boy was a shade better yesterday. Perhaps we have yet to learn what the Great Physician can do – or perhaps it was just a short flash of betterness. Made lace beside my sick boy in the evening as the other patients were well enough to be looked after by an orderly. I have been glued to this base for eight months now, and wish they would send me back to a CCS. Never mind – take your job and don't grizzle. This is a lovely place.

Ill boy still holding his own and am longing to know how he is this morning. Lovely summer's day yesterday and many off-duty people bathed. I was not off till the evening, then went for a long walk with Matron and Toby. Rested in a hayfield on the cliff top to enjoy the view, then came back just a breath late for second supper. This 'early saving bill'* is most misleading. It was really 4.30 a.m. when I got up and very cold, and is now only 5 a.m., calling itself 6. The sea is dead calm and there are salmony-pinky coloured clouds warming up to full day. It is frightfully tempting to run out for a dip but rules are so strict not to go without a boat! Excitement is growing among the people here and they think the war will end in or before September. Please may they be right!

July 21

My ill boy is going to die after all. He is simply being poisoned by his own system. I suppose the lump of lead is making havoc of the lung and that is going bad and poisoning him. He talked more yesterday than ever before, but does not look right and has such a quick pulse. I think he will die quite soon. Yesterday was a gloriously fine day. I was off in the afternoon and many of us bathed, and one, Miss Andrew, swam out into the strong currents and was nearly drowned – she sank twice, then the boat got her. It is a pity to swim out too far as it only means more rules being made for everyone. Ill boy still alive, but very, very ill indeed. Lovely day today and off in the afternoon, so we bathed. The sea was so clear we could see the under-sea part of people swimming far away – and could see the bottom easily in water deeper than ourselves. Maxey, Constable and I took tea on to the cliff – watermelon and rolls with tea – very good. New Assistant Matron arrived, who has been jumped from Staff Nurse to this present job.

* In order to help the war effort by saving energy, the Summer Time Act of 1916 followed the example of Germany and many other European countries by advancing the clocks for one hour between 21 May and 1 October.

July 24

A heavy convoy is coming in this morning, so we must all be up for first breakfast. It isn't to be wondered at after the fighting there has been the last two or three days. We took La Longueville, then the Germans got a footing in the north of it again, and before 5.30 yesterday another village had changed hands.

July 25

Busy day yesterday, a convoy of 450 arrived at 9 a.m. We took in 80 and sent 22 on to England, and a further 20 to a general hospital. Poor wretches! One cannot help feeling sorry for them. While they were waiting for their car to take them to their destination, two of them added to their troubles by getting away and drinking brandy. They were found drunk and put in the guardroom, where they became violent and smashed everything they could. I wonder why they have sunk so low – they may have the kindest natures, and a whole lot of good in them. When I told one old sergeant to change back quick to khaki to go home to England, he laughed and sobbed and thanked me, all in one. He had been through many 'thick of its' and had not been home to his wife and children. I told him it was the MO who was sending him back, not me, but they so often think it is we sisters who send them – but after all, what could we do without the signature of the MO in charge, and of the CO. My ill boy in status quo.

July 26

Lovely day yesterday and many of us bathed and enjoyed it very much. In the evening the sky and sea were a picture of beauty and soft shadows. This morning is just right too, but the silly boat will not be out for sure. Later I risked it and found the boat *was* out and had the bathe of my life. The water was as clear as glass, and when quite far out of my depth I could see the pebbles below as clearly as in six inches of fresh water. Collins came too but the others will be sorry they did not come with us.

July 27

My ill boy may be dead by now. He was dying yesterday and knew it. I stayed with him until 11 o'clock and he implored me 'not to leave him in the night' – but that would be impossible. I only hope the poor little creature is happily away. The English patients were to go at 4 a.m., so I expect the men were all up then and are too tired. Epilepsy is very much like being possessed of devils. While I was on late duty one epileptic had a succession of about four most distressing fits.

July 28

My poor ill boy did not manage to get away yesterday, but he is terribly feverish and weak and keeps coughing up stuff from fresh abscesses – as soon as one dies off, another starts. Lena Ashwell's concert party were here and gave us a charming selection of songs and violin and piano pieces. Yesterday was muggy, and everywhere shrouded in white mist – and today bids fair to be the same. The sea is just right for a dip, but I have not the least doubt that the men of the boat will say it is too foggy. Any excuse is better than taking the boat out. I had a pathetic letter from my boy's mother last night – poor thing, she is suffering far more than he is.

July 29

Ill boy in status quo. There was a heavy sea mist yesterday, but I bathed in the afternoon, then went for a walk with

Matron and Toby after supper. The lights and shades and various effects were wonderful. All the country, even close round, was blotted out, and the opposite cliff and the church were not to be seen at all. Only the little crescent of houses and bathing huts were visible. Out to sea, there was a magnificent sunset in progress but only at the brightest part was it able to glimmer through. The sea, dead calm, managed to get just a few of the sunset rays to play with – very curious and wonderful.

July 30

The boat did go out and we had a glorious bathe, but a French girl went out too far and got into trouble. A Frenchman in all his clothes dashed in after her first, then one of our orderlies went to the rescue. By the time we had floundered up she was out, had returned what she had taken of the sea and was feeling better. If only they would bathe nearer our boat! Off in the afternoon and went with Maxey to a glorious garden where we cut flowers to our hearts' content, and when we both had double armfuls we asked the old man how much. He, with an apologetic look of 'hope it's not too much', said, '*Deux francs les deux*', so then we did the flowers in both churches, took bundles to the ward, gave some away and still had enough left for our own rooms.

July 31

Not a glimmer of hope for my poor boy Lennox[*]. He has a generally poisoned condition and is daily weaker and worse. He has been good, but now is so tired I think he will

[*] Through research, Edie's family learned that this was Rifleman James Lennox of the 12th Battalion, Royal Irish Rifles. Lennox, who was 24, came from Harryville, Ballymena. Diary references to him begin on 13 July.

be glad of a rest. I was off duty last night and went for a lovely walk with Matron and Toby, over the golf links cliff as far as the first coastguard station. We climbed down to the shore and found to our great surprise that Miss Wallen's hut was right there, and not miles further on, as we had thought. The evening was the sunniest and hottest we have had, and she was just going for a bathe, and I so wished I could too. She was undressing like lightning to go out in a little fishing boat, that was just starting out. Matron had a brainwave and said, 'Why not hurry up and have a dip? A boat is a boat, and that is enough to swear by.' So I borrowed a gown and had a delightful bathe, all far from Étretat and everyone, in this wild little bay. Never enjoyed a bathe more in my life.

August 1

A convoy of 380 arrived soon after 8 o'clock yesterday morning and my share made me up to a family of 69, so instead of a bathe it was, 'Convoy, Sister please', and first breakfast. I got up soon after 5 o'clock by mistake, but am glad, because I saw a queer thing out at sea. Quite what the break of white was I could not make out, but she was going at a decent rate. I imagine it was something to do with the excitement of yesterday. All the morning and up to teatime, four or five hydroplanes and the airship were scouting busily. Then at tea time there was an explosion, which to those who knew was unmistakably a shell bursting. We were both startled nearly out of breath, and went out to find ... absolutely nothing. No-one even seemed to have heard it or wondered what it was. When I went back to the ward all the men said that it was a bursting shell – perhaps a shot from a naval gun at sea or a bomb dropped for practice by an aeroplane. One man told me he was quite sure he had seen a submarine. In the evening we heard from the coastguard on the cliff that the aircraft had been scouting for a submarine all day, and one of them had dropped a bomb on it. If so, good luck – and I enjoyed the noise!

August 2

Yesterday was the hottest day this summer ... lovely. The ADMS has received orders to prepare all base hospitals on the super-expansion scale for the next big push, which means we are to be ready to take 1,600 without turning a hair – any number at a push.

August 3

The afternoon was so hot, all I felt equal to was a bath and then to sit on the shore and watch the bathers. The women finish at 3 p.m., then patients, orderlies, officers, and all and sundry have their innings. There must have been well over 100 of them and all but about 12 could swim well. They looked like so many seals swarming round the raft and diving off in all directions! My ill boy Lennox has got a surgical emphysema, which shows that lung destruction is going on and I am afraid he cannot put up a fight against that.

August 4

Had a letter from the mother of my ill boy. She asks that he may write just two words to her and she will feel more content. So I went back to the ward last night, in case he is not there this morning, and helped him do it. It is a poor little five-word scrawl, but I hope it will please her poor soul. The hospital sports are to be held tomorrow, bar convoy, etc. There are two items for us sisters – an egg-and-spoon race and a table decorating competition. Our mess is giving the prize for the tug o'war.

August 5

Ill boy very sick and sore all day and getting worse. No other special news – three sisters are already up and away to gather flowers for the decorating of their tables this afternoon.

August 6

The sports were a great success. All went off well and the ordnance band was a great treat to us all. Both my VADs went in for the table decoration competition, and one got first prize and the other second – so that was not so bad for the old annexe. One of our orderlies took two prizes and came fourth in the three-mile race. I did not join them until the evening, but it seems it was all very pretty and good fun.

August 7

Ill boy even worse. Two or three sisters were promised 'long days' but at suppertime a telegram came telling of a convoy of 400 coming this morning, so it will be 'Convoy, Sister please' and early breakfast. The port has been closed for three or four days owing to submarines. A merchantman with ammunition arrived safely three days ago, but the vessel behind him was blown to bits and he was unable to help. I expect the spies keep our enemies well informed of when ammunition is sent. The submarines have probably been caught now, as there was a delivery of mail last night.

August 8

A convoy of 400 in, and we sent an English convoy out, so I am left with a family of 64. None seriously ill, except poor

Lennox, who really seems to be chained to Earth. He is so utterly weak, that even to turn his head is hard work. I wrote to his mother and fiancée for him again yesterday, and wanted him to tell me his own words, but all he said was, 'I don't know what there is you could say.' I knew his mother was his greatest anxiety, and so wrote, 'I am no stronger at all – but I have tried my hardest to take all my food and medicine, and to get well.' He said, 'Yes, say that I wanted her to know just that.' I don't think he will be detained longer than this week, and hope not, for his own sake. Was not off duty, but went for an hour's walk with Matron from 6.30 – about which I am sure I shall hear from my MO. If ever I am off in the evening he tells me I had a half day off – the old silly. He likes to come at the same time, sit in the same chair, and find the same person writing the night report every night. I suppose because at home he finds the same person to talk to, he thinks he ought to here.

Ambulances in Étretat in the early years of the war. Edie refers several times in her diaries to the *chauffeuses* or VAD drivers. The woman seated at the wheel here, however, is not a driver but a QAIMNS nurse.
Photograph courtesy of Brian Dunlop

August 9

It is getting uncommonly parky in the early morning – and of course we must not forget that 5.30 is really 4.30, so it would be cold. Yesterday morning something rather interesting crossed our path. A biggish steamer, evidently wounded, was towed backwards past here towards Le Havre. There were two mine-sweepers just in front and an additional tug in attendance. Some people say there was a submarine alongside, but personally I did not see that. If that was the case, the steamer had probably been torpedoed ineffectually, and the submarine had been taken. I had a terrible fierce lecture from my MO last night, on not being married. He is a dear old thing, and says he has found marriage an undiluted success, so I told him, with the saddest look I could raise, that 'my day was done' – it was *too late*!

August 10

I had a half day yesterday, so Matron and I took tea to the beautiful solitary bay where Miss Wallen has her hut. She is very kind and allows us to use it and all her things, so we only took milk and eatables. First we bathed, and the sea was dead calm and warm – then had tea of hard-boiled eggs, tomatoes, cucumber and bread and butter. We started for home and met Miss Wallen, who was having two of our sisters to supper – and she has asked us to go some time.

August 11

Not off yesterday, as my ill boy was too ill. I thought he was going to manage to slip away – but no, he was not allowed to, poor boy. He will be vastly happier when he does. I hope he will be alive this morning, all the same, I have a letter from his mother that he will like to know about.

August 12

It's 31 days since Lennox came in, and he is still not able to get away. He won't be long though, as the bad chest attacks are more frequent now and poor dear, he will be so grateful to be gone. The last two days and nights have been sultry, and I have been glad of my morning dip to cool me down. Poor old Major Martyn has to bathe all alone after us, as he can't get any of the others to come out. He is a married man with a large family, so I don't see why he shouldn't come with us. Went for short walk with Matron last night, then back to the ward. Toby is ill and we think he has been kicked. One of my corporals, an old vet, is attending him and he is getting better. Yesterday he gave him a dose of Epsom salts, turpentine, iodine and olive oil, all mixed up together and he was much better for it. We hear that the three bursts of heavy firing we heard two nights ago, at 9 p.m., 10 p.m., and 2.30 a.m., were from some of our boats, probably firing at Zeppelins on their journey to and from England.

August 13

Hottest day we have had, and we bathed before breakfast and in the afternoon too. Captain Scott came to examine Lennox in the evening – I wish to goodness he would leave him alone.

August 14

The firing and explosion we heard about four days ago was a steamer of ours being blown up by a submarine; there were six hidden away there and our vessels fired at them, but I don't know if any have been caught. The port has been closed three days now – more submarines about. Maxey,

Constable and I took tea to a cave and were cool for once. It is underwater at high tide and the water was dripping through the rocks all the time. It is a huge cave and could hold 100 people without turning a hair, and we just sat and looked across at the heat and Étretat, and got cooler and cooler. It was a very fairyland of a cave, with all sorts of anemones and small shellfish clinging to the rocks – when we touched the anemones they let out tremendous squirts of water at us!

August 15

Yesterday was quiet in the hospital. Matron is on the sick-list with an over-strained heart. We are all terribly sorry, but I do not in the least wonder at it after all she has gone through and done, and the little leave she has had. As I know her, I am doing her washings and bed-makings, morning and evening, while my wards are not busy. She and Lennox are my two 'bad' patients. Some English patients left yesterday, although the port is still closed.

Five former colleagues, Palmer, Allen, Ginboal, Smith and Leedam, visited us from the *Asturias* – they are looking fat and well. We hear two submarines have been caught – so I suppose there are still four more to be rounded up. However, the port is open and we had a huge mail in last night. The early mornings are getting very grey. It is low tide and the men are crab-hunting on the rocks. They look like big crabs themselves, creeping about in their red sail-cloth garments. Yesterday was a scampering, busy day for me – up early and did Matron for the day in the time when I was due to be off. Then had to be back in the ward for Major Martyn and Captain Scott to explore Lennox's chest. In the evening bathed Matron, then flew on duty again. Poor Lennox is bad and everything is up and down in the two houses I have open, but when no one watches, if you take the stairs at the

bounce they are not so tiring – and I am more than pleased
to do all I can for Matron.

August 17

Lennox is worse, but Matron the same. It was a glorious day
and the bathing boat was out again – but I was too busy.

August 19

I see by yesterday's casualty lists that four nurses have been
wounded. I knew one of them – Miss Tunley was Matron at
No. 10 Stationary Hospital when I was there. Funnily
enough, while we were there she was told by a fortune-
teller that she would be sent up the line and would be
wounded! That was nearly two years ago and she has been
to Egypt in the meantime. Eight VADs were to have had
days off today, but a convoy is expected, which will put the
lid on that.

August 20

We had a convoy of 450 in on Saturday, making my family up
to 79. As we have only two orderlies, we were quite busy
enough. Matron is still my out-patient. She has improved
much in her week of complete rest, and may be allowed to
wash herself after today. Poor Lennox is even worse – only
his heart and eyes are alive, but all the rest of him is dead,
poor dear.

August 22

Matron was up for the first time yesterday. She looks none
too well, and my private opinion is that she ought to be sent
away for a long rest. Major Martyn has fixed a good map of

the Western Front on the wall of my bunk – so now we shall know all about where we are!

August 23

Lennox died soon after 8 o'clock last night. Never have I seen such a slow, painful death. It was as if the boy was chained to Earth for punishment. Towards the end it was agony for him to draw his little gasping breaths and I felt I must clap my hand over his nose and mouth and quench the flickering flame. I am very glad for the boy to be away.

August 28

Have earache and spent a day fomenting my ear. Yesterday morning Major Martyn opened the swelling with a knife, since when it has been vastly more comfortable, but I'm now as deaf as an adder in both ears – one because I have wool in it, and the other because I have a cold. There is going to be a 'board' on Major Martyn today, to consider the advisability of giving him three weeks' sick leave, as his heart goes wrong at times.

September 8

I have not written my diary for a while because my ears have been bad and I have been a very miserable person, just creeping out of bed in time for breakfast and spending all my free time in my bed with poultices on my ears. Yesterday I had a half day and took Matron in the car to Yport and other pretty little places along the coast. After that Maxey and I walked to Miss Wallen's hut for a bathe. Unfortunately she was giving a tea to a large number of French people, so we quickly changed our plans and trudged along the beach to some huge rocks. The tide was rough and high, but we undressed into our bathing gowns and played the mermaid in the rock pools and over the rocks. It was great fun and we had a good buffeting.

September 9

The Colonel is away on urgent family affairs, Major Martyn is on sick leave for three weeks and Matron off duty. Truslove went sick yesterday so our staff is far under number, so heaven help us when the expected rush does come.

September 11

We had a convoy of 399 in yesterday, but only 70 wounded. By far the majority of the sick were suffering badly from shellshock. It is sad to see them – they dither like palsied old men, and talk all the time about their mates who were blown to bits, or their mates who were wounded and never brought in. The whole scene is burnt into their brains and they can't get rid of the sight of it. One rumpled, raisin-faced old fellow said his job was to take bombs up to the bombers, and sometimes going through the trenches he had to push past men with their arms blown off or horribly wounded, and they would yell at him, 'Don't touch me,' but he had to get past, because the fellows must have their bombs. Then he would stand on something wobbly and nearly fall down – and see it was a dying or dead man, half covered in mud. Once he returned to find his own officer blown to bits – a leg in one place, his body in another. Another man told me quite calmly, 'Our Div was terribly cut up, because we had to be a sacrifice to let the others advance . . . and they did advance all right.'

A Canadian said to me yesterday he didn't know how the British Tommies had done what they did. They had advanced uphill and taken dugouts that were like underground fortresses, some as much as 60 feet deep, and well fortified. They all think the next advance will be less difficult than the last, and also that Fritz's number is up. *May they be right.*

September 12

Yesterday I sent 17 of my shellshocks off to Le Havre, where they are to receive special treatment. I should have liked to keep them here, treating them would be very interesting. In the afternoon took Toby for a walk over the cliffs to Miss Wallen's hut. I was quite alone there and enjoyed it immensely. I bathed, sat with not much on and my hair loose and read, then a heavy rain shower came and we sheltered in the hut. While I was there an aeroplane flew past so low over the water that the man on board waved to me.

A mine-sweeper put a boatload of men ashore for provisions. Such a relief to see the blue uniforms! The sailor boys looked such young clean creatures! Lena Ashwell came with her party yesterday and gave us a most excellent concert – quite the best so far. She is a true artist in the way of reciting and acting, and the men loved it. There were two short acts – a funny one something to do with a bathroom at 8.30, and the other was entitled 'The £12 look', in which Lena took chief part. The men were like great children when they came back. They trooped along after me, all talking at once! One boy knew Mr Ben Field, the principal actor. Apparently he had taken boys' parts with him before his voice broke.

The tales the men from the Somme tell are terrible – how some poor fellows go mad, and some die from fright or shock –

One of the most celebrated actresses of the day, Lena Ashwell
pioneered the concept of touring theatrical entertainment
for serving troops in the Great War. This postcard was
part of the popular Rotary Photographic Series.

and all swear terribly. One very quiet man told me swearing
was not his habit, or any joy to him, but he swore as much as
any man when shells were coming over. 'It helps one to bear
it quite wonderfully,' he said. One time they were following
the 1st Warwicks and the Black Watch and had to advance
over No-Man's-Land, strewn thick with our own dead and not
a square yard without a dead body on it. The Warwicks had
been almost entirely wiped out and the Black Watch nearly as
bad. And they always say, 'We took what we had to.'

September 14

We had a sudden hurried order to clear the hospital
yesterday, so we have. I have only 20 patients left – it should
have been 19, but a sergeant threw himself into the water

and is now a prisoner patient. It was sad to send so many to convalescent camp who have only been in four days, they were not well, but just too 'nearly well' to go to England, and they will be wanted back up the line as soon as possible.

September 15

Hospital now reduced to 13 patients as we are awaiting the great push. Matron is supposed to come back on light duty tomorrow. I fell down last night and cut my knee and broke my watch.

September 17

Had the day off yesterday. Indeed, I think about half the staff did too as we have so very few patients in. I went for a walk with Wood and Maxey over the cliffs and lunched with Madame – crab, roast mutton, grilled potatoes and salad, then a delicious sort of cheese that is traditionally eaten with sugar then cider, and all followed by coffee. At 1 o'clock Matron, Maxey and I started off for Caudebec en Caux, but we broke down five minutes after we started out and went back for a fresh car. The journey was a joy of beauty, bathed in sunshine. The Seine was most picturesque, with all the trees and hills along its banks just beginning to turn to autumn. We looked all about Caudebec and much enjoyed the oldness of it all, especially the church, then had tea at the Hotel de Marine.

September 19

We were called at 4 a.m. yesterday to admit a heavy convoy of wounded from the latest action. There were only 115 walkers, all the rest were badly wounded. Among mine there is one boy with his leg in such an awful state that I think it will have to come off, and on his chest there is a deep, wide wound about eight inches long, and both his arms are wounded. The two beside him have wounds right through the chest, and another man in the same room has his intestines sticking out through his ribs. However, they all seem very cheerful about things.

A company sergeant major (CSM) told me that these new guns that go with them in the advance are a tremendous help – they crash along over German trenches and the Germans really fear them*. The Germans have been giving themselves up in groups and will come over and help any stretcher-bearers, or do anything they can to not be killed. They are quite right not to expect mercy, because they have been doing the despicable thing of killing our wounded! The CSM has an excellent photo of the Kaiser and some of his officers, which was given him by an old, old man for sparing his life – but he need not have given it. The sergeant major said he could never have killed such an old man. They say the numbers of German dead are appalling!

So far the Germans seem to be living right well and the Tommies have found wine, cigars, soda water and other comforts in their front-line trenches. Evidently they considered their dugouts absolutely safe, because they had their wives and families to stay with them there, and often our people have found women's bodies among the dead. Their dugouts are like wonderful underground hotels with bathrooms, hot and cold water, electric light and more! The CSM told me about one very young and ardent Tommy who yelled down into a dugout, 'How many of you?' They, hoping to be spared, said, 'Five *Kamerad*.' 'All right,' says Tommy, 'here is one each for you!' and sent down five bombs! Just one would

---

* Edie is referring to the use of tanks, which were used in combat for the first time in September 1916. Edie mentions them again on 14 October, this time referring to them as tanks.

have done it, and the stink and smoke was awful – but the sergeant major could not help laughing.

We were supposed to get another trainload in last night (including 15 stretcher Germans for me) but the last we heard of it was that it had been derailed and we were not called up. We are living through one of Étretat's special storms – sea where it shouldn't be and things blowing about – and all we can do is to batten the windows and hope for the best.

September 20

Our train met with a second accident – the engine went wrong – so all on board were put off at Rouen. We didn't lament it, as we had quite enough to do already. I was locked in the one and only lavatory in the house yesterday afternoon for quite a long time, with not so much as a pair of scissors on me. The wind had broken the connection between the handle and latch, and after thumping and banging until I was tired, I espied a hook in the wall and in desperation took it out. With it as my tool I picked my way out – then the door immediately banged behind me, shut as fast as before. So in the evening I got my own back and finally wrenched it open with the kitchen poker – a hefty three-foot one with a chisel end. It was no ordinary lock, it was not in line with the crack of the door, which made it well nigh impossible to open from the outside. A shout of joy and triumph went up from all present when they saw the last signs of resistance give way!

September 21

One of my DIs died yesterday. He was one mass of very putrid rottenness long before he died and was oozing everywhere. The smell was so very terrible I had to move him right away from everyone, and all one could do was dress and redress. Happily I don't think he could smell it himself, but I have never breathed a worse poison. Another of my DIs has the Distinguished Conduct Medal (DCM) and *Le Croix de Guerre avec Palme*, both won at Loos where, when the French took a fright, our boys rallied and helped them to gain their objective.

September 23

Spent most of yesterday in the office, doing pay-sheets and writing letters to the relatives on the SI and DI lists – we did 60 before lunch. Matron invited Wilson, Maxey and me for a drive in the afternoon and we went through tiny country lanes, so small that even donkey-carts had to turn into the fields to let us pass, then came home via Yport and the coast.

One of our sisters told us how she was in charge of a train which was held up for a few days for repairs at St Pol. She had heard that Arras was only 33 kilometres away, and thought it would be short-sighted to miss seeing it, so one night she told her CO not to worry if he did not see her for the whole of the next day, as she was going for a tramp. She left at 6 a.m. and walked where she had to and got a lift where she could, and considered herself lucky in riding the last few miles in an ambulance which was going up to fetch wounded. She alighted in the town of Arras and was nearly petrified with fear at an awful, indescribable rumbling noise, as if an earthquake was in progress. She asked the officer in the ambulance what it was, but he was nervy and frightened and said, 'I don't know. One never does know what is happening.' She left him and asked a Tommy the way to the square and cathedral, noticing all the way what a dead city it was – not a soul about except on-duty Tommies, who were hurrying to do their job and get back. One Tommy told her she mustn't mind the noise, as it was only our own guns.

She was much enjoying the sight-seeing and picking up souvenirs in the interesting ruins when a new and terrible noise alarmed her. There was a sickening shrieking whistle overhead, then an explosion and the rattle of falling masonry. She knew it was a shell and thought she should go. On her way a nun saw her from a cellar and called her to join them, so she lunched with them then went out to find a way back. At last she was promised a lift on an ambulance, which had to go to the trenches to get its wounded, and finally had among its load the driver and officer of the car that brought her in. She was told to walk slowly on and the car would pick her up. When she got to the Divisional Headquarters, a brass hat* spotted her and questioned her narrowly as to who she was and how she'd come. Then she was left alone and her ambulance arrived and picked her up. On account of being in sister's uniform, not a single sentry had challenged her. Meanwhile, the brass hat had telephoned to the OC of the train and told him to send out a picket to escort an arrested sister back, then he chased after the ambulance, arrested her and took her in his own car to meet the picket, which escorted her home. She put up with much unpleasantness and was threatened with being sent to England, but in the end she was sent here ... she supposes for the duration of the war.

September 26

The last two days have been quiet with no convoy, but there are still many very heavy cases in the hospital. There was a case of diphtheria in No. 5, so the ward was closed and disinfected, and the sisters are having today off.

---

* A senior officer.

September 28

Had the half day off yesterday and because it was raining, Waite, Thomson, Maxey, Constable and I had the Ford and went on a joyride to Caudebec. The rain stopped soon after we left, so everything was bright and beautiful, and everyone in good temper. The country was looking lovely – just getting the autumn colourings. We stopped at Lillebonne to look over the ruined Roman theatre, and the old man there knew his history well and made it all most interesting. The whole amphitheatre is fairly intact, all being built of thick grey stone. He told us that the area towards the theatre was stalls and seating, but in case of invasion from the Seine, it could be used as a fort. During a siege it was used for refugees to live in and there are beautiful Roman baths and a well in the pit of the theatre, that were built for them. They have found all sorts of treasures – beautifully carved ivory and bone pins used by the Roman ladies, old bits of crockery bearing Roman inscriptions, and so on. There is a tiny tomb – a thick square of stone, with a well about a foot deep by one and a half long and a foot wide – and in it they found the ashes of the body of a baby, put in a bottle, together with all its possessions – a tiny bracelet, a silver spoon and its toys! We saw the fine old Roman tower where William I stayed in 1063, then we dashed on along the banks of the Seine to Caudebec – all very beautiful. We arrived at 5 o'clock, just in time to see the cathedral and a shop or two before starting for home.

September 29

Quiet day yesterday, so I helped in the office, gathering and writing up particulars of leave. Does that mean leave is going to start? I wonder!

September 30

At 9.30 last night there was great excitement along the sea front. It was pitch black darkness and a siren was being blown about once a minute, at what sounded around a mile out. No light showed from that area and the sea was very rough. A man just along the shore was waving a lamp seawards and another in a little boat 100 yards out to sea was doing the same. They thought it was a fishing boat trying to get in. Poor things, I hope they managed it – it was such a rough dark night. It was very weird and horrible to hear that siren scream of distress, repeated and repeated in the pitch darkness. It may be that the waving lights were all they needed to show them where Étretat was.

October 1

We learned that it was a fishing boat in distress the other night – a big lugger that had become water-logged – and she blew her siren until some of our Étretataises went to her assistance and brought her ashore here. We had a convoy of 347 in yesterday – *badly* wounded with only a dozen walking cases among them, so although numbers were not high, there was a great deal of work and we are all going on after first breakfast. I only took 43 patients – German prisoners. They always fall to my share. Six were slight cases, but the rest were shot to rags and putrid! Really the smell of gangrene, added to the always unpleasant German smell, was a trial to one's stomach. As I was the only trained person available to do the dressings, it meant my doing dressings all the morning until lunchtime, finishing them afterwards, and then immediately starting a most necessary second round. Most of them are Prussian infantry, with some Württemburgers and some from Saxony. One poor Saxony youngster got his wounds from his own bomb – he'd held it too long after the pin was out.

As before when I had the German patients, the whole population of Étretat turned out to see them carried in (37 were on stretchers), and they made themselves such a nuisance that I closed the ground-floor shutters. The youth of Étretat have been parading in front of the house, whistling and singing the 'Marseillaise' for the benefit of the Germans, and our own people are as bad. I find bunches of strange orderlies gazing at them, and I make myself thoroughly unpleasant and banish the lot. I'm not going to keep a peepshow. If they want to see Germans, I tell them to join an infantry regiment and they will get all the Germans they want. One man gives me the creeps to look at – he seems so like Beelzebub, which is caused by scarring on the outside and an evil spirit inside. Our boys do their work very thoroughly judging by the Germans' wounds. They are not at all a brave set this time, and they whimper and cry over their dressings before they are even touched.

October 2

A rampant day yesterday, and I sent 16 of the least bad Germans to the Canadian hospital at Le Havre. They were not pleased to go. They looked really quaint in their funny old brown civilian tweed caps. They really looked like robbers, and there were some poor, cringing creatures among them. Those remaining are stinking with gangrene and ought all to be operated on, but they must wait until our own Tommies have had their turn in the theatre. Even now there are quite 30 urgent English cases still not treated, and the theatre people are working night and day as it is. I gave each VAD an hour off duty and the orderlies a short spell too, but I can't get off as I have no one to leave in charge.

October 3

The Port of Le Havre has been closed for about four days, so I am having to keep my *Allemand* prisoners. Six are too ill to travel and one of them is going to die – the whole ward smells worse than a bad drain of him – and there are two very gangrenous ones which I expect will be struck off the list too. A sergeant major among them told us the war would not go on through the winter, he thought it would end next month. We asked him who would win, and he said, 'Not us.' I expect he thought he was throwing sand in our eyes, but on principle I don't believe a word they say.

There was a report of a Zep having been brought down over London, and one of the orderlies told the Germans

Zeppelins were shot down both on the continent and over England. This is German Zeppelin LZ 77, which raided eastern England in 1915 and was shot down by anti-aircraft fire over Revigny in France on 21 February 1916.
Photograph © IWM Q58481

about it. The Saxons rejoiced, and one Prussian said '*Das ist nichts.*' So I said, '*Ja – das ist nichts*', and explained to him that it happened too often for it to excite us any more. (One of them speaks English and has to interpret for us.) Another Prussian asked if it were true, and if so when and where, then went to sleep on the facts without commenting. Some of them are very young – two say they are 18, but don't look it, and some say they are 20 and 21 but look 18 or 19 at the most. They are also very lousy and we who are looking after them have to hunt carefully every night. We go on duty louse-free, but regularly after a few hours feel things chasing up and down our spines, and the remainder of the busy day they do not rest. If only they would have their game and go to sleep for a time – but no – either they never rest, or they must take it in shifts to keep us well-tormented.

I am sad to say a petrol boat has been sunk with considerable loss of life. However, I fancy their adversary must be dead too, as the port is to be opened today, and that would not happen with a submarine at large. Major Martyn has a long extension of leave, and I very much doubt if he will ever come back. I am very sorry as the present company officer is too slow for the job. He is MO of my division and very good-hearted – but is as slow as a funeral. A very charming lad of 18 who was badly wounded died at the officers' ward two days ago. His mother was here, poor thing, she lost her husband killed in action and now this boy, and I think one other. She now has only one son left, and he is in the navy – she knows not where. There is a sergeant attached to this unit who has lost six brothers killed in action, a child and both parents since the beginning of war . . .

I think leave will be started soon . . . ish. My German prisoners are as happy as sandboys – they sing and laugh and talk and some seem to be really nice men. They are most grateful for all that is done for them and their stinking wounds are cleaning up wonderfully.

October 4

Still no sign of shifting my prisoners. Day after day I hope for a boat, but none comes, and still the port is closed. I shall be glad to pack them off. One of the seven, too ill to travel, is going to die I think, but the rest are doing well. I took two hours off yesterday and sat on the beach, watched the bathing and drank in clean sea air. It was such a glorious sunny afternoon.

October 5

The night super came to me and said there was going to be an evacuation soon after 6.30, so I dressed and went with great joy and fixed up 20 of my Boches for England. Twenty-one were to have gone, but one was too ill. I am now left with seven – five shot through the lungs, one with his whole shoulder joint removed and many other wounds and *very* gangrenous, and one trephine, who has fits. After getting those 20 really heavy cases away we were much lighter.

The orderlies had a busy day ridding us of the creepy crawlies – 36 beds, mattresses, pillows and blankets all had to go to be baked. Of the men who went to England some were pleased to go, but some would rather have stayed here. One old man was shaking with fright, he thought they were being taken to be shot. The rest were all profuse in their gratitude, one man stopped his stretcher by clinging to the seat in the hall as he passed, seized my hand, and shook and shook it. Another, quite fierce man with black, bolt-on-end hair made me quite a long speech

of thanks and presented me with his identity disc as a
souvenir.

Last night when I was doing their dressings they were
roaring with laughter at a cartoon of the Kaiser in the
Tatler. I told them they ought not to laugh at their own
Kaiser, but they said even people in Germany considered
him very eccentric. They told me with great pride that
the Kaiser's *mother* was our King Edward's own sister. I
don't know why they should, but they do all seem to
envy England and the English. One of those who went
to England yesterday left a notebook in his locker with
much German writing that no one could understand, and
a map of Metz, showing where the barracks were. It was
most interesting and looks as if airmen would strike military buildings in whatever area they might drop bombs –
the place was almost covered with them. The map and
notes have been sent to the Intelligence Department. I
only hope that our young feather-pates think to tear up
or otherwise destroy any maps or notes they may have
on them when they are captured. The hospital is still
heavy – six of the last convoy are dead and others are
dying.

October 6

A much more peaceful day yesterday, and the Boches quite
happy. The one I think is going to die is quite off his head
and wanders. I don't know what he is talking about, but just
catch odd words like 'infantry' and 'Metz', so I suppose he
came from there. Was off yesterday afternoon, so unpacked
Red Cross stores for Wilson. She is looking very tired. Letter
from Matron – am glad to say she is better, and very much
hope she will soon be back.

October 7

Still have my seven Boches, but four of them are fit and marked for England. One looking at the *Daily Mail* yesterday was trying hard to understand the headline: 'BRITISH EXHAUST 256,000 GERMANS . . .' in however many days. He could understand British and German and the numbers, but was much worried over the 'exhaust', and much surprised when I told him what it meant. Apparently they get no news of failures of any kind in the trenches. He is a clever keen boy of 19, very polite and quite happy.

October 8

All my Englishmen left yesterday so now all we have in the way of patients is seven Boches. I feel they will never go and are here for the duration.

October 10

Had a man brought in who was so badly wounded across the shoulders that both arms were entirely paralysed. His story is pathetic. He was servant to a major and at the attack they were both wounded. They were together getting over the parapet, and quite soon the major was hit in the lungs. Mac carried him to the nearest shelter – just a shell hole – but soon found that unsafe, so he carried him further back. He settled him in a little nook then sat close to shelter him. After a bit Mac got hit and found he was unable to do anything for the major using his arms, but he stayed on, although he might well have walked to the dressing station and had his own wounds attended to. He stayed, doing what he could for the major by nosing round him like a dog and using his teeth, and eventually after 12

hours the stretcher-bearers came. They took the major
first – and he was caught by another shell and killed. When
the stretcher-bearers went back they found Mac unconscious, having been hit again. When he reached here he
asked if his major had come down on the same train and
asked Constable to write to a lieutenant who would know
what had happened. He wrote back and told Constable the
whole story of it – and he wrote to Mac too – such a nice
letter:

> Dear Mac
> I have heard from your nurse and am glad to hear you
> are getting on well, though I am afraid the Boches made
> a bit of a mess of you. Still, you mustn't mind that. I'm
> afraid though I can't send you cheerful news in return.
> Major Sands was killed at the aid post, either by the
> shell that laid you out, or one immediately after. We all
> knew what you did for him and are grateful to you.
> Such bravery will not go unrewarded. You must not
> worry too much about Major S. He was too great a man
> to be stopped by a little thing like Death, and is
> carrying on somewhere, although we don't know how
> or where.
> Yours,
> Yoxall

Went to Le Havre yesterday to get the pay – a big lot –
because now the VADs are being back-paid all their field
allowance since June, when it was stopped.

October 11

Went for a lantern lecture on Lourdes last night given
by the Roman Catholic padre in his chapel. Most interesting pictures were shown of the little shepherdess

Bernadette[*], seeing the vision and scratching the ground where the spring of healing waters came up, and of people who had been cured there.

October 12

We had a convoy of about 400 in yesterday. Many very bad cases, with one dead and one dying. I took 53 English and two *Allemands*, who were sent to the Canadian hospital at Le Havre as they were slight cases. They were standing laughing at our badly wounded, so got short shrift from me. I bundled them into bed at once and told them they were not going to stay with us – instead they were to go to the Canadians. It made them jibber, the cowards, because they are terrified of the Canadians.

October 13

Sent 12 patients to England and my remaining Boches are marked 'E', so will also go soon. Some of my men were very bad with shellshock. One poor child, looking not a day older than 14 but who said he was 18, was very bad. He was too conscious and could not forget for a moment what he had seen.

October 14

In the afternoon I went with Wood to put the big church in order and to arrange flowers there and in our little chapel, in case I have no time today. I learnt from one patient yesterday that a 'barrage' is when all the batteries fire as fast as

---

[*] Edie is referring to the 14-year-old Bernadette Soubirous (1844–1879), who claimed to have seen a series of visions of the Virgin Mary in 1858, which led to Lourdes becoming a major site for Catholic pilgrimage.

they can at the same time, and that it is often used to stop the enemy's advance. Where he came from, there were two tanks out of action – in one the bodies of two men apparently burnt to death.

October 16

Calm and peaceful yesterday, capped by an agreeable surprise. At 5 p.m. my MO told me the Germans would leave at 5.30, so with great joy I fixed them up and had them ready. We are having much more bracing weather now – bright sunshine, sharp showers and a blustering wind – all very welcome after the weeks of 'mug'. This morning the sea is a clean blue-green with salmon-coloured waves reflecting the clouds. The beauty of the sky defies description.

October 17

Two more patients to England, and condensed all but eight into Annexe D, and am hoping for the best. It is too much for two orderlies to keep four large homes clean.

October 18

I saw a thing that interested me much and of which I still do not know the explanation. Maxey and I were walking through the valley towards the shore, and I was ahead, looking at the sea. Suddenly my slow-working brain said to itself, 'Funny – that wave seems to be staying up in a spray ... It is not spray – it looks like steam!' I waited to show it to Maxey, and by the time I had directed her attention to the spot, flames were leaping out of the water, just one at a time, then going down. Quickly seven mine-sweepers came from the north and placed themselves round the spot, like people playing rounders. I dashed up the cliff to the French sentry-box for information – where I found both men the worse for drink, cooking a rabbit in a shed. They hadn't seen anything of it.

October 20

Very busy day yesterday. I took only 19 men, but they are rotten with gangrene – and German. All but one – a Prussian – belong to the 111th Baden Regiment. Some are very badly wounded, and four on the DI list. Were their consciences tender – if they have such things – that they were such terrified creatures when they were admitted? They are settling down now – despite all they might know, we still don't want the nasty job of killing them.

One man is simply entered as 'German prisoner, name unknown', as he has a bullet in his brain and has been unconscious all the time. He probably does not even know that he is a prisoner. Another arrived with both legs badly gangrenous, and one has been amputated high up. The other may clean up – or may have to be taken off. Another has the flesh torn off his thigh so deep that one can see the femoral artery, and he is lying dead still in the hope it won't bleed. If it does there will be little chance of stopping it, as the wound extends to his stomach. The forth DI has three gaping wounds across his back into the lung. Five of the less bad ones were sent to the Canadian hospital at Le Havre. Among my English patients I have a young thing of about 17 – a short, baby-faced creature, who makes us laugh with his stories of the trenches. He said, 'Fancy, a big fellow, putting up his hands to me and crying, "Mercy, *Kamerad*", but they do, to a little fing like me! He was so big that I was frightened too, but when I saw he was frightened, I wasn't any more, and then someone else shot him.'

October 21

When I went on duty I received a message that English patients were to go in half an hour and I said they would be ready, knowing quite well that their half hour would be more like one and a half hours. Even so, we had to chase to get ten badly wounded men – each wounded in many places – with their wounds dressed, properly clad, and on to stretchers in the time. But we were ready all right. It is an extraordinary thing that the Germans rejoice to go to England, and many talk of settling in England after the war – but I don't think they will. One of the slightly wounded, marked for the Canadian hospital at Le Havre, was left behind as the hospital was full. He asked me where he was going and I told him, 'Le Havre'. He was very grumpy about it and tried to be very ill to get marked 'England' – but to Le Havre he will go. Some have even asked if their wound is a 'Blighty' one! Of this last lot, not one speaks French or English – which sometimes makes it a little awkward. For instance, one man asked me for a cushion under his buttocks (probably because I had just put the man next to him on an air-ring), and from his pantomime description of what he wanted I sent the orderly to him with a bed-pan, much to his disgust as he did not want it.

October 22

Sunday, and I have just come back from 6.30 service. Everything is white with frost, and glistening in the pinky morning sunshine. All is very beautiful and very cold. My head-case Boche was operated on yesterday, but will die soon.

October 23

The 'unknown German prisoner' died yesterday and one went to Le Havre. Of the remaining five, three are DI and two are marked down for England.

October 25

Two Boches have left for England, so now I have only the three DIs left, and so far they are doing well. A great flutter was caused in the dovecote by the reinforcement of an old rule: 'No meals are to be taken in the sisters' duty room', because as a rule we have a mid-morning cup of tea and a biscuit, and invite our MO to join us, but in some wards they have exaggerated it to a huge feed that takes far too much time. There was the usual complaining and grumbling and 'we ought not to sit down under it', but in time they will get used to it – after all it is an army rule.

October 26

Yesterday walked with Waite to the lighthouse and called at Miss Wallen's for tea. She lives quite alone, with just one servant, in a fairly big old French house, far away from everything and everyone except a few odd farms. The house is immaculate – beautifully polished floors, old French furniture, brasses and bronzes. We were overtaken by darkness long before we had crossed the country between the lighthouse and the Le Havre Road, and at last decided to make a straight cut over hill or dale, ploughed or sewn, and eventually we struck the road. It was pitch dark and we were miles from home when heavy rain came on and in two minutes we were soaked. Luckily, after a bit one of our ambulances overtook us and brought us the rest of the way back to bath, supper and bed.

October 28

I am afraid one of my Boches will lose his left foot, and his right leg was amputated the day after he arrived here.

October 29

My very DI Boche is, if anything, better. There is rumour of a naval battle[*]. We heard that a hospital ship has struck a mine[†], and 30 RAMC drowned, but the sisters were all saved and one is at No. 2 General Hospital, Le Havre.

October 31

Big storm raging and I have been hopping in and out of bed, trying to hit the happy medium between the stuffiness of my tiny room when entirely closed and being blown out when there is the smallest crack of window open. Now I have cleared the decks and am letting it all come in. Had a heated discussion yesterday with my washerwoman on the treatment of ill Boches – she thinks 'kill the lot'. Bought a pair of sabots yesterday and am longing for rain to wear them.

November 1

All Saints Day yesterday, and some of us went to the 6.30 a.m. service. In the afternoon we put flowers on the

---

[*] This was the Battle of the Dover Strait two days earlier, when German torpedo boats launched a raid to try and disrupt the Dover Barrage, a large area of steel nets and mines designed to keep the German Navy out of the Channel. The Germans managed to sink the destroyer HMS *Flirt* and a number of other vessels before being repelled.

[†] This was HMHS *Galeka*, which indeed did hit a mine while entering Le Havre, but she was not carrying any passengers at the time and the number of medical personnel to die was 19, not 30.

graves of some of our men. Had the half day off yesterday and Maxey, Waite and I walked over the cliffs and back home by the beach – where we got drenched with sea water. *Tres bon!*

November 3

Two days ago the port was closed, but big boats are heading for Le Havre this morning, so perhaps it is open again. Yesterday, one boat got across because she did not catch the wireless message sent soon after she left, that she was to return to port. Seven of them started and were called back because a French boat was blown up just outside Southampton.

November 4

The chief event of yesterday was that Major Martyn returned, to the great joy of us all, and brought me the most beautiful pair of black silk stockings that I have ever possessed. Great care must be taken of them.

November 7

The last three days have been quiet with just one convoy in. Among my lot were three Germans – one badly wounded, two not so bad. Shall I ever be quit of Germans? I wonder. Concert last night given by the staff, male and female, was quite good. After it went for a walk with Maxey in glorious moonlight.

Yesterday morning there was word of evacuation so I went on duty early. I dressed the men and got them on to stretchers and gave morphia to the painful ones, then word came from Le Havre cancelling the order, so back to bed they all had to be put. I don't think I shall ever be without Germans.

We spent a pleasant evening at the officers' mess last night –
music and bridge all very enjoyable.

November 13

Am nearly driven crazy with these 150 terrible Austr-I-lians.
They are not ill and are the dirtiest and most untidy men I
have ever had dealings with. All that and only two orderlies
to cope with the lot.

November 14

The place is still seething with Australians as only 15
went yesterday to convalescent camp. On Sunday night
they broke out all over the town, taking no notice of the
police. They went to the cafés and generally made nui-
sances of themselves. Two arrived home next morning
dead drunk – they are horrid men. It was so strange this
morning, I was sitting at my window in the dark, drinking
my tea and brushing my hair. The washerwomen were
already at work by the dim light of dawn, washing at the
sea's edge, and the men were drawing the day's supply
of water from the tap. There was so much going on in
the dark.

November 15

This morning at 5.30 the place reminded me of a fairytale.
There was brilliant blue moonlight, and the stars were glittering, the air frosty. Again, the washerwomen were all at
work on the shore, and the water-carriers were filling their
containers for the day. It all looked so eerie in the moonlight
and everything cast sharp black shadows on the ground. We
are still seething with Australians – I have 100, but they are
getting less unruly now, thank goodness. I was off yesterday

afternoon, so went for trudge along the shore with old Waite. We wanted to go through the cave that comes out at the station, but the tide was too high for us to get in. Major Martyn announces that he would like to come and see you and stay for a few days after the War. I said that I was quite sure you would welcome him, Mother.

Volume Four

1918.

Tréport. June 21st

I returned to Abbeville from leave. June 15th & found
orders awaiting me to proceed forthwith
to No 3 Gen. Hosp. –

They seemed a sad little group at Sick Sisters &
the Home – & I was sorry to leave them.
There was very little work being done & why
they don't close both places remains a mystery.
I did not proceed at once. I wanted a few
hours to say Goodbye & collect my odds &
ends. – So – postponed the procedure to next
morning.

Major Jolley of the R.A.F. very kindly lent a
tender to take me – instead of going by train
& we made a good spin of it round by
Dieppe etc – a good day & I enjoyed the
trip, but not the arriving at a fresh hospital
there is nothing I hate much more than that.
– The hospital is splendid – partly in a huge hotel
perched on the top of a high cliff – In a way it
reminds me of when we (No 3. C.C.S) were
in the International Lunatic Asylum at
Bailleul.

1918, Le Tréport

June 21

I returned to Abbeville from leave on June 15 and found orders awaiting me to proceed forthwith to No. 3 General Hospital. I did *not* proceed at once, as I wanted a few hours to say goodbye and collect my odds and ends. So I postponed the procedure until the next morning, when Major Jolley of the RAF* very kindly sent a tender to take me, instead of going by train, and we made a good spin of it round by Dieppe. It was a good day and I enjoyed the trip, but not the arrival at a fresh hospital. There is nothing I hate much more than that. The hospital itself is splendid and is partly in a huge hotel, perched on the top of a high cliff†. In a way it reminds me of when we of No. 3 CCS were in the International Lunatic Asylum at Bailleul. I arrived in time for second lunch at 1 p.m., and then, not being wanted for duty, I made myself scarce in my room for the rest of the day, picking the lock on my trunk and sawing the padlock off my kitbag, as I had accidentally left my keys somewhere.

* The RAF had been formed on 1 April 1918 by amalgamating the Royal Flying Corps and the Royal Naval Air Service.
† This was the enormous and very luxurious 300-bedroom cliff-top Hotel Trianon, built in 1912, which became General Hospital No. 3 during the war. The hotel was destroyed by the Germans in 1942, on the grounds that it could be used as a useful landmark by Allied aircraft.

I have a ward of 60 beds in the big building, all acute medical and surgical cases. At present there are only 40 patients in it, but some of them are pretty bad. It felt a little strange at first being back to large numbers, with big wounds and the smells of gas-gangrene, pus and antiseptics, but my nose is getting used to them now. One poor fellow died a couple of hours after being admitted, and I am afraid two more are following him. One is badly gassed and the other was in the CCS suffering from trench-fever when it was bombed. He has lost an arm and one foot is useless, and I am afraid he will not get over it.

Every day I have been for a long and lonely walk – a big mess is a rare place for making one feel desperately alone, but as I enjoy my own company, all is well. Yesterday and today have been very stormy and I can hardly see the vessels at anchor for the storm of mist and spray over the sea. About 14 small steamers came in to anchor this evening, and it is rather a pathetic sight. They all seem to anchor near some-one else – presumably so that there will always be someone to rescue one if the other gets hit. Up on this cliff there are four or five hospitals and no other camps within about two miles, but we know the Boches so well now that every hut is being sandbagged as a protection in the event of an air-raid. I have been down into the town once, a rather dirty little place was my impression. There is a funicular railway down the cliff, or you can walk down the 365 steps. I chose the steps, as there were people I had never set eyes on at the railway – sisters! Terrifying people! The MO of my ward is a Yankee – young and quite amenable and consci-entious. No. 2 Canadian Hospital had a convoy in today and I think we take the next. The last one we had was chiefly wounded – many of them badly.

The grand and imposing Trianon Hotel,
where Edie was based, with the tents of the hospital
camp on the clifftop around it. The building was later
. destroyed in the Second World War.
Photograph courtesy of Jean-Luc Dron

June 24

My ward is lighter than it was as we have sent about 16
patients to England. The poor gassed boy has died, but the
one with bomb wounds is better and may live, although he
is still quite off his head. It is very interesting to listen to the
men's conversation – their opinion on the situation in
Ireland[*], how prisoners should be treated, and the general
situation. I wonder if there is any truth in what they say
about the bombing of hospitals – that in German territory
the flying men have seen what are without doubt aeroplane
hangers and ammunition dumps marked with huge red
crosses. They are not near a railway and are so placed that
they simply cannot be hospitals. I suppose they think we do

* The British Government's decision to extend conscription to Ireland early in 1918
met with widespread resistance.

the same and they bomb us on the chance of it. Of course we bomb their hangers and dumps – we should be fools if we didn't! I am quite sure though that they do know what is a real hospital. They can see the wounded men walking about and some lying out in beds. As a nation they are dirty dogs! In one CCS a German spat at a sister and the Tommy nearest him hit him over the head with the butt of his rifle. Then *he* got punished – though he ought not to have been.

June 25

Shrieks are coming from the plot of grass just below the ward – some VADs are out early, practising cricket for the match tomorrow. The patients were well satisfied with the news in the *Daily Mail* yesterday: 'Get the Austrians to give in, and we'll see this war over by the end of July.' If only that would happen! Anyway the Austrians have made a bit of a failure of their offensive so far, and for once the weather favoured the Allies. Rain came down in big storms and swept away the bridge across the river and made it impossible for the enemy to bring up supplies or guns. The night super, Tilney, got orders last night to report at Abbeville. In a way I envy her, but believe in taking what comes.

June 28

We had a convoy in yesterday but I only took eight patients. There were some nasty wounds, two with appendicitis and one a New Zealander who has been in the war since 1914. He thinks my brother must be at Doullens, as all the New Zealanders are there[*]. I hope he is, as at the moment that

---

[*] Edie's youngest brother, Alfred James Appleton, but known as Jim or 'Taff', was born on 19 January 1887. He went to South Africa and later made New Zealand his home.

part of the line is quiet – if you can call *any* part of it quiet.
A sad tragedy happened at five yesterday morning. A mental
patient – a lady driver – managed to dodge her special atten-
dant and fling herself over the cliff. Her body was soon
picked up, quite smashed in every part. She evidently meant
to do it as she had left letters for people telling them so. It
is said she had a similar attack a few years ago and her father
insisted on her coming out to France to work. He thought
the complete change and occupation would cure her. I think,
if he knew her tendency, it was wrong to allow her to be in
charge of helpless men at any time.

The cricket match was much enjoyed by all – but no one
seems to know quite who won. They all turned up smiling
for a strawberry-and-cream tea after it, so I think no one was
badly beaten. Have found one nice country walk, but must
look for others. I usually take myself for my walks as I don't
know anyone here and naturally they all have their own
plans and friends. Anyhow, what is the matter with a walk
alone? I enjoy it. It is evidently calmer this morning as the
crows were able to do their drill and they had fine fun –
whereas during the stormy weather they could not. They
would start off from the edge of the cliff and see who could
stay like an aeroplane longest, without moving tails or wings.
They are funny creatures.

The other end of Le Tréport is like the south end of
Deal, and is very typical of French seaside resorts with
gay, quite gaudy little houses in all odd shapes and forms,
very gimcrackily built and painted all colours, spanning
the seafront which runs from our cliff to the next. I was
interested yesterday to watch the visitors – well-off people
with nice, smartly dressed children, who are staying along
at Le Tréport. Their little youngsters have to play in their
smart clothes, and you hardly ever see a child dressed for
digging in the sand or doing just what it likes, as they do

in England. The lads in the ward are still satisfied with the
news and we are all hoping hard that Austria, Bulgaria
and Turkey will negotiate themselves a separate peace.
Then, according to yesterday's speculation, Russia would
not mind coming in again and having another go at the
Germans.

June 29

When I got down to breakfast yesterday, everyone asked if
I was kept awake long by the air-raid warning – a bugle call –
and saying how many hours they were awake. I lay low as I
had slept through it all. The morning before I was wakened
by Boche planes passing overhead, and that is a noise once
heard, never slept through I think. Tonight I was up like a
bird at what I thought was a bomb, but as I heard no planes
or other excitement, I think it must have been a door banging. It ought to be a punishable crime to bang a door these
days. This morning the sea is like glass with a light haze over
it – going to be a hot day I think. Got a letter from Major
Martyn – he has broken loose from his moorings and is to
report to Deputy Director of Medical Services, Étaples, for
a fresh job. I hope it will be somewhere nearer than his last
one.

June 30

The poor suicide girl was buried yesterday, and to my way of
thinking far too much of a pageant was made of it. There
was a long procession headed by the convalescent camp
band, then the ambulance with the coffin, smothered in
flowers, then all the drivers – about 40 of them. There followed the girl's own car, also full of most lovely flowers, then
big contingents of MOs and sisters from 47 General
Hospital, our own hospital, the Canadian and American

hospitals, men from the convalescent camp, then our own Colonel and the Surgeon General, then the three commandants of the drivers. Must have been about 300 people. The French photographers were all over the place taking photos for postcards! If I were her people I should be heartily disgusted at the whole thing. A quiet funeral would surely have been more comely. It reminded me of when the bomb victims were buried at Abbeville. I was on my way to the station with some patients, and the area all round the cathedral was absolutely blocked with the debris of fallen houses. There were about 20 hearses, gaudily trapped, carrying the bodies of the dead, and hundreds and hundreds of civilians seething round. Our Military Police (MPs) were keeping order and sending all traffic another way.

Yesterday I had a half day off and went with three others to Bois de Cise – a very pretty wooded little place about four miles along the coast. We walked by the main road and the flag was flying from the Tank Camp, warning us that they were practising firing, so it was not safe to walk seaward of them. The camp is a school for officers and men for instruction in the working of tanks, and we passed right through it. It is very well laid out with blocks of huts divided by broad roads, each one named after a battle. In front of the huts the ground has been worked into little flowerbeds with big green tubs, and every hut and tub has a yellow tank painted on it. We had our tea at a restaurant in Bois de Cise, and like everywhere else near here, it was *thick* with officers, sisters and Tommies. For my own part I would rather take tea and have a quiet picnic where no other folk are. Luckily we took a loaf with us, which came in very handy for our own and other people's tea, as they had very little there.

Two New Zealanders were visiting someone in my ward and told me that the New Zealanders were due to go over the top last night, and I am wondering if my brother Taff was going with them. I hope he is all right. I am longing to hear from him. The whole line seems to be livening up a bit and the Germans are preparing for an offensive again. Hope they will fail as badly as the Austrians did. There is a very virulent form of influenza spreading like wildfire among the hospitals and ours is nearly full up with them, all with temperatures of anything up to 104° or 105°. The good thing is, it is usually over in a week, but if everyone is going to get it, we shall have a long time of it.

July 1

Today is Dominion Day for the Canadians – which probably accounts for the band and cheering I heard a short while ago at 6 a.m. Yesterday a procession of sisters, officers and men, headed by their band, marched to all the cemeteries where Canadians are resting, where they held a short service and sounded the Last Post. The sisters marched well and looked rather pretty in the distance – quite a long line of them four deep, all in their bright blue dresses and white caps.

July 3

The Canadians' sports day went off well and they gave a good concert in the evening. Tomorrow is Thanksgiving Day, so the Americans will be *en fête*. I went for a walk yesterday nearly as far as Eu. The country is very beautiful and in places quite scarlet with poppies. The one drawback is when one meets Portuguese soldiers – they are an ill-mannered lot and very objectionable. The colouring at Étretat was about triple what it is here, the sunsets, sunrises, clouds and sea were all far more glorious there. I had heard it said that this was so, but never believed there could have been such a great difference.

The funeral of an English officer – part of an evocative series of
contemporary postcards depicting Le Tréport during the war.
Photograph courtesy of Jean-Luc Dron

I love watching the life on the strip of sea opposite me.
There are hundreds of fishing smacks out, just now a line of
steam trawlers is heading out to sea and there is a tiny tug
with three queer-looking lighters hurrying after them. I
sometimes wonder if I properly realise that I am living in
one of France's smartest hotels. It is beautifully situated with
good rooms, wide corridors, bathrooms galore – and I always
choose a room that looks towards the rising sun and over the
harbour and town. It is so quaint and beautiful in the early
morning – and it is all free of charge!

The Boches have scuttled another hospital ship, the *Llandovery Castle**. It was on its return journey from Canada, so

---

* On 27 June HMHS *Llandovery Castle* was torpedoed by German submarine UC-
26, despite being clearly marked as a hospital ship; 234 lives were lost.

fortunately it was not carrying patients, however, it was fully marked as a hospital ship. They didn't take the trouble to board her – just torpedoed her without warning and then fired on the small boats full of survivors, because they thought there were American airmen on board. There were none – but of course that was a mere detail to them. They are asking for trouble and they will get it – and it would do them good. I find it soothing to see the men's faces stiffen when they read a thing like that, and the comment I heard many of them make was, 'and all those sisters gone'. It was only 14, after all, but the men are so wonderfully chivalrous. Then you hear them say 'H'm! Catch *me* taking any more prisoners – we don't want them and they have to be fed.' It doesn't matter what nationality they are, their blood is up, and they are going to remember this.

July 5

A great blow! Someone is now sharing my room and it makes early rising rather an agony as I am afraid of waking her. She is a staff nurse – quite nice – who objected to sharing a room with the one she was supposed to (who is a Bart's contemporary of mine and an absolute prize grouser), so if I get tired of this child I know what to do. I'll start bemoaning my fate and perhaps she will again ask to be moved.

Yesterday was the Yanks' great day and they held a baseball match and invited all of us and the officers to it, and then to tea. I went to the match but did not stay to tea, which I hear was a feast to remember, with cocktails, iced tea and coffee, and wonderful cakes just like in pre-war times. The Yanks at play are most un-English – they lose every scrap of self control and act like so many lunatics. Not knowing the game I can't judge it, but it gives me far greater pleasure to watch a good game of rugby than baseball any day. They are queer folk – the sisters and orderlies were all crowded together and standing on their seats and yelling for their side. The town was full of tipsy Yanks by 2 p.m., so I tremble to think what they were like later on. Major Martyn is working at Étaples now at No. 24. He says he likes the work by day but does not like spending hours in a dugout at night.

July 6

Had a delightful day off yesterday. Breakfast 8.45 a.m., brought by my kind ward VADs, then I sewed and enjoyed myself until 10 o'clock. I dressed and prepared lunch for Hansard and me and we set off for a long walk to the woods of Eu. The post arrived just as we were starting, so I took my three letters, unopened, to enjoy at leisure! The woods themselves are *ex*quisite. The property belongs to the Compte d'Eu – there are very large and beautiful grounds and woods, and a fine old château! The count is poor, so has let the place to the English, but as far as we could see, no one was in it and we seemed to have it all to ourselves.

We chose a pleasant slope under some pine trees – the pine smell pleased us and the midges and flies do not like it. A squirrel was very busy in the tree above us and quite big sticks and all sorts of debris came hurtling down round us. After a lunch of ham sandwiches, cheese and tea, we sat and enjoyed our surroundings for an hour and a half, then walked on to Eu. It is a quaint, very old place, and I should think very gay in ordinary times. Close round the château are many very fine old houses with large grounds, then beside them there is the small village, the college and its chapel, and the old Notre Dame church – a very fine structure. The only date we could see anywhere on the building was 1308.

*

The view out of my window at the hotel is a never-ending joy to me. The colouring at eventide is not a patch on Étretat, but it is very pretty, and we look right down over the shipping. In the evening we saw a large convoy of about 30 steamers – big merchantmen – a fleet of them heading for England. There is always something going on.

July 7

Yesterday I took myself for a long country walk and gathered an armful of poppies, cornflowers and white wild flowers, so today the ward is a mass of red, white and blue. The 'up' patients wear blue suits with white shirts and red ties, and with the huge vases of poppies, daisies and cornflowers dotted about, it all looks very gay. Most of our influenza patients are a good deal better, but a few are still very ill indeed.

July 9

Yesterday was a boiling day, and the sea dead calm, so I took my first plunge – and much enjoyed it. A1! On the spur of the moment I bought a bathing gown from Sister Hansard. She is about two sizes taller and bigger round than me, so I cut off a good bit of the skirt of the coat, made a deep tuck in the body of the trousers, and made them short enough – but never thought about the elastic being too loose, so when I began to swim the pull of the sea nearly washed them off. I had to swim two strokes then pull up my breeches – two strokes – and so forth, but they just about stayed on all right. I hope the rumour is true that the Germans are suffering so many men lost through influenza that they cannot attack. The more the merrier, I say, because in the meantime the Americans are still arriving.

July 14

On Friday another sister and I took some patients who were for England to Abbeville to join the ambulance train there. We had a fine run and at one point came to a field so blue with cornflowers that we had to stop and gather armfuls. I spent five hours visiting friends at my old hospital, then the other sister who came with me arrived back with a high temperature and influenza, so has been a patient in sick sisters ever since. I had a strong feeling all along that I had been sent in disgrace from Abbeville, as it was so sudden and unexpected. I heard while visiting on Friday that it was the matron of the home who had me ejected. She told Miss McCarthy that I influenced the staff so that she could do nothing with them. The truth is that she tried to boss me and run the hospital when I was in charge. I would not have that, and told her so – after all, when I am in charge it is quite sufficient for me to boss the staff. She hated me for not allowing her to do so, and got me thrown out! The dirty dog! However, being in disgrace does not sit heavy on my chest.

Austria seems to be in a fine old muddle! The army is in retreat and losing heavily and the Germans are anxious to put Germans in command – but the Austrians say that, as they have never sent the 12 divisions they promised, they refuse to have German generals over them until the divisions are sent. They are sensible folk and, poor creatures, their plight seems to be deplorable. Today is a national *fête* and all ships in the harbour are decked with flags – and those poor dears in the cemetery had another service held over them! The Canadians held one on 1 July, and today it is the French and Americans. I think it is the anniversary of the taking of the Bastille.

The hospital has been terribly slack this week, and it has

been difficult to find enough for the staff to do, let alone
myself. Colonel Barfoot, the ADMS of Étaples, is in here as
a patient. He has had a rough time through the war and very
little leave, and now he has been spitting blood and is to go
home. Miss Baldry, the matron of the home in Abbeville,
came to me on Friday and behaved as if she had never been
fonder of any one, but it didn't last long as I was duly polite
to her but saw as little of her as I could. She knew she had
done wrong, and so did I!

July 16

I took only 15 patients from the convoy, but most of them
were badly wounded. One poor thing had a shot across the
back, from side to side, and it seems to have left a furrow
of about four inches across and very deep. He is DI, but
very cheerful, lying on his waterbed. He says he is as comfortable as a ship at sea. Another one, SI, has a gash across
the left chest and a biggish piece of shrapnel in his lung.
He belongs to the Tank Corps and says that going over the
top in a tank is 'great'. Telling me about one attack, he
said, 'A hundred tanks went over, and each one has a crew
of six, plus one officer. Each man has his allotted job and
we just go on until we see the infantry held up somewhere. Then we make straight for that place and fire on
the machine-gun nest – and if they won't shift, we ride
over them.'

One sergeant brought down two beautiful little photo
maps taken from the air, which show the country round
Hamel. Nowadays, when they are ordered to take a certain
position or space, the sergeant is given one of these maps
showing his objective. The maps or photos have been useful
in another way too – they have shown how very distinctly
even tiny footpaths show up – and of course when the
Boches take photos, he sees them too, and can often gather

from them where one of our batteries is. He thinks paths to batteries are to be camouflaged now, and rightly too. People living on the other side of the house say there was a heavy bombardment two nights ago, and patients from this convoy think we are going to make an attack soon. The Boche devils have got a new gas, which is odourless, and its effect is to paralyse people. The first they know of it is that they have lost all voluntary power in their muscles.

July 18

The Boches opened up on a 50-mile front on July 15, against the French and Americans. I think they made a poor show as they threw in 40 of their best divisions, but did not progress much. By the end of the first day the attack was counted 'broken'. I think the French airmen didn't give them much chance to bring up supplies and reinforcements in comfort, and the Americans made a brilliant counterattack and drove the enemy back. Our preparatory artillery fire seems to have upset them too, and killed large numbers of them who had assembled to make the attack – but I hope before the end of the battle they will get more than that. I read in yesterday's paper that America has a great number of bomber planes ready to come across – and that will not make pleasant reading for the Boches[*].

July 20

We sent several patients to England today, so shall be pretty slack, bar the arrival of a convoy. My half day has been a dead failure – so least said soonest mended. A sister whom

---

[*] In fact the Americans relied entirely on British and French-made planes.

I do *not* like tied herself around my neck and would not be
shaken off. Poor thing! Nobody likes her as she talks nothing but unpleasantnesses about everybody and anybody –
which is very boring for folk who are forced to listen. I
wasted good afternoon hours in a dreary slouch round the
dirty little beast of a town and tea in a horrid place, instead
of having a decent country walk. This person said she was
coming with me, then after the first few steps was too tired
for the country. 'Oh, *do* come to the town!' The Boche offensive seems to have met with a speedy nip in the bud. The
French and Americans have done magnificently, and today's
paper says 17,000 prisoners and 360 guns have been taken!
That really is good. Naturally, all Americans have been on
tenterhooks waiting and wondering how their men would do
in an important affair. They need not fear now, I think.
Their men have done capitally.

July 23

Up to the present the news remains good. The British are in
it now near Rheims, and are doing as well as the French and
Americans are to the south. The total of prisoners in the
paper two days ago was 20,000, and nearly 400 guns! We are
using a deadly gas that eats through the German helmets,
but I really wish both sides would give up gas, it is a devil-
ish way of fighting – indeed, it isn't fighting. One patient
told me yesterday that once when they were using this gas,
a German rushed across to give himself up and said it was
terrible – that they couldn't stand it. He died almost at once.
One poor creature in the ward is very ill indeed. He is DI
and has gas-gangrene. He wrote home yesterday, 'Dear
Mother, you will be pleased to know I am wounded in the
left leg and am in hospital.' I have never yet known a man
write a letter home that could worry his people. They are a
wonderful lot.

July 26

Our last batch are doing well. The mother of the boy with gas-gangrene is here, and the one with the bad chest wound is extraordinarily better, in spite of having, as shown by X-ray, a large piece of metal near the first sacral vertebra. This has fractured one of the bones of the pelvis and there is another biggish piece in his chest. They cannot possibly operate until he is able to breathe a little better. The news still keeps good! What a thing to be grateful for – and how *very* disquieting *pour les Boches* – if they know.

Many of our orderlies have been taken away and we have heard that a general hospital is being mobilised to be sent with the 47th Division to Russia*. They say three general hospitals are going, and I should like to go too – unless I could be somewhere where I could see something of brother Taff.

I watched the French army tailors at work the other day. They are established in what in my own mind I had always called the swimming baths. The room I looked into was about 60 feet long and wide in comparison. It was filled with tables running nearly the whole length of it – and all tables had the light blue serge of the French service uniform running the whole length. I tried to count how many thicknesses and came to the conclusion there were 24! On one table a girl had a trolley laden with a huge roll of the stuff, which ran up and down on rails – the same way as a breakfast tray on legs is laid across the patient – and as it went, the roll of stuff unwound on to the table. Two girls followed it and laid the material smooth. The middle table was already covered with its 24 layers. At a single small table a tailor was

---

* In fact the 47th Division remained on the Western Front.

chalking out the pattern of a greatcoat, and at the table nearest the window the cutter-out was at work, using a truly
wonderful electric apparatus.

There is a great, steel, hand-shaped plate, very thin at
the far end – that runs under the part that is to be followed by the knife. Then there is a deadly sharp blade
that I imagine is worked up and down by electricity –
although it appeared only to shiver! Finally there is the
handle the tailor uses to push it, and it is connected by a
flex to a battery somewhere. He changed some part of it
while I was watching, and it seemed to burn his hands as
he put it down in a mighty hurry. He was a careful cutter,
and a lot of little bits from the pattern were cut into small
squares – perhaps to go behind buttons. Behind him came
a girl with a huge armful of calico, and she tied all the different parts in bundles. Then came a trolley and neat
bundles of front sleeves, back sleeves, shoulder straps,
backs and fronts were piled up on it to be taken to the
machinists.

July 27

Yesterday Sister McCorqudale and I had a half day and
packed our tea and went for a most glorious walk. First to
Eu by tram, then straight out and up, up, up – first through
cultivated land, then woodland. When we had walked what
seemed to us about four miles, we came upon an old man
tidying up a château garden. The château, like most, is
closed. We asked if we were nearly at La Madeleine – our
destination – and he laughed and said he hoped we were
not in a hurry as we had *'encore cinq kilometres'*! More than
three miles more! We had plenty of time, so didn't mind a
bit, and we continued uphill for a little way – then a gentle
down, through heather-clad moorland. And then, La
Madeleine, which is a huge forest owned by the state, rich

in pines, larches, oaks, mountain ashes, birches – every sort of tree.

The pines and larches keep very much to themselves, and it was like walking on velvet going through them, the ground thick in last year's needles and the scent so refreshing and good. The mountain ashes were just red, and it was very pretty to look far into the depths of the forest where all the tree trunks were covered in brilliant green moss. The bright red berries of the mountain ash peeped through all the many tints of greens and browns – and above was the violet-blue sky with perfectly white clouds.

There is only one house, and that is a trim red-brick one with lots of quaint old out-houses. The head forester lives there, and the wife and daughters run quite a good-sized farm. We had tea there (saying nothing about already having had one at 4 o'clock by the road side). We had fruit and cream, with rusks and butter and tea. They put a bowl quite full of cream on the table and were hurt if you didn't finish it – so we did.

The view of the place on the way back was interesting, with the church, the many fine old châteaux, the rambling quaint old town, and what looks like another busy town outside. There are camps upon camps upon camps of Belgians and Americans, all in huts. There is a war on, but we might not have known it from the blessed peace and quiet of our half day. We got to Eu just as the tram was starting and, with the rest of people anxious to ride to Tréport, threw ourselves at the door and were successfully packed in, pressed on or off our feet by the crowd behind. I should think there were about twice too many people on board. I was standing with the knees of a sitting Belgian shoving me into the middle of the car, and the behind of the very fat Frenchman standing behind me shoving me towards the Belgian. I was carrying a huge bunch of mountain ash and other branches and had to plant both hands firmly on the wall over the Belgian's head to keep myself upright. The berries hung just where they hit his nose every time the car rattled, and he did look cross – but as he might have at least offered me his seat, I left things as they were.

While we were waiting for our tram in Tréport, a lorry arrived from Amiens, bringing in 20 officers on a few hours' leave. In a nearby café some tables were occupied by soldiers, and at one were two girls, dressed and painted to a high degree, 'playing cards' and laughing loudly. They did not seem much interested in their game but the lorry-load of clean young officers soon gained all their attention. There are hundreds of such in every big French town. I asked the lorry-driver if Amiens has been much knocked about and he said not so much – although the cathedral had been hit once. I marvelled at that, then he told me that we had billeted German officers there! Oh, clever thought! I would pack it with them! It is such a beautiful cathedral!

July 29

Sister Woods, an old friend of mine, appeared here yesterday. She is going on leave from her train which brought us a convoy last night. She told me they had been having disturbed nights, and they were never allowed to sleep on the train when there were no patients on board. Wherever they happened to be, they would be sent off either to someone's dugout or with blankets and pillows to the fields! This moon has had greater decency than last month's in the way of shrouding its treacherous face. I'm sick of the moon – it seems to be always there. Abbeville and Étaples have been raided again too, as it is the railway they want.

*

There are a great many of the Guards out at rest at Mesnil-Val. Grenadiers, Coldstreams and Irish. We notice how dearly they love us to say even 'goodnight' to them. One man said, 'I was hoping you were going to speak. It is 18 months since I heard an Englishwoman talk.' They do like to hear our voices. There is a man here – a Colonel Boden – who started the war in the munitions department, but he has become a specialist at the job he is doing now. He is in charge of making light railways, and trucks and cars to run on them, all the way from the base to Candas. There is an 'up' rail and a 'down', and innumerable junctions and by-rails. They say it is a marvellous organisation and saves a tremendous amount of traffic on the main railway. Ammunition, supplies, patients, troops – all can now go up on his railway, so leaving the other less congested and also greatly relieving the lorry traffic and leaving the roads clear – *très bon*.

July 30

Yesterday was calm and two trawlers and three aeroplanes were very busy looking for a mine or a submarine, so instead of going out, I stayed at my window and watched them. The aeroplanes reminded me of seagulls over sewage – they would swoop down and along, almost on the water, then up, circle round, then down again. In the meantime, there was a great deal of tooting going on from trawler to trawler and they were steaming round in what looked like circles. I don't know if they found anything. Twenty Canadian sisters were added to our strength yesterday – for temporary duty! It is a great education and I am sure very good for us to rub shoulders with all sorts. In my ward I have two sorts of Americans, and now we have a Canadian, as well as English, Scottish and Irish.

July 31

Yesterday was wonderful from the point of view of spectacle. The sea, for all the enormous spread of it that we can see, was like glass. Hundreds of fishing boats were out, chiefly sitting in one place with all their sails up, but not moving an inch. They are about the size of Deal luggers and have sails of all colours – blue, red, brown, white. Think of them all in reflection! If it hadn't been upside-down you wouldn't have known which was boat and which was reflection. Some drifted home to harbour, and as soon as they were near enough they sent a long tow-rope ashore in a dinghy, and a line of men and women would pull them in with a fine catch of mackerel.

August 2

Yesterday a non-bathing friend and I walked to Mesnil-Val, where there is a huge convalescent and rest camp. The water there was thick with bathers, but we turned sharp to the right and walked along to where there was not a soul on the shore, and lovely little cliff caves to undress in. On the way we passed three Canadian sisters sitting on the beach – two non-bathers and one pining to go in but not liking to do so alone. I was expecting to bathe alone, but we went together, I vastly prefer someone beside me in the water. The sea looked calm but there was a very strong current and we were out of our depth before we knew it. We are busy now as we have had a convoy down every day for the past 12 days, however, news in the paper is still good. Von Somebody – a big German in Moscow – has been assassinated*. As one of my men says, he

---

* German diplomat Count Wilhelm von Mirbach, who was assassinated at the request of the Central Committee of the Left Socialist-Revolutionaries, a group opposed to the Bolsheviks. They hoped the assassination would restart the war with Germany.

does not like murder, but thinks it quite a good thing for some of these influential Germans to be put aside.

August 3

I heard yesterday that Boulogne had been badly raided the night before. The Boche got through the barrage and did pretty much as he liked, burning the Hotel Devereux (DMS's HQ) to the ground, along with a food-store and a detail-camp. Luckily there was very little loss of life, which is something to be grateful for.

August 4

On Saturday Sister Payne and I took tea to Mesnil-Val, and walked there over the cliff and back under it until we found a quite deserted spot. The tide was at its lowest, but after walking for what seemed like half a mile over sand, rocks and pools, I came to a deep basin into which every wave dashed. I bathed there and had a thorough swirling – it was lovely. We thought it looked to be working up for a storm, the south-western sky was deep violet and spreading – so we decided to walk home by the coast as a short cut. However, every inch was over rocks and pebbles, which made it seem much further. The storm raced us, and gave us a thorough drenching before we got home. My coat now looks like nothing on earth.

We still feel like holding our breath about the latest news – up to yesterday it was still excellent! Long may it last! Soissons has fallen to us and we are near Rheims! All the Allies seem to have fought splendidly, including the Americans, who of course *ought* to, as they are using the cream of their men and they are fresh to the war. We are getting a convoy of wounded down every day now as the

Étaples hospital is not being used. I suppose it is still out of action from its last bombing raid. Wish I could hear of or from Taff – I am wondering very much where he is in all this.

August 5

Since the last entry we have been fairly evenly busy with a convoy every day but one. I heard that a million men were to go over the top. Good luck to them. The dining hall gave a huge tea the other day for their boys and kindly invited all of mine, who were able, to go. They had an excellent tea of salad, cakes, jellies and fruit. After tea there was an impromptu concert got up by a sick officer who, when he is not fighting, composes music. Judging by his appearance and the way he sings and plays, his peace-time occupation suits him better than his present one.

Yesterday I went out with a sister who plays golf – she wanted to practise, so I did too! My! It is not a bit like it looks! It's unbelievable how hard it is to hit the ball – and when you do, it goes and hides itself so cleverly that it takes ages to find. But I can quite realise the fascination of the game for one who can play, and I may try again one day.

For about ten days I felt positively ill – like influenza, but with a stiff neck and left arm. Nothing did it much good and rubbing and applications both failed, so I had settled to calling it 'chronic rheumatism' and letting it take its chance. It is a good bit better now, but I can't look sideways very well. Then two days ago I met a sister on the stairs who looked about 100 years old – and was very stiff. She had just the same thing as I did and was having the next day off. She felt so seedy, she said, she was going to spend it in bed. Then last night I heard of another nurse with a stiff back and another with stiff legs, so now I believe there is some sort of a germ going round.

*

Some of my own patients were on the *Warilda** when she
was torpedoed, and I was very thankful to get a letter from
one of them yesterday – a boy who had been on the DI list
for some time and whose mother came out to visit.

August 10

The times are stirring and it's been an exciting week. I think
yesterday was top day! When I went on duty at 8 a.m., I was
met by a patient who asked if I had heard the news – we had
broken through at Albert and in front of Amiens, and had
advanced nine miles. A little later my Yankee MO arrived,
flushed and excited. Had I heard – we had taken prisoner two
divisional generals, lots of big guns and two complete CCSs?
Our tanks had done wonders and we had taken lots of
German tanks. The ward is full of men who had taken part
in the push. Some had got only as far as the German first-line
trenches and some to the second and some to the third – and
they were perked up and longing for more to arrive to find
out if the wood near the German side of the third-line trench
had been taken. Our tanks did good work – they went over
five to a battalion, and when they got to the German front
line they turned and paraded up and down, firing all the time,
which made a good protection for our infantry. The weather
was misty two days ago and our big bombing planes could not
take part, but yesterday was clear and I expect they did.

We have only had slight cases down so far, but during the night
more trains arrived, and today there will be more again, which

* On 3 August, the HMHS *Warilda* was transporting wounded soldiers from Le
Havre to Southampton when she was torpedoed by a German submarine despite
being marked clearly with the Red Cross; as with a number of other hospital ships torpedoed during the war, Germany claimed the ships were also carrying arms. The
Warilda sank in two hours with the loss of 115 patients, one nurse and one medical
orderly.

will probably bring the severely wounded. The spirit and cheer of the men is unbounded. You hear them talking about it as excitedly as if it were a game of football and once the tale is told, they go off into such a sleep, there seems no wakening them for anything. Sometimes I wish I were up at a CCS, but then again, I don't think I really do. They say the British – by that I mean all English-speaking troops including Americans – have done the real work so far. The French are held in readiness, resting with their very best cavalry, and when we are tired out the French are going to make a dash and carry on. That is the plan – let us only hope it will carry through all right. They say our casualties are light – one serious to five slightly wounded, and not a heavy toll killed. Thank God for that.

August 11

Yesterday was a good, old-time busy day with convoys in and out, patients going to the theatre and others to be X-rayed. We had some very badly wounded in – those who were left behind in CCSs when we got the slight ones yesterday. The bad ones were all very exhausted, poor dears – tired from the fight, as well as having in most cases lost a lot of blood – and what a quantity they drink! It is the very best thing for them and their natures evidently demand it – but what an agony of thirst a wounded man, out of reach of water, must suffer! There is one youngster with his leg off above the knee, who says that when the doctor comes round to mark them for Blighty, he wishes to be sent to Brighton.

The reading in the *Daily Mail* was thrilling yesterday, especially where the cavalry and Whippets* charged ahead

---

* The new Whippet tanks, introduced the previous year, were designed to be lighter, faster and more mobile than the earliest models.

of the infantry, who opened out to let them pass. The tanks really did marvels, and some of them went so far into the German lines that they paraded the streets of a village occupied by the enemy and fired their guns, point-blank, into rooms where officers were feeding, dressing or working. Truly a great surprise for them! Surely the Germans cannot stand such treatment for long. I got a letter from Taff yesterday written on the 3rd – it had been held up by way of censoring probably.

August 14

This push is a very steady-going one, and we have had three and four trains a day in since it began. Everywhere is crowded out, and those fit to travel go almost straight on to Blighty, but we are accumulating a heavy residue of those 'unfit'. In my ward I have ten DI and SI, including three bad spine cases and one fractured skull, so the work if anything

Patients arriving at Le Tréport by Ambulance Train were transferred to General Hospital No. 3 by motor ambulance.
Photograph courtesy of Jean-Luc Dron

becomes heavier. We also have a great number of very badly wounded Germans, and I hear from Major Martyn that 24 General Hospital is full of them. By what the men are saying, as well as from the papers, the enemy resistance is stiffening considerably, and our casualties are less light in consequence. The weather I think has favoured us – but I wonder how long they can keep up this pitch of warfare!

August 16

My ward is rather a sad place just now – so full of extremely badly wounded. There is plenty of gas-gangrene and two fractured spines dying in a room which is very difficult to ventilate. One feels the horrible smell in one's throat and nose all the time. Poor old things! One died yesterday – an Australian. His leg was very gangrenous and had to be taken off high up, but it was too far gone. His constant cry

Le Camp Anglo-Canadian – Départ de Convalescents

Moussi photo. du Funiculaire

Convalescents departing Le Tréport for embarkation to England.
Photograph courtesy of Jean-Luc Dron

was to get up and go out – that he was quite all right – then about half an hour before he died he settled down and said 'I'm done. I'm dying fast.' And he was quite right. It is very sad for these colonials with their people so far away, but when he was off his head I think he thought I was his mother, from the way he hugged and kissed my hand. So long as he does not get a great disappointment in a lucid interval, I do not mind. The news is keeping very good – long may it last.

August 19

Our last convoy was a heavy one of gassed men. I only took 11, but 11 such as they were, added to my already very busy ward, meant a lot. The two poor spines are dying so slowly – one, an old sergeant, is quite happily rambling on to his wife, a queer old fish who looks almost reprovingly at him for dying, and keeps saying in broad Lancashire, 'I didn't think he would die.' The other is an Australian and really a most handsome fair lad – 24 years old yesterday. His mother and fiancée are in Australia, but I hope to get his aunt from England to see him. He is a marvel – can't feel a single thing below his chest, but his upper part is always happy, content and cheerful. A sister of another ward, who comes from nearly the same part of Australia, comes and talks to him when she can. Another Australian told me that they were obliged to take more prisoners than they wanted, because they were too tired to bayonet any more. They came over in shoals and the Australians bayoneted and bayoneted until they could do no more.

The gassed patients all say they're using quite a new sort of gas. Their eyes are all swollen, bloodshot and streaming – and their skin and tender parts of their bodies are burnt a copper colour. The gas does not take effect at once, but

comes on by degrees. As a preliminary symptom they may
be sick after their first meal – then their eyes begin to prick.
By the time they reach the base they are extremely ill,
breathing like a person dying from bronchitis with a horrible
discharge pouring from nose and mouth, a temperature
about 104° and pulse of about 140.

My own MO is on leave, and taking his place is Captain
Randle, a Bart's man who was with a battalion until a few
weeks ago – I like him. It seems they did well, but were terribly cut up, so the remnant was sent to the base to be quiet
for a bit. I said I thought not one person, if they spoke the
truth, would say they wanted to go back to the front, and he
quite agreed. However, he said he knew just one man who
was an exception – a major in his battalion. He was a big
man, very slow of speech, but who was absolutely fearless.
Once, when the Germans had advanced, he went back to
where the battalion had retreated from to get some information for his colonel. He found out what was wanted, and
then went down to one of their old dugouts, where he knew
there was a telephone back to HQ. He rang up his colonel
and told his tale, and the colonel asked him where he was.
The major told him and the colonel said, 'Thank you very
much for the information, which will be most useful. Now,
will you please come back as quickly as you can?' The major
answered in his usual drawl, 'Very well, sir. I will if I can, but
there are rather a lot of Boches about – I can hear some talking outside the dugout.' He got back all right. Apparently he
was always loathe to take leave and had to be sent. Someone
showed him an account in a paper of some of his exploits on
the Marne – no name was mentioned, but it was 'a major
who has won the DSO and Military Cross, both with bars'.
The exploits left no doubt it was him, and he was extremely
angry about it.

*

In my ward I have a sergeant with 14 years' Army service who's rather a character. He was in the navy for two years, but didn't like it, he said, because 'You get beaten every time you dare speak to an able seaman', so he swam ashore to Plymouth one night, bought himself some clothes, took a train to London without a ticket, and immediately enlisted in the army. He was caught and court-martialled two years later at Malta, but seems to have got through all right. This is his sixth time of being wounded, and he has two bits of shrapnel through his lungs, but he thinks that if he starts deep-breathing exercises, he will be better soon, and he is accustomed to doing them every day.

I sat out on the pier-head yesterday afternoon and it was gloriously breezy. I was much entertained watching a Belgian officer making love to a Belgian lady, who seemed far more taken up with keeping her skirts from being blown over her head than with him. As it was, her little powder puff blew away and two small boys had a fine game chasing it until it finally dodged through a porthole and flew out to sea.

August 22

Saint Bartholomew's Day. I wonder if the children will get their buns – I don't suppose there will be many plums in them, if any – but it is the bun that is the joy! One spine case died yesterday. His wife was with him, dear simple soul, and it was very pathetic. She suffered untold anguish but grief is strange – the heart enveloped in it is constantly finding little peepholes of comfort, and occasions for rejoicing. The poor thing would weep that she was losing a good husband, then say, '. . . but his colonel was proud of him, and is going to write to me, and then it'll all be in the paper!' Then she would cry again . . . but then say, 'All Accrington will know of him – it'll all be in the papers.' And, 'Ah well, I'm glad

I've seen the last of him – I shall be more content.' Sergeant Partlin* was only 35, but I thought from looking at him he was about 50. War does age them so.

I heard a good argument from the sergeant who ran away from the navy in favour of being two parts drunk when you 'go over the bags' – and he is a man who has done well and won medals. To begin with, if you're wounded, you don't bleed as much, and secondly, you are quite sensible enough to know what is expected of you and you do the job with a crest-high spirit and daring – but minus fear. He told me that in one big attack, at their first objective they found a dugout where four German officers were lunching on bread, ham and plenty of wine. They killed the Germans, ate the lunch themselves, and then had a good drink of rum – of which they had found dozens of pints, decanted into our English Bass bottles. First of all he and four other sergeants tucked in, then an officer joined them, then the colonel – and when they had finished, they sent the men down for their rum, and after that took another 90 yards in a brilliant dash. The sergeant is a man of fine physique and goes in for long-distance running, deep breathing and all sorts of exercise. When he is in the line he takes two meals a day and his rum issue, but when they are back for a rest, he eats three meals a day and drinks three pints of stout every night at the estaminet before going to bed.

*

---

* A visitors' book entry on the Appleton website reveals that this was Sergeant James Partlin, from Accrington, Lancashire. His wife May had left their five children to travel to France to be with him. May was proved right; his commanding officer, Lieutenant-Colonel Bradley Williams, did in due course write to her, praising James's work highly, and the letter made its way into the local papers. 'I feel sure that if your husband had not been hit so soon in this tremendous battle which had been going on on the Western Front, he would have proved himself one of the most gallant N.C.O.s in the regiment.'

My gassed men are terribly ill – every one of them the colour of a dirty penny, pulses rocky, throats raw, eyes streaming with swollen lids – and all off their heads at intervals.

August 27

The battles are raging, hot and strong, and up to yesterday there seemed to be no holding the Allies back – God speed them still! Our boy Taff is in the thick of it at Bapaume – at least so I imagine, as a New Zealander I have in told me the whole division was there, which of course includes Private 54268. It is a difficult part of the line and I'm wishing the whole bloody war at an end and all the boys safely home.

The ward is a shambles of men with broken skulls, legs off and spines broken – and it is also a shifting scene of ins and outs. Every day, two or three trainloads come in, and every day those who are at all fit to travel go out. Roll on the war and why, oh why – since you have to squeal for peace – don't you wretched Boches start squealing now? We are getting hundreds of Boches in – many mortally wounded – so no time for me or such things as diaries. If there were, I would just say how pretty the sea and sky are this morning – blue and copper!

August 30

The news keeps good, thank God, but we have no breathing time between trains. My ward is full to overflowing all the time and many have their relatives wired for by the War Office. Really it is heart-breaking, one dear old lady came all the way alone – and she had never travelled in her life before – to see her youngest boy. Fathers, mothers, brothers, aunts – all kinds of relatives arrive.

September 2

Bullecourt has been taken – and lost – but Peronne is ours, and lots of other places, including Roye, Noyon, Mont St Quentin, and many prisoners taken. Still the tide of wounded comes in and passes on, either to England, or to its last resting place. September is here and the war not nearly ended – God speed the Allies to do something to stop it before its fifth winter!

A corporal in my ward tells how a 'Chink' was killed in an air-raid*. The Chinese compound was close to a huge cage of German prisoners, and at the death of their man they broke bounds, got to a bomb-dump, equipped themselves and left not one German alive in the cage. We are still flooded out with Germans, and talk about the 'Blighty smile'! It sits as surely on the face of the prisoners going to England as on our boys. Yesterday I saw a huge bus that carries about 40 sitting cases. The two last rows were Boches, and they were all smiles and just as excited-looking as our own men.

September 4

The battle proceeds, all along the line and in Russia. One feels breathless and nervous of shouting too soon, but up to yesterday the Allies were sweeping forward. All hospitals are kept at top speed, receiving and passing on wounded. Even so, they say that thanks to aeroplanes and tanks, our casualties are light for the victories won. The Germans got wind that we were bringing out a new tank, so our people wrote many accounts of the 'Whippet' – a small new one currently in use – to throw dust in their eyes and divert attention from

---

* The British government recruited Chinese workers for manual labour and support work. They became The Chinese Labour Corps.

the *real* new ones that we are now using. They are large enough to carry 15 infantrymen as well as their own crew, and are so big that up to the present they have not come to any trench too big for them to cross.

We are absolutely flooded out with Germans, and I imagine hundreds are being killed. A Canadian I had in yesterday was surprised when I told him how many we had – he said they had orders to kill as many as they could … God help us. I went crabbing last night with a VAD. It is great fun – you scramble about over rocks and poke them out with a stick. We brought home about nine of an edible size.

September 11

The busy time continues, although the last two trainloads have had quite a percentage of what we call 'ICT'* – that is such things as poisoned sores, or tears from barbed wire. All the same, an empty bed is still an unknown thing. I don't know how the soldiers keep it up, as I think hospital staffs are beginning to feel a bit done in – but still we would much rather they get on with the war if it means ending it any sooner.

We have got the funniest old Scot in the ward – he's shot through the stomach and has to be dressed often. He knows each time exactly how he wants to be laid and tells us, 'on ma right side – with ma bottom theyre' – or sometimes he does not say which side. 'Poot ma bottom theyre, and I'll be right.' So we do exactly as he says and he is quite content. Rogers, a man from Sandwich, is still running a temperature between 103° and 105°, but I hope he will pull through.

*

* Inflammation of Connective Tissue. This was an umbrella term covering a range of conditions affecting the dermis, from impetigo through streptococcal infection to severe ulceration and gangrene.

The news in the papers is good still – but we don't seem much nearer the end of the war. Still no news of Taff – I suppose he is still in the thick of it. Quite a well-off relative of one of our wounded said she would like to send me something for the ward. I warned her that I really did not know the prices of these things, but said I should like a gramophone – and she has promised it. I hope it is not too expensive.

September 12

Pouring rain! This will put a stopper on our 'push', but I fancy we are in a better position than the Boches. Looking down a row of beds yesterday, number one was an Australian, the second a South African, the third a New Zealander, the fourth a Scot, numbers five and six Canadians, the seventh Irish, the eighth English, the ninth Portuguese – and after that it became more monotonous.

September 13

Very rough weather and I was in and out of bed a dozen times shutting the window against rain, and eventually opening it again, knowing it was only heavy showers. Yesterday's paper reported the Germans counterattacking. I do hope we shall get St Quentin before the winter sets in. Miss Eardley and I went for a rough and muddy walk last night and got caught in two deluges. Luckily we were in a cornfield at the time, and buried ourselves in the sheaves. We were coming home by a straight narrow lane which was muddy everywhere, with ponds in parts, and we scrambled along the upright banks past the puddles. An old, old Frenchman was coming towards us and was evidently very anxious to help us over the difficult bits, from one side of the lane to the other – perhaps a tiny shade less muddy than the one we were on.

Rogers is still critically ill. I had a letter from his father yesterday, and a box of chocolates from the fiancée of poor old Limbrick (now dead). Really this push makes one's correspondence a bit heavy, but the DI's relatives do like to hear from those who nurse their dear ones.

September 19

The last few days have been quieter, although busy. All our American sisters and three of our own have been taken away, and an old friend of mine of 45 CCS days has come here for duty. She went on leave from her ambulance train and asked for a move when she came back, as the strain was too great for her, spending most nights in dugouts, and with no steady work to counterbalance things. I had two spine cases in a month ago – apparently wounded the same and paralysed the same. One died in a few days, but the other is much better and going to England today. We had three head-cases, all looking to be equally wounded – one got (apparently) quite well, one became childish and travelled home (well, but ten years younger than when he came out), and the third is dying by quarter inches, poor fellow! Both his mother and wife are in New Zealand.

September 24

The morning is beautiful. Golden-red clouds making golden-red patches on the steely calm sea, and little ships sailing past. News up to date is good, but work is steady, and quite enough of it.

September 25

Had a half day off and in the afternoon went to the pier with Sister Payne. It was wild and glorious there, and the tide was very high and rough. The end of the pier is dangerous and railed off, and each big wave made it wheeze and creak, but many people were fishing on the main pier. There was a school of sprats in the sea and it was a case of catch-who-catch-could between the fishers on the pier and the porpoises in the sea. The fishers used no bait – simply lowered a line with many hooks on, then drew it up with the little sprats hanging on!

The harbour is a joy at high tide with all the steamers and fishing boats in, and it felt very tempting to step on some vessel or another and fly the country! In the evening Miss Williams (our Assistant Matron) and I walked to the country where we gathered flowers, picked mushrooms and returned in time for first dinner and an early bed. A convoy was scheduled to arrive during the night, so we may expect a busy day today, and my ward is already pretty full. The mornings are getting very dark now and I shall be quite pleased when the clock is moved back in five days' time.

October 1

The weather is cold and stormy and I thought even this great hotel would be blown away last night – but after all it has stood six years, so perhaps it will manage one or two more. We are very busy all the time, and they keep taking from our staff to reinforce up the line. News is A1 up to date, and the men say the newspapers do not exaggerate! The casualties are the sad, tragic part – whatever the papers say in that direction, the men say we have lost a terrible lot killed and wounded. Leave is still being granted, and quite right too, because if the fighting goes on all winter we shall never get any leave if we wait for a calm period. The 47 General Hospital – a hut and tent camp beside us – was all blown down last year. I wonder if it will fare better this year!

*

Poor old Sergeant Chitty – fractured skull – died two nights ago, but the second spine case I had in ages ago went to England, and is now marked for Australia, his home. We had one man brought in dying two days ago, but something is very kind to the dying. He laughed and seemed delighted to see us, and said, 'Oh it's good to be here', and he died smiling. He must have thought we were his home people. I have just taken a poor old Irishman from the mental hut. He has one leg off at the top of the thigh, the other foot wounded, one hand wounded and one eye, and his throat is badly cut. He did that himself as he lay on the field. He had lain there a long time and couldn't move on account of his wounds, then he heard a creeping barrage coming towards him. He couldn't bear it, so he groped for his razor, cut his throat – and knew no more. I don't blame him and nobody would, but of course he is now under arrest. Anyway, he is getting on well now.

October 2

I am enjoying myself very much this morning. It is still grey dawn, the clouds as yet have not a tinge of colour, but soon they will be putting on little dabs of gold and heliotrope and all sorts. A brig has taken the lucky chance of high tide, and with no one looking, has quickly left the harbour and is speeding out to sea – FREE. Two men, looking very friendly, walking in step and rubbing shoulder to shoulder have just passed. When they were opposite my window I saw one was a Boche prisoner and the other his guard – so in the darkness even enemies may be friends! In daylight the Boche walks in front and the guard behind, carrying a fixed bayonet, but there was no bayonet this morning.

Dare we feel that there is one small chip of Peace? Yesterday's paper talked about the Bulgarians' unconditional surrender – peace on the Allies' terms and an armistice to be arranged at once! Thank God for Peace, even in one small part. Now, of course, Turkey will not be able to get ammunition for her big guns through from Germany, so perhaps she also will sue for Peace. Peace deserves a capital letter every time it is written! Our last load are very badly wounded. Half mine were either DI or SI, and some will die. Their poor, poor mothers. It's not as bad for the boys themselves, as they die happy, but the relatives are left so wretched.

October 6

We are living through stirring times. Yesterday, 'Turkey is going to give in', and today 'The Central Powers have asked President Wilson* for a two-months' armistice'. They *must not* be granted it! Oh, I do hope *no*-one will be in favour of that! Just think how they would prepare and dig in, and then at the end make our task twice as heavy as it would be if we kept straight on. No! For all our sakes – and tired as every one is – I do hope we shall keep on until he asks for Peace, and that in a rather less arrogant tone than appears in today's paper.

A Jewish padre from 24 General Hospital called on me two days ago. He was most interesting. He said the Jews would still be in mourning in spite of Jerusalem being taken, until the Temple was rebuilt. The Jews already have a vast amount of money for the rebuilding of it. Apparently an English Jew and German Jew were in hot conflict trying to

---

* Thomas Woodrow Wilson (1856–1924), 28th President of the United States. His famous 'Fourteen Points' speech of January 1918 prompted the Germans to sue for peace, although the terms were dictated by Marshal Foch and the British with no American input.

kill each other when they both thought their last hour had come, and they both repeated three lines of verse in Hebrew*. They heard each other, stopped fighting – and saved each other! Part of the Jewish creed is that a man must repent the day before he dies, but as he never knows the day of his death, he must repent every day.

Oh, I do wish the fighting could stop! We are all wondering if Turkey will stand with Germany whatever happens, or if she will sue for a separate Peace in the event of us not granting the two-months' armistice. We put our clocks back an hour last night and now at 1800 (army time), it is getting quite appreciably dark.

October 11

We had some cavalrymen down with our last batch, and one told me what a surprise they had given the Germans at the turn of the tide of war on the Amiens front. There were four divisions of cavalry following the infantry, and as soon as a breach was made, through they went and had a clear run of nearly nine miles. Then they dismounted and dug themselves in, the Germans apparently ignorant of their having broken through. They saw three Fritzes bicycling towards Amiens, so they took them and found out from them where their Brigade HQ was. They found it and captured it, then they found a 'leave' train full of men going home. They shot the engine driver and made all the men prisoners. They also found an ambulance train, and again they shot the driver and took the complete train. Apparently there were chiefly sisters on board and no wounded, so the sisters

---

* Edie is referring to the Shema, the central prayer of the Jewish faith. It is recited at least twice daily, in the morning and in the evening, as well as by the dying. The opening words are 'Hear, O Israel, the Lord is our God, the Lord is One.' (Deuteronomy 6:4)

were sent down the line and subsequently returned to their own land.

Another man I had in – with a knee so bad that he will most likely lose the leg – told me that he was a prisoner with the Germans for a few days and he was never given so much as a drink of water the whole time, and his wound was not dressed. Hence how bad it is. That I forgive them – they probably do as we do and dress their own first – and God help them, do they ever get to the end of their own? Whether they left their worst for us or not I don't know, but they are blown to bits and torn to ribbons, inside and out.

We had an unusually busy day and I have only one staff nurse and two VADs at present, but on that particular day, my staff nurse and one VAD went sick and two 'blue boys'*, whom we have taught to help us with the dressings, had to be kept in bed with high temperatures and sore throats. However, the two General Service VAD girls – which were all I had – turned up trumps and we got through all right. Our whole hospital is very understaffed with only 20 trained people for about 2,000 beds. Thank goodness my VADs are good, in fact they are splendid. Nicol, a 45 CCS friend of mine, is now on night duty here, and yesterday I was glad to hear that Hamilton Watts – another of our 45 staff – is at the hospital adjoining ours.

I went for a walk along the sea front at Mers-les-Bains yesterday and saw a French hydroplane broken on the beach. It had come down at sea and evidently sent word for help, and it was towed in here at about 3 p.m. It looked pretty badly smashed, but it was very interesting to see it. The car was of shining aluminium – no wonder they shine like silver birds

* Patients who were well enough to be up and dressed were given blue suits to wear, known as 'hospital blues'.

when they are high up! I thought the seafront quite a
respectable place to walk alone in the evening, but evidently
it is not. Every Frenchman who was by himself cooed at
me – a sort of 'tweet tweet' noise – so now the clocks are put
back I can't walk alone at night. I suppose they thought I
was on the lookout for a companion! Not much! They evidently don't realise the bliss and joy of being quite alone
when you live in a hum of many voices.

Sadly I have taken my beautiful winter coat to be made
hideous and regulation – silly fools with their rules!

October 14

Great excitement yesterday over the newspaper headline:
'Kaiser's Cabinet Gives In' and we are all wondering just
what it means. The Hun is no more sorry for what he has
done now than he was four years ago, of that all are certain –
and as for saying he agrees to vacate Belgium! The fool! He
agrees! There's not much 'agrees' about it. He is being made
to do it, and at top speed. They want an armistice and time
to prepare some foul new device of Satan to launch at us.
Yesterday an arrogant Prussian officer here was saying, boast-
ingly, 'It has taken the whole world to move us.' Prussians
are dirty dogs, every one of them.

   We had an airman officer to dine with us last night, and he
says there are no first-class Germans now and their planes
are made of bad materials. The propellers are made of coarse
rough wood instead of polished mahogany! He was a gentleman and not one to speak evil of his kind, and he did say
that in the early war days the German flying men showed
considerable chivalry, but that now that was sadly lacking
and they play some very ill tricks in the air. He said they had
great fun dropping their first bomb on Lille. They floated
over the place several times and finally dropped it. The Hun

saw this object descending and flew for shelter, and many were still fleeing when it arrived, plumb in the middle of *La Place*. It bounced a few times and finally stayed still. Little by little the Hun became brave and ventured to look at this unexploded object – and found it was a football with the message 'Love from the RFC' tied to it. He said they did not bomb places like Lille more than they were obliged to. However, we English have got a diabolical new bomb which makes an unearthly siren whistle on its way down. I believe its moral effect is very far reaching.

October 15

Peace talk seemed all fizzled out yesterday and now the popular opinion is two years more! It is no good going by papers or popular opinion and we must just wait and see. I thought, as we sent patients out the day before and no convoy was announced, that we should have a few empty beds yesterday, but a convoy of men from the Douai region came in unannounced. They say the Germans are making a bit of a stand there, but that we have both sides of it covered.

Rogers, who has been DI for such a very long time, and still is, has taken a most funny turn and makes the men roar with laughter. He mimics my voice to a T. It quite made me jump when he began it, because I recognised myself quite well. He calls the VAD 'Nurse', but lately it has been 'Miss Welford! I want you.' I suppose he is only partly sensible and doesn't really know.

October 18

Not using newspaper talk, or authorities' ideas or thinking it out one bit in my own brain, but I hope we shall *not* give the Germans peace yet, for the one reason that the men, one and all, are fiercely against it and it is they who bear the brunt. If they feel they can stand a little more of it, why should they be held back? They feel they have not yet hit back hard enough for the dirty, mean, brutal tricks played by the very dishonourable enemy. Given another few months they may make a far more satisfactory job of it.

The CCSs are playing a great game of leap-frog and just occasionally something stirs in my blood and I wish I were back at one, advancing every few weeks over the heads of all the others, then feeling annoyed when they get ahead again – and then taking our turn to jump when it comes again. I loved it all – except the shelling and bombing, which was horrible. It must be very interesting just now, as they are following up the armies over the new battle-fields – and unsalvaged battlefields tell such thrilling tales. On the whole I believe I should welcome orders to go up – but it never pays in the army to ask for anything at all. There has been an unending stream of men through since July, but we are glad because all the while the news is good! No-one knows the difference in nursing men from a successful and unsuccessful battle, except those who have done it. Ill as they are, these men are happy and cheerful. The German sisters must be having a hard and sad task.

October 19

Last evening I went to town to collect my modified coat. There were huge flags flying and I wondered what on earth – but then I discovered that the people were rejoicing over the retaking of Ostend, Bruges and especially Lille. Little urchins were marching through the town with impro-vised bands of drums, voices and whistles, and it sounded joyful. Many of the inhabitants here are refugees from places that the Boches invaded. The tailor who altered my coat, and who now lives in a tiny house told me that he came from La Bassée where he had a big shop and, as he said, 'beautiful things also', and many assistants.

I hear rumours of 11 sisters coming – please may it be true! We could do with double the number. We had a poor youngster from the last convoy with a ghastly shoulder wound and I do not expect to find him there today as it was all gas-gangrene. We have an anti-gas serum now, but to do any good it must be given at the earliest stages and this boy was too far advanced when he came. His mother was told she might come, but I doubt if she will arrive in time, poor dear.

October 23

The news yesterday was good. The French are at the Danube so Germany cannot send to Constantinople by that way – in fact, all ways except by Russia seem to be barred now. We had a very heavy convoy in yesterday – most of them from the front near Cambrai. They say there are hundreds of civilians in the villages we are taking now, and one boy said the people had been told that the 'Tommies' were coming. The people were delighted when they arrived and as this boy said, some of the chaps who speak French learned that the Germans made the civilians do all the cooking and slapped them if it was not well done. Lots of the girls and women had been taken to 'work' for the Germans. One old man over 80 didn't seem to know what to do – he walked up and down, half laughing and half crying. Many civilians have been wounded and are in our CCSs.

I had a terribly sad case in. He was such a nice cheery man – a gentleman farmer – who was brought in with a very deep thigh wound. It looked fairly clean and he was all right in himself, except for a bad headache (a great symptom of gas). He wrote to his wife saying he hoped to get to England soon and was constantly rejoicing at going back to his wife and child and farm. But there was gas-gangrene in the wound, and he died in less than a day. I saw in yesterday's paper that we have captured a 15-inch gun on the Belgian coast that was used for shelling Dunkirk. The Fourth Army are 'at home'* today, and if I can I shall go.

October 24

Miss Williams, our Assistant Matron, and I went to the Army School 'at home'. The first part was quite interesting when they showed us the school mascot – a boar which they had brought with them from Fliers Wood – and when they showed us photographs of the battle areas taken from aeroplanes. Tea was all right and there was a band which played outside the mess during tea then later in the lecture hall, which was a large hut with a splendid waxed floor. British nurses are not allowed to dance – but the Canadians and Americans are. That explains our misery in a nutshell – OUR PEOPLE DANCED, and it is Miss Williams' duty, being in charge of the party, to report it. If she reports it officially, it means drastic punishment for the offenders. If she does not, she has not done her job. The moment we spotted three of ours in full swing we fled from the hut and spent the rest of the time wandering anywhere that was not near the dancing. We talked the matter through inside out and came to the conclusion that the thing to do was to tell Matron unofficially and pretend we did not see it – but to warn them if any one dances next time, no further invitations will be accepted. Do you wonder I asked not to be charge; in some ways it is a grisly, policeman's job.

*

* An open invitation to visit, the host or hosts being present to receive guests.

We saw an interesting photograph of where the Americans had been holding the line. They had to advance over a canal which ran underground for about 2,000 yards. The Yanks dashed straight ahead over the canal, never thinking to guard the two ends of the tunnel. The Boches were lying in wait in numbers along the towpath in the tunnel, and when the Yanks were well over, they came out with machine-guns and killed most of them. The Australians came over after the Yanks and the Germans bobbed up and gave them a bad time too.

October 25

The British are making a fresh attack round Valenciennes, and are having a stiffer job than over their last attack. The place is bristling with Boches, and I'm afraid our casualties are heavy. A while back, an airman came to visit his brother, who was dangerously ill in the officers' ward, and he dined with us. He came over again two days ago and did some marvellous low flying, and dropped a message for his father and mother who are visiting the other son. We thought he would graze the huts he was so low! He started back when it was dark and hard to see – and crashed to the ground and was killed. It really is very sad for his parents, poor dears. They have already had one son killed, a second is a prisoner in Austria, the third is here DI, and now this fourth one has been killed. He had only been married a short time, but he looked so young I couldn't believe he was old enough.

October 27

Some Canterbury Infantry Regiment came down on yesterday's convoy – and that's who Taff is with. One of them told me they left their resting spot last Tuesday night to be ready

for the attack on Wednesday, when they had a hard time. I
wish he knew Taff, but he doesn't.

October 28

Sister Nicol had a letter from an officer who passed through
Achiet a little while ago and who was a patient of hers there
in 1917. He said, 'I spent the night where the old 45 CCS
used to be. It is now a scene of devastation and ruin – it
made me feel very sad. The officers' ward where I spent
so many happy hours is just a tumbled ruin. The only
recognisable thing was the fireplace, which I remember
being built, and the two little chimney corner seats. The
mess was marked "Believed to be mined – not to enter".
The hut where your room was had been removed bodily
and a disused machine-gun post had been blown up
there.'

The Assistant Matron brings round the bundles of mag-
azines sent to the hospital. One day she came in from the
huts looking like I don't know what – drenched and blown
and her sou'wester on any way but straight. She didn't mind
a bit what figure she cut when a man bobbed up in bed and
said, 'Here comes the Sketch'. She heard and enjoyed the
aptness very much. I think they love the *Sketch* the most of
all the papers we get.

October 31

Sister Nicol has gone back to a CCS so why haven't *I*? I
wrote to Miss Wilton Smith yesterday and asked her not to
let me become a shirker at the base where I have had over
a year now. A new Red Cape arrived yesterday with orders
that she is to be Assistant Matron. That means the present
one must go and everyone will be terribly sorry.

＊

The news seems good and I believe the heads of the nations are conferring in Paris on the peace problem – good luck to them! I have got a sailor in my ward – a stoker from a collier – and I was telling him something the paper had reported from Norway. 'Don't believe a single thing any Norwegian tells you,' he said*. He says that they are the biggest lot of spies imaginable. They were caught carrying letters for enemy subjects, to and fro from England. Now, when a Norwegian vessel enters the Humber, or any other port, the pilot who boards the ship has to take all binoculars and telescopes and lock them up until the vessel is out of port again. That is certainly not done on a British vessel.

November 3

Sadly our Assistant Matron is being moved to 72 General Hospital at Trouville – all thanks to those young villains who let her down by dancing the other day. She and Matron and I went to La Madeleine for tea on All Saints' Day. All the people were dressed up, finer than on Sunday, and were going in huge groups and families to honour their dead. The cemeteries were a blaze of flowers when they had finished. The news of the surrender of Turkey had come on the same day, so they ended up making it quite a day of rejoicing, and French, British, Belgian and American flags were flying everywhere.

November 9

There is a whole lot of peace talk going on but they don't seem to be getting on with it. The news has been absolutely glorious and yesterday we have had lots of convoys down – chiefly not

---

* Norway, although neutral, was probably the most pro-Allies of the Scandinavian countries. Sweden was very pro-German and this may be what he meant. Norway had only gained its independence from Sweden in 1905.

very severe cases. My head has been too much like a pumpkin with neuralgia to tell a single word of anything that may have happened – new cases have swarmed in and swarmed out and some have had influenza and all are very cheerful about the news. Apparently the German Navy has mutinied – badly[*].

November 12

Peace! Thank God for that! It feels very queer too, as if your elastic had snapped.

Matron and I took some sick sisters to Abbeville yesterday, and the moment we stopped at the siding we were pounced upon by the ambulance drivers and told we were much behind the times for not knowing the news – *they* had been told the night before. We went back to the nurses' home – my old billet – and told them the news, then to the sisters' hospital to tell them. We stayed there for breakfast, then walked around Abbeville, where I showed Matron the air-raid damage.

Evidently the folk everywhere had heard the news and French girls were embracing Tommies, and French children blew kisses to us as we passed. French soldiers waved ecstatically, and looked as if for two pins, or if we were not going so fast, they would climb aboard and kiss us. We came back to Tréport just minutes after the news broke there, and in less than an hour the whole place had gone stark mad, with flags of all nations flying everywhere and sirens blowing. All the bands turned out and processed along the camp, with convalescent patients and oddments of French following. Ambulances bedecked with flags and streamers – which are

---

[*] On 28 October German sailors refused to obey orders to launch a last-ditch attack on the Royal Navy for the honour of the High Seas Fleet. Germany, Austria-Hungary and the Ottoman Empire were already in talks with the Allies about armistices and the attack would have been a futile gesture.

normally allowed to carry eight sitting or four lying and one sitting – carried about 16 inside and as many as could manage to stay up on the roof. Then they paraded solemnly round and round the roads, the men cheering, shouting and waving flags.

In the afternoon I think many had drunk the good health of the occasion and the spirit of *entente* was well to the fore, with French soldiers, Tommies and French girls walking about in long lines, locked in each others' arms. Even the motor lorries were decked with flags.

In the Music Room we bought six bottles of good port and when the lights were up we made our longest-staying patient (a sergeant of the Naval Division) give a little speech. Then they all drank – to *Peace*! We are to have one more convoy, direct from the line – and then local sick.

Here endeth the fighting part of the war – GOD SAVE THE KING!

Nation	Entered war	Armistice signed
Bulgaria	October 1, 1915	September 30, 1918
Turkey	November 5, 1914	October 31, 1918
Austria	July 28-29, 1914	November 4, 1918
Germany	July 28-29, 1914	November 11, 1918

November 16

A few days ago I was detailed to escort a wounded officer, Hendry, who was being transferred from here to a hospital in Paris, where his people lived. We had a reserved carriage and no change, which was a blessing, and the stretcher rested well along one seat while I had the other to myself. The train was slow and took six hours to do the journey, but with a nice luncheon hamper and books, the time passed all right. Paris looked fine! Such wide streets! A clean-looking city and flags, flags, flags, everywhere. We drove right through and it was all brightly lit with hundreds of beautiful cars dashing about. I should very much have liked to do some shopping, but had no spare time.

The Hendrys live past the Bois de Boulogne, beyond the city gates, and have a delightful house, where they gave me a small suite of rooms. Mr Hendry was a charming host and took me to the station next morning. We started early and he drove me all through the Bois de Boulogne and round all the principal parts of Paris to let me see everything there was to see. There were hundreds of German field-guns – *Minen-werfer** – French mortars, one big gun (not a Bertha), a whole long line of Boche aeroplanes, a Boche tank and a sandbag air-raid shelter, quite the size of our house at home, was hung thick with Boche tin hats! The Statue of Liberty was draped in the National Flag and everyone seemed gay. They are going to have a great *fête* day on Sunday.

November 18

Thank the good God, we are nothing like as busy now. Twenty of my beds have been taken down and put into store, so now I have only 40 beds and 40 patients – and some of them will be going soon. They say, 'as thy day, so shall thy strength be', and while we were so busy we could have any number of badly broken people each with five or six wounds and just get on with it – but now it almost bores me to put on a simple fomentation.

November 19

What a difference! We have – and shall have for some time – heavy surgical cases in, but it is a very different matter nursing

---

* Literally 'mine launcher', used by the Germans to clear close range obstacles, such as barbed wire, that long range artillery could not accurately target.

them when they are well established and have no shock to contend with, and we have no convoys in khaki all smothered in mud and blood, straight through from the fight. They all come down nicely washed and in pyjamas now, and they don't mind half as much being marked 'Base' or 'Con camp'. I have not sent any patients to England for four days now – and we are starting having days off. My last VAD has hers tomorrow and then, if all be well, I shall take the next day. Think of it! A whole day!

November 20

A very sudden and merry thing happened last night. Ten of the MOs took themselves to a 'Peace dinner' in the town, and the rest were a little hurt that they were neither told about it nor asked to attend it, so two of them fled to Matron and asked her to come and bring seven sisters with her to an impromptu dinner. As I was on my way to dinner, I met Matron wearing a worried look trying to find a seventh, so instead of dinner at 7.15, I flew back to my room, changed and was down before half past to join the rest at the 'Impromptu'. It was great fun! The ADMS and the DADMS were both there and enjoyed the fun like anything. After dinner some of us played bridge and some played the rowdiest game of *vingt-et-un*. At 11.15 in came the diners-out, and their expressions were a study!

Mr Marriott, who took me in to dinner, has spent 17 years in China, and is most interesting on the subject. If a Chinaman who is sentenced to death can raise 50 dollars, he can always get someone to take his place. Many of them will accept 30 dollars and give up their life in exchange. Also, if you tip the executioner highly enough he will do the job at one blow – otherwise he is not so particular. The Chinese like us British, and most important ports where Mr Marriott has been are held by us. He says the British prestige is very high indeed since we have beaten the Germans at their own game of war. During the war the Japanese have been on the fence, ready to side with the stronger power – now they have plumped for the Allies*.

November 22

Yesterday my kind people sent up breakfast from the ward, then until 10 o'clock I chiefly slept – it was too cold to put as much as a nose out of bed. Then I got up and Swanzy and I went to the Casino to lunch and after joined several folk who had a half day off, and walked through the tank camp to Bois de Cise. It was a frosty afternoon with golden sunshine and the autumn tints showed up to perfection. We went for tea to a quaint little hotel which is kept by a charming old man and his wife. They are rather a picturesque couple and he played the gramophone to us while she prepared tea. The great excitement in Tréport yesterday was the huge catch of herrings. The sea was dead calm and boat after boat came in to harbour laden with them. Barrows, barrels, baskets full of them and some just heaped on the sails were being sold and everyone from toddlers upwards seemed to be carrying herrings away.

November 25

We sent off a batch of wounded to Blighty two days ago and filled up with medical cases yesterday. What a difference! What a mixture! We still have nearly a dozen wounded left who are too bad to be moved – the rest are strained hearts, bad ears, boils, etc. Rumour is about the busiest element in camp just now – one day we are to stay as a demobilisation base, the next we are to disband within a month, and the

* In fact Japan declared war on Germany on 23 August 1914.

next to get out of the building (the rent of which is enormous) and move into the huts and tents.

November 26

I got orders to proceed at once to No. 7 Stationary Boulogne for duty, so I had to make a sudden ending at Le Tréport. This new hospital is a camp, high up and about 40 minutes' walk along the Boulogne–Calais Rd. What a change on a wet day, from living in a smart hotel with a roof over one's head all the time, to living in one hut, messing in another one a muddy walk off, and working in two more a longer and muddier walk off! Instead of a private bathroom, one has to walk a fair distance through the camp to a general bathhouse, common to all. It is a ramshackle camp but everyone seems quite happy. I have charge of a couple of surgical huts, and the MO, Major Martin*, is quite a pleasant young man. There are scores of 'birds of passage' sisters here, waiting for distribution. Many have been sent to Bruges to nurse the Belgians and some will be sent into Germany when the places are ready for them.

November 30

Quiet day yesterday – four patients went to England and four fresh ones took their places. They say our Cavalry Division, which is to be part of the army of occupation, is a glorious sight. Beautiful horses, equipment the last word, and new lances for the lancers with new flags bearing the King's and Queen's heads on the top of each one. At present it is on show in Paris, and I should very much like to go and see it.

---

* Not the Major Martyn who was Edie's MO at Étretat and whom she was to meet again shortly after this entry. An odd coincidence that Edie should have worked alongside two different MOs with such similar names.

December 6

Boulogne – what a life! I was just starting dressings in the ward this morning when Matron came in and told me to go *at once* to 42 Ambulance Train for temporary duty, so I had to take off my rubber gloves and fly to my room to pack up all my worldly belongings and join this train, taking with me hand luggage only. The longer one lives in this war, the more one learns to take less about. I took no blankets and very few clothes with me – wrapped in a groundsheet, as my hold-all may be anywhere in France.

This is the top-dog of ambulance trains – the very latest out from England. The sister-in-charge had a telegram from home and has gone on a fortnight's leave and now I feel like a fish out of water who doesn't know his job – but it is a fine train and it is A1 having a compartment quite to myself instead of half a beastly little hutch where you could hear every word spoken in the beastly little hutches either side of you. Major Martyn came to tea on Tuesday, and it was nice to see him again. He was coming over again tomorrow but I have sent him word that I shall not be there. I hear we are to go to Étaples to take a load to Calais.

December 7

We got to Étaples at 11 last night and loaded at 3 a.m. – 291 patients (chiefly stretchers) and 90 repatriated prisoners of war, one of whom was taken prisoner in 1914 in the Battle of the Marne. They do not seem in a bad state. We can order a special diet for them – bacon for breakfast and milk pudding and fruit for dinner, sardines for tea. Also, they are given an extra ration of cigarettes and matches.

At Calais harbour there were lots of German trains there and hundreds of guns – our own and captured German ones – and gun carriages by the hundred! I suppose all that war

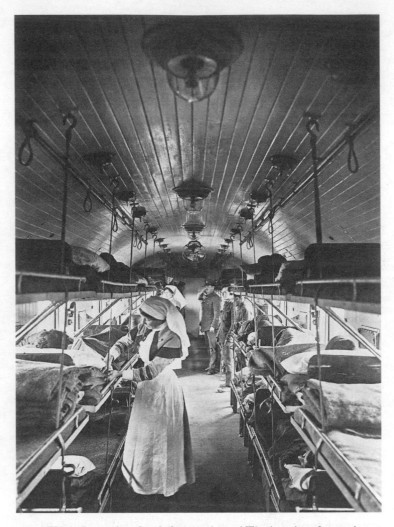

'*This is the top dog of ambulance trains . . .*' The interior of a ward
on a British ambulance train showing the narrow aisle and
triple bunks with nurses, patients and orderlies.
Photograph © IWM Q8749

material is being collected at the different ports to be
returned to *Angleterre*. One man died on the trip last night –
he had a gun-shot wound in the neck, and his carotid artery

had been tied, but it broke down. The MO did his best, but
it was a very quick and quiet ending. Mine is like a first-class
carriage one side and the other has a wardrobe and dressing-
table. Of course there is precious little room – you almost
stand on your other foot when you walk – but it is very comfortable. The French have been very busy all afternoon
mending steam pipes, etc. It is quite funny to do nothing but
listen to the engine whistles and the hooters of the men guard-
ing the line. You could not stick a pin between the hoots and
shrieks! They say we are to go on a long run to fetch POWs.

December 8

Sunday. This morning reminded me of 1914, the morning
we arrived at Ostend. I awoke and found the train still – not
a sound of any kind to be heard – then soon the clang of
church bells and I knew we were at a big town. We are currently lying in a siding and our engine has left us, so perhaps
we shall be able to get out and look at the place – Tournai.
It looks a very big, important town and from the number of
rail lines and telegraph lines, must be a big junction.

On days when there are no patients aboard, we live like
millionaires! We stay in bed until our batman calls us with
tea, have a leisurely breakfast no earlier than 9 o'clock, and
then out to see the place! This morning was glorious – sunny
and clear. Church bells sounded joyful and a train-load of
Tommies passed us on their way to Blighty – everything
seemed happy. The church parade came our way and we followed them to the garrison church, which is the cinema at
other times. The church was packed – there must have been
nearly 1,000 men. The music was a good brass band, the
padre was a fine fellow, and everything went with a swing, as
services up the line usually do. One thing impressed me,
although I think it happened more by accident than intention. In the responses before the *Venite*, the music and

congregation could not get together in 'As it was in the
beginning is now', etc, and only a few sang it – but when it
came to the last one, 'The Lord's name be praised', the clar-
inets and all the band were full blast and the men sang it at
the tops of their voices. It fitted the day and the sunshine
and the war being over well.

They wanted us to sit in front with the officers but we
couldn't face it and went to the gallery, as we were the only
two women there. The result was that many of the
men were screwing their heads round to have a look at us.
After the service the troops all assembled in the square in
front of the cathedral and marched off, headed by a fine
band. They looked splendid. Tournai is gay with flags –
especially one huge Belgian national flag. The King and the
Prince of Wales and Prince Albert* were here yesterday and
had a great welcome and acclamation from the people. An
RE officer showed us the belfry and all the bridges that had
been blown up by the Boches a few days before they left.

December 10

We have stayed at Tournai all night, so have had a lovely
undisturbed sleep. In the afternoon yesterday, Mr Lowery,
our American MO, took us out again, and we visited the
cathedral and stayed to a service. The music was glorious,
and the pageant very magnificent, but we didn't understand
it. I thought the cathedral quite the most beautiful I have
seen in France – no tawdry decorations and the stonework
and sculpture are very good. The windows are beautiful old
stained glass and the organ a great joy. Then to tea at a
hotel – tea without milk – and biscuits. In the evening we
went to a performance at the cinema, which was quite amus-
ing. It was packed with Tommies and officers, and a few of

* Later King George VI (r. 1936–1952)

the men had brought French children, or women with them. They seemed highly amused at it all. The piano was being played all the time, and every time a well-known tune came up the whole house whistled or sang to it – it was fine.

In one shop the woman told us what greedy brutes the Germans were. They swarmed into her shop in large numbers and while she was serving one, the rest would take all they could find. She had sham packets of chocolate made – piles of them – and no real sweets at all, so when they stole they were only the better off by so much paper and firewood. All honour to our airmen – they did their bombing here most scientifically and kindly. There is hardly a house touched. The beautiful cathedral is not minus as much as one pane of glass, but by the station and the bridges! God help those who were near – they are blown to blazes. Yesterday, Sister and I had to walk over a temporary railway bridge as our train is on the wrong side, in a siding. It was just beams, planks and rails, with huge gaps looking down to the road beneath, and big enough to fall through. We had gone a little way when suddenly both took fright and could not budge another inch. Luckily a Tommy came along and said, 'It's all right. 'Ere, I'll take you.' He took my hand and I had Sister's and we got over safely.

We got orders to load up and then to go to Villeneuve d'Ascq, where we took on patients and set off. We pulled in to the main station at 11 o'clock and soon after an RE came on the train and told us to open all our windows as they were going to blow up a bridge just behind us. We had hardly got them all open when the explosion went off and the bridge and a mountain of smoke and muck flew up into the air. They blew it up twice and as we had to have our windows open, the whole train was filthy with debris. We stopped at Ascq for about 120 more patients. One or two seem rather poorly but on the whole they are a very convalescent bunch.

Our load tonight consists of three Chinese, 12 Frenchmen, two Germans and 56 POWs, and up to 600 ordinary hospital cases. The CO says he expects trains soon will be running right into Germany.

The POWs tell endless tales. Some of them have been in Germany over four years and most complain of ill treatment, and of being shockingly badly fed. The officers in charge of the camps used to take most of the food out of their parcels from home and send it to their own families. The Germans complain that it was the English who caused all revolutionary riots in Germany. They claim that an English dreadnought sailed into Kiel harbour flying a red flag, and that was a signal that there was revolution in the British Royal Navy and that they were to do the same. I asked our boys if they believed that of the navy, and they said, 'No! We knew it wasn't true.'

One of them had been working in a bakery and he said they put a large quantity of sawdust in the bread. He showed me a piece and true enough, there was sawdust and quite visible sized flecks of wood too. They said that when the armistice was signed, the German people flew flags and decorated the place – they would not have stood another winter of war.

December 11

We came to Lille after making short stays at St Omer and Hazebrouck. We are supposed to be leaving at any minute for Ath, which is a fair way beyond Tournai. I can't see much of Lille from here, but it looks a big place and not at all smashed up.

December 12

We left Villeneuve d'Ascq at 9.30 this morning and are now on our way to Tournai for a load. We look out of the window at the myriads of railway lines and wonder why they hold us up every half hour or so to let some train pass – the lines look all right, but the Boches apparently rendered them useless by taking out all bolts at the junctions and breaking off about six inches at the end of each length of rail. These Belgians are such *thieves*! There were many coal trucks standing alongside us this morning and I was amazed to see an army of Belgian women and children arrive with sacks, barrows and perambulators. They climbed into the trucks, filled their sacks and cleared off with any amount of *our* coal – and two Tommies were helping them! Our OC says in some places the thieving is so bad that they keep armed guards by the coal trucks.

British Tommies – these are men of the 57th Division –
marching through Lille, accompanied by a young boy holding
a rifle. Edie writes earlier in her diaries of the French
children playing at being soldiers.
Photograph © IWM Q9586

December 13

It is 3.30 a.m. and I am taking the second half of the night duty this trip. We are nearing Calais, which means we shall reach Boulogne about 7 a.m. I have just made my round of the train – quite a walk from one end to the other. There are 16 coaches in all, of which 12 are wards with 36 beds in each, although we carry more than 432 patients. In wards where we keep the stretcher patients, we sometimes have all the beds full and a dozen stretchers on the floor, and where the wards are used for 'sitters' the beds are put back and they pack 60 to 80 in a coach. Tonight we have a light load – only a little over 300. It is an interesting study to go along and see them all asleep, there they lie looking perfectly happy. We have about eight French, eight Moroccans, one Indian, five Germans, many Australians and a vast majority of British.

While we were loading at Tournai, No. 35 Ambulance Train passed us, also with a light load, having been to a place 20 miles beyond the German frontier. We unloaded at Wimereux and started off again a few hours later on a different run. This time we are bound for Montigny, just beyond Douai. The night is fair and Étaples was a wonderful sight as we came through. The vast expanse of hut and tent encampments, all brightly lit, looked like a massive town. A trainload of Yanks passed us outside Wimereux – either a medical or flying corps unit with truckloads of stuff all packed for transport – it was a whole unit on its way back to America. Several of their hospitals have already gone, and five ambulance trains have been demobilised already.

December 14

We were at St Pol when we went to bed last night and expected to wake up at our destination Montigny, but to our surprise we were still moving, and looking out found

ourselves passing through a vast coal mining district. Sister
said, 'It looks like Valenciennes' then the first name we read
was 'Jemeppe'. Looking it up on the map we found we were
nearing *Mons*. We badly wanted to see this, so we dressed in
double-quick time and watched as we made our way
through that ever-famous place. It is huge and the station a
very big one with myriads of platforms. We spent the morning glued to the windows, leaning out then dashing across
and looking out of the other side.

They have not had many ambulance trains through here,
and as we pass the villages the inhabitants line up and wave
and bow to us and shout '*Les Anglais!*' We waited quite a long
time in Charleroi and we two sisters got off the train and had
a good brisk walk up and down. We passed a newly made
line of trenches – the last the Boches made in preparation for
retreat. At Charleroi our orders were changed and we are
now on our way via Namur and Liège to Herbesthal, just
across the German border*. I imagine we are to bring back
prisoners being repatriated.

Several times on our journey we have met German
trains – both passenger and goods trains – *laden* with
refugees from Germany. In some of the vans women were
cooking and men and children were huddled around eating.
There were lots of civilians – men, women and children –
and French and British soldiers too. Such long train-loads
and such quaint luggage, chiefly huge bundles tied up like
washing. We have seen hundreds of Boche trains today –
one quite new one was brought into Charleroi while we
were there. It was clean and empty and the Belgians
cheered as it came in. One thing is very striking. Every new
place we come to, the first thing we notice are British
Tommies and REs, with our British lorries, mending the
damage everywhere. Twice we have been assailed by

* Now in Belgium.

Belgians – the first an officer and the second a well-dressed lady – asking us to take them with us. Not much! In any case it is not allowed.

At one stop of the train, Sister and I hopped out and were grubbing over the debris of Boche aeroplanes and a destroyed ammunition train, intending to pick up a souvenir. All the shell-cases were badly scorched and not much use and we were still busily culling when Mr Lowery yelled to us that the train was off. It takes a little time to get up speed, so we chased and caught her quite easily – but it was just a bit thrilling.

Beyond Mons and Charleroi there are large areas of hundreds upon hundreds of ammunition and supply trucks, all blown up! Never was there such a scene of desolation. One supply train – a very, very long one of over 100 trucks – was burnt right out and the only thing that showed what it had been was a truck laden with burnt and twisted steel helmets. There are shells by the thousand – some lying about unexploded – and whole tracks have been blown up, their sleepers and rails all standing on end. Our OC says they must have destroyed about £1 million's worth of material. We are through Namur now, another big place and a fine station. From the train these places all look much the same style, but the scenery is beautiful here – on one side high, beautifully overgrown rocks, and on the other the river, gay with barges. Some of these, very heavily laden, were being towed by a man wearing a sort of harness across his chest and straining all he could, managing about half a mile an hour. Some were drawn by two women and some by a pair of boys.

At Charleroi we saw any number of destroyed German aeroplanes, and at the moment we are passing an orchard with a large number of German field-guns. At Namur there were lots of big German guns, festooned with moss and stuff that looked like green seaweed – there were

Minenwerfen, trench mortars and all sorts. All round Douai, the line was very dicky. Every bridge had been blown to bits and the train had to go over temporary bridges. The train had to go dead slow and very gently all through that part and it was very bumpy – it was the worst knocked about part of all.

We are waiting at Liège now. An official has been along and taken the number and letter of each coach and the number of the train, as this is the last big station before we cross the frontier. The OC thinks we are the first ambulance train to do this trip and all along the people wave and shout '*Vive l'Angleterre!*' There is a New Zealand division stationed along this line and I have gazed and gazed so as not to miss a glimpse of dear old Taff – but no luck.

The Germans have not spoiled these places and they all look in perfect order. The people look well fed and in good health, and the shops we could see from the train seemed well stocked and the gardens full of vegetables. Even the refugees from Germany did not look at all bad and were neatly dressed – our Tommies and the French soldiers looked the hungriest. At Charleroi there was one poor old Belgian man who made me feel very sad. He looked frightfully thin and ill, but was so polite to us. I do hope to goodness he has enough to eat.

We are 40 kilometres from our destination, Herbesthal, and now as the first ambulance train this side of Mons, there is a whole lot of red tape to be arranged. We go on two stations further, then are to be handed over to the Germans – either we take a German engine and crew or take on a German pilot. It was very interesting to look out at Liège and to remember that it was the guns of her forts that first held the Germans up in 1914 for nearly a week, and so gave time for the French to mobilise and our men to come out. We remembered Mons as the first place we lost –

and the last we won. For miles and miles we seem to have been passing through coal and iron mining districts and there are wonderful overhead railways and all sorts of clever machinery.

December 17

It has been a long and weary journey for the poor patients – two whole days – but with luck we should be at Boulogne shortly. They took us just across the border into Germany and left us there half the night, then took us back to Pepinster where we loaded up and have since been trying to get back. At Mons we were diverted, owing to a smash on the line, and we were constantly held up. At one place we waited and waited until at last Mr Lowery walked along to the signal-box to ask what was holding us up. He found two Jocks having a nice little tea-party with a couple of French girls, and we were quickly on our way again.

The La Bassée Canal is beautiful, although the place itself is no more. Absolutely every building is razed to the ground, and the station too. I thought of the little tailor at Tréport who altered my coat, who had a large business in La Bassée and hoped his house had escaped – but no chance. We are carrying lots of POWs from German hospitals. The poor things! They look like raisins and are all skin and bone, and their thighs are not as big round as my arm. Their wounds are foul and their backs in a horrible state with bed sores. Their digestions are so upset by starvation that they can only take little drinks and tiny little bits of bread and butter or jam. They certainly can't digest meat. Their foreheads and noses look huge as the rest of their faces and necks have sunk right in. They had their dressings done only once in four days. We have several fractured femurs, and all the extension they had was a couple of bricks tied on the leg, with no splint at all, so consequently their legs are in very bad shape and will mend short. We also have an attempted suicide officer on board. The poor thing went so far it is a pity he did not finish it, as his brain is oozing and he is paralysed all down one side.

I noticed many New Zealanders at Huy and asked one if he happened to know Taff. He did not, but has promised to find him and give him a message from me, as they are all together there. I was talking to a New Zealand boy through the train window and when I came in a sergeant major said, 'Excuse me – were you asking for a machine-gunner?' I said I was and he said 'I trace a likeness. Is it Appleton?' He told me what a fine set of men they were, and said Taff was thin but hard as nails. He thought very highly of Taff. It was very tantalising to be so near the boy and yet so far – they are supposed to leave for Germany today.

When our prisoners asked for more food they were told it was England's fault, because there was a total blockade. Bravo for the navy – they did their job very thoroughly. I asked one man what he got to know of the war news, and he said they thought we must be winning because one day they heard some German orderlies talking about an armistice and then they took down a big calendar with the Kaiser's picture on it, tore it to bits and trampled on it. The prisoners who are up and dressed are not as underfed looking – but their clothes! Russian trousers, Belgian coats and waistcoats – French and German civilian clothes and any old cap! They look like so many Bill Sykeses*. They say the soup they had was only cabbage water and they thought themselves very lucky if they found any little bits of anything floating in it. But they said the German civilians looked absolutely starved and wretched too – and were wearing clothes made of paper and wooden shoes.

Our REs have an endless task in repairing miles and miles

---

* The rough and dishevelled robber in Charles Dickens's *Oliver Twist*.

of broken railways. At Ath Jerry had evidently meant to spoil the whole system, as at one point the line was blown up by mines every 20 yards. There were about 20 lines abreast and every one was blown up and the rails all twisted and broken. Our track was the only repaired one and we had to go dead slow as it ran on plank bridges over the mine craters. The bridge they were blowing up at Tournai is quite down and looks a ponderous wreck.

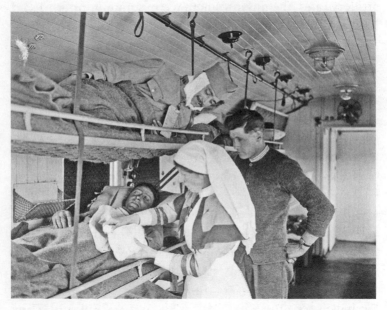

'... *a long and weary journey for the poor patients* ...' French and British wounded having their wounds dressed in a British Ambulance Train near Doullens.
Photograph © IWM Q8736

December 18

We are being punished today for our sins of yesterday. Our OC had a bit of a row with the Railway Transport Officer at Boulogne and our train was not ready to start at its appointed

time. Consequently we lost our '*marche*' in the heavy traffic
and are now waiting in Tournai Station. At this rate we shall
be about three days on the outward journey.

December 19

At three this morning we stopped at Charleroi and took on
a fresh engine and a vastly better driver, and after that we
made good speed. In one place we saw some New Zealand
artillery, and the infantrymen were standing around the
houses as if they were billeted there and not yet under way
for Germany. I waved hard on the off-chance of brother Taff
being anywhere near and reading our large '42 AT' number-
plate. They looked fine men, and made a good show.

At 9 a.m., here we are across the border again and the
square-heads are everywhere. Some wear white armlets – a
sign that they are in favour of the revolution, I believe.
There are girl engine-cleaners, dressed in ordinary men's
clothes – dirty old trousers and boots and coats and caps.
None of them look the least bit hungry ... A troop train has
just passed us – a German train with German driver, crew
and guard, but all the vans and coaches are packed with
laughing, irresponsible British officers and Tommies enjoying themselves.

We have spent the whole day at Herbesthal waiting for an
engine to take us to Cologne. In the morning we went for a
short walk along the lines, not daring to go too far in case the
engine arrived. After lunch we turned out our six Canadian
visitors and took them for a brisk walk up and down the line.
One of them had a camera with one film left, and we had
great fun having a snapshot taken. After that, Sister
Summers and I set to work in earnest to make paper flowers
for Christmas, then we made ourselves smart and went to tea
with the Canadians. The Canadian sisters are a cheery crew

and we had a very gay tea-party. Another troop train went past while we were at tea, and as each coach passed our window, the men shouted to us and cheered loudly. Tonight I saw our own Tommies pilfering lovely big cabbages from two German trucks. Fraser, the OC's batman even brought one in to show me and told me they had not nearly finished yet – they had only taken four so far!

December 20

We lay at Herbesthal until 4 p.m. and then were taken back to Pepinster again to load. I think the Germans working in offices round about have done very little work – they have been much too interested in all the happenings. Every hour or two a troop train has passed on its way to Cologne, with trucks for the Tommies and coaches for the officers. The Tommies all seemed in high feather. We always stand at our window and wave to them, and as each truck passes they cheer like mad and sing and wave back. On one train some were waving Union Jacks, one was ringing a big bell, while others were cooking and lots were eating.

Taff is due in Cologne tomorrow and we might have met, but I have left lots of messages for him and have asked the sister in charge of 33 to mother him for me. She is an old and good friend of mine. I called to a New Zealander early this morning and asked him for news of Taff. He had seen him yesterday and says he is very fit and well. It is provokingly tantalising to just miss him each time. I spoke to a New Zealand evacuation officer, and he is going to try to see that Taff gets leave whenever Ambulance Train 42 comes up to Cologne. He was a very charming officer and stands *no* nonsense from the Boches. He was sleeping on the floor of a hut here last night and this morning told some people here that he wanted a decent room. They said, 'By the terms of the Armistice, no claim can be made on private property.' He answered, 'Give me a key and the room, instantly', and he said the key was not long in being handed to him. He *loathes* the Hun, and so do I – they don't look a bit repentant, or even becomingly thin or poor.

We had great fun this afternoon. An engine came to take an ambulance train to Namur. First he hitched on to us, then for some unknown reason the Germans put him on to AT 33. Then all the staffs of both trains came out and had battle royal. Each said *they* were to go to Cologne. Of course orders are orders and in the end it was we who were ordered back to Pepinster. Whether they will go on or not is a matter of conjecture – things are in such a muddle and there is no co-operation between the Germans and this side of the border. I understand Taff is due to entrain at 1 p.m. tomorrow at Herbesthal for Cologne.

I am on night duty, we have about 400-odd on board, and are to fill up at Huy in about half an hour. Our OC is an old bachelor – deaf and rather inclined to be strong-minded – and one of his fads is to visit each man, ill or well. In the sitting wards the men are thick on the ground and it is nothing to see him take one man's card and ask the questions of quite a different one. Tonight, with a card in his hand, he went to a fellow and said, 'Any diarrhoea?' 'No, sir,' said the man angrily. 'Any sickness?' '*No*, sir.' 'Any pains in the stomach? Put out the tongue.' 'That ain't my complaint, sir – I got an 'ammer toe.' Then he finds he has been reading the card belonging to the next man ...

December 21

We made a good run and were well through Namur when I went to bed at 3 a.m. We stopped at Huy for a load – and to our surprise found no patients. The CCS had moved the day before and another ambulance train had taken all their patients. Today we are going through Douai, Arras and St Pol. The last time I was in Arras and St Pol they didn't look badly hurt, but I expect there will be a big difference now. The RTO at Namur yesterday told us of an incident that happened there in the morning. A supply train was standing in a siding and a troop train came in carrying reinforcements on their way up to Cologne. The troops raided the supply train and the RTO saw a long line of them proceeding back to their train, each with a sack of something – bread, bully, biscuits – anything that could be eaten. That of course meant short rations for lots of people, so the RTO had an inspiration and walked along the troop train shouting, 'All change!' and he held the train back. Out tumbled the men, sacks and all, and he rescued a lot, but even so lots of them got off with pockets bulging.

December 23

The last run was the slowest I have known – the French had taken control of the line the day before and were not quite used to it. We were about 12 hours late and the patients over-tired from their long journey. We off-loaded at Wimereux and just had time to scuttle off and do a little shopping, then on to Étaples, where we still are, but we have just got orders to go to Tréport to take an evacuation load to Le Havre or Boulogne. Sister and I have been for a good walk and fresh air this afternoon, such a treat after being cooped up so long. I went to bed early with a sore throat last night – it is from living this shut-up existence not getting a daily walk.

December 24

It is 4 a.m. and we are taking our load to Calais, which should suit us rather nicely if all be well! We should off-load about 11 a.m., then be free for the rest of the day and have our

Christmas dinner tonight. As I was walking through the train tonight I was greeted with, 'Hello Sister,' and behold – two of my old patients, at last on their way to Blighty.

Christmas Day

A happy Christmas to all. It is 3 p.m. and I am enjoying myself immensely sitting in a comfortable chair in the kitchen. The wide-open window and glorious sunshine make even this wrecked, desolate, uninhabited area beautiful. We are creeping very slowly over some of the most fought-on ground in France, between Armentières and Lille. Everywhere is trenches – now kindly covered in soft green grass – and dugouts, gun emplacements, barbed-wire entanglements – all of Boche construction. The poor trees are all standing, split and dead, and over towards the town is one sad chaos of bricks and mortar, walls and skeletons of houses. I don't see a roof on a single one. Nobody lives here now and the ground will have to be cleared of all sorts of war hamper before it can be cultivated. We are having a very happy Christmastide. Yesterday was our day, but today is for the men. We had a very moving dinner party last night, just four of us – the OC, Mr Lowery, Sister Summers and I.

Soup: Julienne
Fish: Fried plaice
Roast: Pork
Fowl: Roast chicken
Sweets: Xmas pudding – mince pies – jelly and blanc-mange
Coffee
Drinks: Champagne – the gift of the OC

After a long and cheery meal we played bridge and ended the evening at 11.45 with dancing in the kitchen to the

music of the gramophone. We were just outside Calais, and
expected to be left there over Christmas Day, so Sister and
I got up early and went out in search of a church service. We
found a very nice one in the Church Army hut, conducted by
a fighting man who was a parson in China in peacetime, but
during the war he has been fighting in an infantry regiment –
a very nice man.

On the way back to the train, Sister said, 'She's not there!'
And sure enough, she was not where we had left her, and we
thought she had gone and left us behind. Then we saw an
engine and train higher up the line. Cheers! No. 42!
However, between us and her was a goods train about a mile
long. We were going to climb under it, but it began to move
so we hopped on to it and jumped out the other side and
flew to our own train. We found that the engine had come on
a few minutes after we started out and that she was ordered
to leave at 8 a.m. (I thought I felt a little bump, like an
engine coming on, just as we were leaving – but didn't think
they would take us out on Christmas Day.)

After breakfast we dismissed our staff – two cooks and
two batmen – for the whole day and we are running our own
mess. Hence I am able to sit in the kitchen and enjoy
myself this afternoon. Sister and I helped decorate the
men's tables this morning and their coach looks really fine.
When they sat down to dinner we went along to see them
in a procession, OC, Mr Lowery, Sister Summers and I. The
OC made a most kind and appropriate address to them, the
senior man responded, then we had three hearty cheers and
left them to it.

December 26

Christmas was a great success with our men. They had a
splendid dinner, followed by a whist drive in the afternoon.
In the evening they gave a concert to which we were all

invited. Really it is wonderful what can be done in a train. All their festivities were held in 'P' coach, which is at other times a ward of 36 beds. Some of the beds had been unhinged and made into a long table down the centre, and the other beds were folded up. For the concert a stage had been erected at one end of the coach and curtains borrowed from the ward where they are used to divide the half used for officers from that used for other ranks.

The rule of the concert was that everyone had to do something. Some sang well – some *very badly* – and some did card tricks. For me quite the funniest thing was the minstrel troop called 'Corporal Fox and his Lunies'. They were dressed *any*how, in pyjamas, white drills – and their faces were well blacked. One, our cook, played the big drum – a muffled coal hammer on a large round tea-tray. Another played the cymbals, which were a couple of metal ashtrays which he banged together. The small drum was a large biscuit tin and a couple of pieces of firewood. Another beat a huge hanging poker with the small iron used for lifting the round off the stove, one man beat a gong and Corporal Fox conducted. Behind the scenes the gramophone played some gooey piece and the band played to the tune of it. Corporal Fox was funny and the whole thing had everyone *weak* with laughter. At the end, someone seized a big bunch of paper roses on prickly stalks which we had made as decorations and presented them to the conductor. Corporal Fox is really clever and later recited a poem he had made up himself, on '42 AT', with hits at everyone, including the quartermaster, all the NCOs – and of course the officers and sisters did not escape.

Beer, lemonade and sandwiches half an inch thick were handed round, but we had dined too recently to join in. At the end the Chairman, Corporal Hunt, gave a speech, followed by one from the OC – then we finished up with 'The Soldier's Farewell', two Christmas carols, 'Auld Lang Syne' (all holding hands crossways) and 'God Save the King'. As good luck would have it the train was still during the whole concert and only moved on at 11.45, just when we were singing 'God save the King'.

Edie's diaries end here. The subsequent pages, from January 1919 until her demobilisation in December, are missing.

There are very few photos of Edie herself taken during the war years. This one is dated 1917 – ironically one of the periods for which her diary is missing.
Photograph courtesy of the Appleton family

Appendix

British Military Nurses in the Great War: a Guide to the Services

Little has been written about British military nurses during the Great War, and few primary sources have survived, which makes it difficult to piece together even the basic details of the organisation and administration of the nursing services during this period. To understand the situation that existed during the war, it is necessary to be familiar with the different bodies of nurses that together formed the whole; the type of training and experience they had received, and how each one fitted in during wartime. The following is a brief description of the nursing services that worked under the auspices of the War Office during the Great War, caring for members of the British Expeditionary Force and other nationalities in British military hospitals at home and abroad.

1. Queen Alexandra's Imperial Military Nursing Service [QAIMNS]

QAIMNS or the 'Regular' military nursing service was formed in March 1902, as part of a general reorganisation of the Army Medical Services, and included many existing members of its forerunner, the Army Nursing Service, which had provided nurses for military hospitals since 1861. Despite a reluctance in some quarters to welcome female nurses into military hospitals, they proved themselves an asset, both for their nursing expertise, and for their skill in training orderlies of the Army Hospital Corps and later the Royal Army Medical Corps.

From 1902 members of the service were employed in all military hospitals with more than one hundred beds, both in the United Kingdom and overseas. Standards for admission to the service were high, with women required to be between twenty-five and thirty-five years of age, British subjects, well-educated and having completed a three year nurse training in an approved hospital. Most importantly, they had to persuade the Nursing Board that they were ladies of good social standing. In the main they were the daughters of army officers, clergy, professional men, merchants and farmers.

During its first twelve years, the service found difficulty in attracting enough candidates who were able to meet such stringent standards. Consequently it was usually below establishment, and relied on members of the permanent QAIMNS Reserve employed on temporary contracts to fill gaps in home hospitals. In 1903 the War Office produced a list of just thirty-four hospitals in the United Kingdom considered to have nurse training schools of a high enough standard to supply trained nurses to the Army. Yet within a year the lack of applicants forced a rethink, and the entry requirement was lowered to include any hospital with more than one hundred beds, provided candidates met all the other standards for entry. At the outbreak of war there were 297 members of QAIMNS – matrons, sisters and staff nurses – employed in military hospitals at home, and overseas in Malta, Gibraltar, Egypt, South Africa and China. During the Great War the establishment remained unchanged, as it was considered unwise to permanently employ more women than would be needed after the end of the war. Any women who left the service were replaced, but the many thousands of nurses recruited during the war joined on short-term contracts with clauses that enabled the War Office to end their employment at its convenience.

Life in army hospitals during peacetime was very different from that in civil establishments. Military hospitals were, in general, smaller, with the majority having less than two hundred beds, and the patients were mainly fit men under the age of sixty, suffering from minor illness or the result of accidents. No female probationers were employed, with nursing orderlies of the Royal Army Medical Corps carrying out most of the care in the wards. The rather specialised and insular nature of the life produced a nursing service of educated and adventurous women, experienced in the ways of the army, but with little experience in the organisation and management of large, busy hospitals and considerable female staffs. During the war it soon became evident that a small number of these women, who were part of a professional elite in nursing circles, and who coped admirably with keeping order in military hospitals in peacetime, did not possess the skills to manage wartime units of up to 2,000 beds, or cope with the unrelenting pressures of casualty clearing stations. Some found themselves transferred back to the United Kingdom from overseas, to undertake less demanding duties. More than seventy nurses who had resigned or retired from QAIMNS between 1903 and 1914, returned during the Great War to serve once more, with many of the older women among them taking up positions as matrons of the smaller military hospitals in the United Kingdom, thereby releasing experienced younger matrons for service overseas. The size and composition of the service remained relatively unchanged until the summer of 1919, when a steady expansion began which continued through the next half century.

2. Queen Alexandra's Imperial Military Nursing Service Reserve

A permanent reserve for QAIMNS was formed in 1908, but during peacetime recruitment proved difficult, never successfully competing with the popular Territorial Force Nursing Service. It was intended that the Reserve be held at a constant 500 members; in peacetime they would fill gaps in military hospitals caused by the under-establishment of the Regular Service, and, in the event of war, would be available to provide, at short notice, suitable nurses to supplement QAIMNS. Members were required to sign a contract for a period of three years, and paid a retaining fee of £5 per annum, or if actually employed, received allowances on the QAIMNS scale appropriate to their rank. In the event, recruitment was slow and patchy, and on the eve of war there were less than two hundred nurses of the QAIMNS Reserve available for mobilisation. However, the Reserve flourished following the outbreak of war, with trained nurses flocking to join the military nursing services on yearly contracts. By the end of 1914 more than 2,200 women had enrolled in the service, and in total more than 12,000 served with the Reserve at some time during the Great War in all theatres. In the immediate post-war period, members were retained for employment in the increased number of military hospitals and also in Ministry of Pensions establishments. Some were engaged for the regular QAIMNS, their social and professional pedigree already established by their wartime service, but the majority were demobilised between January and September 1919, returning to civilian life to pick up the threads of their former lives, or venturing overseas to seek new opportunities.

3. Princess Christian's Army Nursing Service Reserve [PCANSR/ANSR]

The Army Nursing Service (ANS) was the forerunner of Queen Alexandra's Imperial Military Nursing Service, the latter replacing it by Royal Warrant in March 1902. The ANS was a small service and, from 1897, was supported by members of Princess Christian's Army Nursing Service Reserve, who were used to supplement the permanent members in military hospitals at home and abroad. During the Boer War, 1,376 members of the PCANSR were employed, with 805 seeing service in South Africa. After the formation of QAIMNS in 1902 the relationship between the two services was uneasy, PCANSR being an independent service under the direct control of the War Office, with no official connection to QAIMNS. When QAIMNS's own Reserve was formed in 1908, members of the PCANSR ceased to be employed in military hospitals, and the nurses were graded in order to identify those women who were suitably qualified in all respects to be appointed to QAIMNS if the need arose. Recruitment to PCANSR ceased, and the running down of the service was anticipated. Yet in September 1914 there were still 337 names on the roll, and a number of these women mobilised, wearing the uniform of the QAIMNS Reserve, but still officially part of the PCANSR. During the course of the war all mobilised members signed contracts to serve as members of Queen Alexandra's Imperial Military Nursing Service Reserve, thus erasing the final traces of Princess Christian's own nursing service.

4. Territorial Force Nursing Service [TFNS]

The Territorial Force Nursing Service was established by R. B. Haldane in March 1908 following the Territorial and Reserve Forces Act (1907), and was intended to provide nursing staff for the twenty-three territorial force general hospitals planned for the United Kingdom in the event of war. Hospitals were allocated a staff of ninety-one trained nurses, and, allowing for the fact that some members might hold civilian positions preventing their immediate mobilisation, 120 women were recruited for each; two matrons, thirty sisters and eighty-eight staff nurses. The nursing staff of each hospital was under the control of a Principal Matron, who was a senior civil nurse already based in a local general hospital, and who continued to fulfil her civilian duties in addition to the administration of the territorial unit. This provided a total establishment of 2,760 women, who in peacetime went about their normal duties in civil hospitals and private homes, but with a commitment to the War Office and holding mobilisation orders. The Standing Orders for the TFNS closely mirrored those of QAIMNS, and the standards of entry were similar. The insistence on a full three-year nurse training in an approved hospital remained, though it seems likely that when appointing staff, rather more emphasis was put on professional ability than on social standing.

Although originally intended for home service only, in 1913 members of the TFNS were given the opportunity to notify their intention of willingness to serve overseas if required, and the sudden need for a large number of nurses to accompany the British Expeditionary Force to France in 1914 resulted in some members proceeding overseas during the early weeks of the war. Because of the pre-war method of forming complete hospitals with nurses of all grades, many of the TFNS nurses who served during the Great War had long experience in nursing, holding positions of great responsibility in civil life. Among them were women who, on the outbreak of war, were working as assistant matrons and senior sisters in some of the United Kingdom's great institutions, including St. Thomas' Hospital in London, and the

Edinburgh Royal Infirmary. Despite initial wariness by the two Matrons-in-Chief of QAIMNS, it soon became evident that many of these women coped admirably with the management of large hospitals and female staffs. They quickly adapted their skills to meet the new and complex needs of casualty clearing stations and field ambulances, becoming some of the war's most able nurse-managers. Over the course of the Great War, 8,140 women served at some time as mobilised members of the Territorial Force Nursing Service, and of these 2,280 served overseas.

5. Civil Hospital Reserve [CHR]

During the early years of the twentieth century the War Office realised that in the event of war there would not be enough military nurses to meet the needs of the Army. Queen Alexandra's Imperial Military Nursing Service was a small, select group, and though adequate to staff the larger military hospitals in peacetime, the numbers were completely inadequate for wartime. In 1906 the QAIMNS Nursing Board considered ways to solve this problem and produced a 'Report on the Expansion of the Nursing Service to meet the needs of War'. Their solution was to increase the size of the QAIMNS Reserve, and to make retired members of the regular service liable to recall in the event of war. However, neither of these plans proved successful, and predicted numbers continued to fall short of requirements by approximately eight hundred. In 1910, the War Office appealed to the civil hospitals for help, and, in 1911, this resulted in the formation of the Civil Hospital Reserve, to 'supplement the nursing services in the military hospitals of peace garrisons'. Some of the largest of the United Kingdom's hospitals invited their trained nursing staff to offer their services to the War Office, and a register was drawn up of suitably qualified women who were willing to mobilise on the outbreak of hostilities, on the understanding that their jobs would be protected, and they would be able to return to their former roles at the end of the war. In August 1914, six hundred women were ready for mobilisation with the Civil Hospital Reserve. Although they were originally intended for service in home hospitals only, many soon found themselves serving with the British Expeditionary Force in France and Flanders and wearing the uniform of the QAIMNS Reserve. There was no further recruitment to the CHR during the war, and over the course of the next four years almost all these members transferred, serving under contracts with the Reserve.

6. Assistant Nurses

Before 1919 there was no register of nurses, or national regulations covering standards for nurse training. During the 1860s and 1870s training was normally for one year, and it was considered that most of what was essential could be learnt in that short time. During the last two decades of the nineteenth century the realisation dawned that a longer period of training was necessary to produce a 'professional' nurse. However, hospitals were not compelled to train nurses for three years, with the result that nursing became a two-tier system, with those who had completed three years' training in a general hospital often regarded as 'proper' nurses, while others, including women trained in fever nursing, the care of children and the mentally ill, were sometimes seen as professionally less qualified. During the early days of the Great War there was little understanding of how long the conflict would last. However, by early 1915 it was evident that there were not enough fully trained nurses to staff the ever-increasing number of hospitals and casualty clearing stations at home and abroad, and it was decided to employ partly-trained nurses in military hospitals.

Applications were accepted from women who held certifi-cates showing that they had completed an approved two-year training in fever, children's or mental nursing, or were certified midwives, and they worked under the trained nurses of QAIMNS and the TFNS at a reduced rate of pay. Assistant nurses were not numerous, but their specialised experience proved particularly useful in the nursing of patients with infectious diseases and mental illness, and in the care of the civilian population and refugees abroad.

7. VADs [Members of Voluntary Aid Detachments]

Following R. B. Haldane's Territorial scheme of 1907, new possibilities arose of co-operation between voluntary agen-cies and the Army, and on the 16th August 1909 the War Office issued its 'Scheme for the Organisation of Voluntary Aid in England and Wales.' This set up both male and female Voluntary Aid detachments to fill certain gaps in the territorial medical services, with a similar scheme for Scotland following in December 1909. Detachments were 'organised for their local Territorial Force Association by the Red Cross, and to receive preliminary training in first aid and nursing from the St. John's Ambulance Association', and after October 1914 this responsibility was transferred to the Joint War Committee of the British Red Cross Society and St. John of Jerusalem, a wartime amalgamation of the two organisations. The scheme proved popular, particularly with women, and immediately prior to the outbreak of war, there were 1823 female detachments and 551 male detachments registered with the War Office.

The women who joined detachments were a mixture, being a wide range of ages and with different sorts of life skills. As a group they were very much defined by being middle or upper middle-class – in the main they were the daughters of local gentry, landowners, army officers, clergy, and professional men, and also included a good sprinkling of women with an aristocratic background. The majority were young women who had never had any paid employment, and of those who eventually went on to wartime service more than three-quarters had either never worked outside the home, or had done work which qualified them for payment of a minor nature. Following the outbreak of war members of female detachments staffed VAD hospitals and auxiliary units, and individual members quickly came to be referred to by the initials of their organisation. As the number of medical units both at home and broad escalated, the difficulties of keeping so many hospitals fully-staffed became increasingly difficult. In the spring of 1915 the War Office agreed that VADs could be employed in the large military hospitals at home to augment the trained staff, and by early summer of that year in general hospitals overseas as well. During the course of the war more than 90,000 women served as VADs in some capacity; 10,000 worked in hospitals under the direction of the War Office, and of those, 8,000 served overseas, in France, Malta, Serbia, Salonika, Egypt and Mesopotamia.

8. Special Military Probationers [SMP]

Special Military Probationers were women who had little or no formal training as nurses, and they served under almost identical conditions of service to members of Voluntary Aid Detachments and did similar work. However, these women were recruited and employed by the War Office, and had no ties with the Joint War Committee of the British Red Cross Society and St. John of Jerusalem.

These eight groups of women combined to form a highly-trained and professional body which, for more than five years, met the nursing needs of the British Expeditionary

Force, its Allies, its prisoners of war and at times the civilian population abroad. At a time when trained nurses were in short supply, the British military nursing services never wavered in their commitment to provide the best possible nursing care to sick and wounded soldiers, in conditions unknown to them before the war. The experience was to stand them in good stead for the future.

Acknowledgements

Edie – thank you so much for your diaries. I was the lucky family member into whose possession the diaries came in the late 1990s. After you died in 1958 two of your nieces – my mother, Elizabeth Robinson, and her sister, Anne Stainforth – cleared your home in the Isle of Wight, and the diaries lay safely in a succession of drawers for the next fifty years.

A chance conversation with a neighbour, Margaret Oliver, encouraged me to publish the diaries. So began a long process whereby my Canadian cousins, Jill and Piers Stainforth, and I painstakingly transcribed the diaries and set up Edie's website: www.edithappleton.org.uk. We looked everywhere for family photographs and three more of Edie's nieces, Dorothy West, Shirley Gudex and Veronica Bickford provided family background as did several of the next generation of Felthams, Hyslops, Wests, Dowdings, Robertses, Clarkes, Blandys, McDonnells and others.

I am hugely indebted to many others: Sue Light, an expert on British military nurses, provided endless encouragement and advice; Gerry Hall created the index of all the people mentioned in the diary; Tony Gilbert made sure I learned about the wider context of the 1914–18 war; staff at the Imperial War Museum and the Wellcome Institute helped me access their records. Others, including the archivists at Bart's Hospital, several folk on the Isle of Wight and my techie friend Bill Thompson have also given significant help.

In 2008 BBC Radio 4's *Making History* programme fea-
tured Edie's diaries and later Jo Green of Pier Productions
persuaded the BBC to broadcast three *Afternoon Reading*
episodes in November 2009, repeated in the summer of
2011. Feedback from around the world is recorded in the
Visitors' Book on Edie's website. A handful of people have
recognised their relatives in the diaries and I am hoping
more will be in touch now that we have added to the website a comprehensive index of all the people named in Edie's
diaries: http://www.edithappleton.org.uk/index/names.asp.

There has also been interest in the diaries in France and we
are indebted to Arfa Ridha, Dr Bruno Garraud and Jean-Luc
Dron in Le Tréport and particularly to Alain Millet in Étretat,
who has been tireless in providing essential local information.
Thanks, too, to Brian Dunlop for his Étretat photos.

After the website was established, the possibility of a
book version loomed and special thanks are due to our pub-
lishing agent, Barbara Levy, as well as to Liz Bowers and
Peter Taylor at the IWM who helped to find a publisher.
Kerri Sharp, at Simon & Schuster, and Sally Partington have
been our enthusiastic and patient commissioning editor and
project manager respectively. We were extremely fortunate
to have Ruth Cowen as editor and it has been a particular
pleasure to work with her in condensing the original manu-
script down to a readable 70,000 words.

I felt that several topics in the diaries resonate with
themes in Michael Morpurgo's books about 'the horror and
pity of war' so I was delighted when he responded so warmly
and generously to my request that he write a Foreword to
Edie's diaries.

Many people, including my children Sara, Sam and Katie,
and Sara's husband Paul have encouraged me greatly in the
process of getting Edie's diaries first onto a website and now
into a delightful book; but none more so than my long-
suffering wife, Lisa.

One final heartfelt request: if, by some miraculous chance, you come across the 'missing' volumes of the diaries (October 1914 to March 1915, November 1916 to June 1918 and from January 1919 onwards), please use Edie's website Visitors' Book to let us know.

Dick Robinson
proud great nephew of Edie Appleton.

Edie enjoying a peaceful country walk near Deal with her brother Sydney. This was taken in 1920, not long after she returned to England in 1919.
Photograph courtesy of the Appleton family

Index

Sept.

being taken prisoner. One Canadian was killed – & the rest
were so infuriated – they fired two volleys at them
& killed both officers – One was a very smart person
wearing all sorts of decorations including the Iron
Cross – Our airmen are sorry they were shot, they
think the Germans will make it an excuse for shot
our airmen when they are brought down in German
territory

a child's funeral.

I was watching 5 nuns – & 3 orderlies, who was
soldiers shirts in the Courtyard of the Convent at
No 8. The men were working the washing machines
& mangle – & the nuns – 4 washing in one huge
tub – & one rinceing in another. They were all
chatting happily together – when a bell rang – the
men stopped talking – one Nun said prayers
& the other 4 asked the Virgin to hear them – at the